East In Focus

taneously the world's most controversial,
tood region. Taking new perspectives on
nost dramatic changes, the Middle East in
bin, seeks to bring the best, most accurate
g the area's countries, issues, and problems.
d to be balanced, accurate, and comprehen-
nd analysis presented clearly for both experts

national Affairs (GLORIA)
iew of International Affairs (MERIA)

s Trouble Lands

Chaos
nael Rubin

ab Middle East: The Cases of Kuwait, Jordan, and Iraq

nd American Wars with Iraq

The Middle

The Middle East has become simu
crisis-ridden, and yet least-unders
the area that has undergone the m
Focus series, edited by Barry Ru
expertise to bear for understandi
The resulting books are designe
sive compendiums of both facts
and the general reader.

Series Editor: Barry Rubin

Director, Global Research Intern
Center Editor, *Middle East Rev*
Journal Editor, *Turkish Studies*

Turkish Dynamics: Bridge acros
By Ersin Kalaycioğlu

Eternal Iran: Continuity and
By Patrick Clawson and Mic

Hybrid Sovereignty in the Ar
By Gokhan Bacik

The Politics of Intelligence
By Ofira Seliktar

The Politics of Intelligence and American Wars with Iraq

Ofira Seliktar

palgrave
macmillan

THE POLITICS OF INTELLIGENCE AND AMERICAN WARS WITH IRAQ

First published in 2008 by
PALGRAVE MACMILLAN™
175 Fifth Avenue, New York, N.Y. 10010 and
Houndmills, Basingstoke, Hampshire, England RG21 6XS
Companies and representatives throughout the world.

PALGRAVE MACMILLAN is the global academic imprint of the Palgrave Macmillan division of St. Martin's Press, LLC and of Palgrave Macmillan Ltd. Macmillan® is a registered trademark in the United States, United Kingdom and other countries. Palgrave is a registered trademark in the European Union and other countries.

ISBN-13: 978–0–230–60453–7
ISBN-10: 0–230–60453–6

Library of Congress Cataloging-in-Publication Data

Seliktar, Ofira.
The politics of intelligence and American wars with Iraq / Ofira Seliktar.
p. cm.—(Middle East in focus)
ISBN 0–230–60453–6 (alk. paper)
1. United States—Foreign relations—Iraq. 2. Iraq—Foreign relations—United States. 3. Intelligence service—United States. 4. Persian Gulf War, 1991. 5. Iraq War, 2003– 6. Intervention (International law) 7. United States—Foreign relations. I. Title.

E183.8.I57S44 2008
956.7044'28—dc22 2007027704

A catalogue record for this book is available from the British Library.

Design by Newgen Imaging Systems (P) Ltd., Chennai, India.

First edition: February 2008

10 9 8 7 6 5 4 3 2 1

Printed in the United States of America.

To my sons Yaron and Dror and their families

Contents

Series Editor's Foreword

A huge amount has been written—and no doubt far more will be published—about the events which led to the U.S.-led operation to overthrow Iraqi President Saddam Hussein and the exceedingly complex and controversial developments that followed. But Ofira Seliktar has done something unique and extremely important—evaluating the issue as a case study in intellectual history, evaluating intelligence, and the turning of intelligence into policy. Her work thus has value not only for this specific and very major issue but also more generally for the creation of and response to crises.

Seliktar analyzes the problem as arising from a mystery that has only deepened as alternative interpretations and strategies designed to deal with it have failed. First, why has the Middle East, and especially the Arabic-speaking states have remained so unstable, slow to develop, resistant to reform or democracy, antagonistic to the West in general, subject to the appeal of radical Islamism, and so on? Second, what can be done about this set of problems?

If one were to list the international crises that have beset the United States and the world in general during the last 30 or so years, they would be disproportionately of Middle East origin or location. This shows the urgency of finding the right answer and implementing the best policies to cope with these issues.

There is a dangerous temptation in discussing such matters and concluding that all interpretations and responses have failed. This is somewhat misleading. True, certainly no single viewpoint has gained hegemony in the West and everything about the Middle East remains controversial, though this is often due both to the continuous invasion of the field by the ignorant and control over it by the ideologically biased who seem unable or uninterested in meeting proper intellectual standards.

On the policy level, there are certainly plenty of failures that can be listed at great length but are quite familiar even to a general audience. Moreover, the problems that plague the region have not been "solved," but continue to fester and mutate into new varieties.

And yet it is not true to say that U.S. or Western policies have been failures for two reasons. First, many of the region's problems are very much the result of the societies and polities of the area, beyond the reach of external factors to affect them. Second, U.S. and Western interests have largely been preserved.

But this discussion threatens to take us beyond the intentions of this book. Seliktar has examined the two main paradigms shaping U.S. policy on

Iraq. Briefly, the Saddam Hussein regime could be made harmless to Western interests or at least not damaging to them through engagement, confidence-building, concessions, and cooperation. This failed. The second and ensuing paradigm was that it could be overthrown and replaced with a new democratic regime. This too, at least in part, failed. For, the Saddam regime was brought down but the new order also brought in its wake huge problems.

Clearly, there were not only no easy answers but quite possibly no answers at all. Seliktar examines systematically and in depth the answers that were offered by and to policymakers and opinion makers. The resulting volume does much to address what went wrong in what is quite arguably the most important issue in U.S. politics and intellectual debate since the Vietnam War. What is especially refreshing here is that the author does not fall into the predictable and tendentious partisan debate, which has had far too much impact on the effort to understand and explain the Iraq issue.

BARRY RUBIN

Introduction: The Theory and Practice of Predicting Political Change

Coming at the heels of September 11 that looms large in the pantheon of American intelligence failures, Operation Iraqi Freedom has focused the limelight on the way in which the United States predicts and manages political change.

Prediction and foreign policy making are closely related. Consciously or subconsciously, policy decisions rest on predictions of a likely course of future events. Henry Kissinger (1981, 283–284) equated foreign policy making with "our ability to perceive trends and dangers before they become overwhelming." Officials must act "when the scope for action is often the least; when certain knowledge is at hand, the scope for creative action has often disappeared" and when "judgments about the future cannot be proved true when they are made."

Given the difficulties involved in this dictum, an enormous intellectual effort to identify sources of predictive failures has been afoot for more than half a century. Following the pioneering work of Roberta Wohlstetter (1962) on Pearl Harbor, a large body of literature has dealt with military-strategic as well as political forecasting. While strategic and political change focuses on different dimensions of international reality, they both are susceptible to the same type of predictive errors. Logically conceived, prediction is comparable to a form of statistical inference. In every predictive episode, evidence is assessed and probability assigned to the "hypothesis" that an event will or will not occur. Prognosticators run the risk of committing two types of inferential errors. They can either reject a "true hypothesis," that is, decide that an event will not take place when, in fact, it is going to occur, or accept a "false hypothesis," that is, decide that an event will take place when it will not occur. Experts have worked to eliminate both types of errors, but instances where adverse events were not predicted have, understandably, attracted the most attention.

Failures range from minimal to fundamental and are grouped in four categories. In the first two—known as residuals and errors—the actual prediction of the event is successful, but the time frame is off by a certain margin. The failure in these categories does not necessitate any change in basic theory and/or predictive methodology. In the third category, the miss is known as an outliner—the error is large enough to warrant revision of the methodology and application used by the community of practitioners, but the basic theory is still viewed as adequate. In the last category, the miss is so great that, in terms of philosophy of science, it becomes an anomaly. An anomaly casts doubts on the underlying theory used by practitioners, and triggers a revision at the epistemic level of knowledge, commonly referred to as a paradigm.

The role of such fundamental failures can be best understood in terms of Thomas Kuhn's analysis of revolutionary change in knowledge. In his famous work on the structure of scientific revolution, Kuhn postulated that in routine times, a set of agreed upon fundamental concepts are used to analyze a situation. These deep-seated concepts known as master theories or paradigms dominate the field of a given intellectual endeavor and dictate the standards of rational inquiry. They form the "entire constellation of beliefs, values, technologies... shared by the members of a given community" (Kuhn 1970, 175). The dominant paradigm ordains what question will arise, what form of explanations will be accepted, and what interpretations will be recognized as legitimate. As long as the paradigm is not challenged, its normalcy is accepted widely. In the wake of a severe crisis though, the dominant paradigm is questioned and overthrown. These paradigmatic battles, which are fought at the very frontiers of rationality, dictate how the community of practitioners looks at the relevant reality. When a new paradigm wins, its novel and "revolutionary" perceptions become routine and "normal."

Although Kuhn was primarily concerned with the scientific community, his work can be applied to the study of prediction. The assumption here is that foreign policy practitioners use paradigms to analyze political reality, present and future. As one scholar put it, without such paradigms—a set of rules and standards for evaluating facts—"the policymaker is lost... all problems, approaches, facts and possible courses of action seem equally plausible" (Shafer 1988, 34). Another added "even the naïve practitioner who insists that he makes every decision solely on the facts at hand operates with an implicit assumption of what the future will be like" (Rothestein 1972, 159).

Discerning how paradigms may shape perceptions of political reality, however, is not easy. Traditional models of foreign policy decision making do not focus explicitly on the epistemic of "understanding" that is so crucial to this endeavor. The rational choice model, the bureaucratic politics model, and the crisis behavior model have either emphasized the political, environmental, and structural dimension of policymaking or have analyzed the process through which a collective understanding of a situation is reached.

The cognitive approach is closer to the issue of epistemology as, in the words of a prominent scholar, the belief system of foreign policy practitioners is a "set of lenses through which information concerning the physical and social environment is received" (Holsti 1962). But even the leading researchers in the field have failed to agree on how the two elements in the "cognitive map" of actors—broad fundamentals and the more narrowly proscribed instrumental beliefs—interact in discerning changing realities. A perusal of the cognitive belief literature hints at the source of these difficulties. A dominant assumption of this model is that key decision makers in charge of appraising the situation can be identified readily, and that their beliefs and perceptions can be deduced through cognitive mapping, simulation, or other analytical devises. Yet from an epistemic standpoint, this assumption is too static and limited. Studies on how bureaucracies "think" reveal that a collective understanding of the situation is arrived at, as a result of the performance of a large number of individuals who apply concepts from an "analytical communal inventory." Such inventories are formed through complex and ill-defined intellectual interactions among foreign policy actors, bureaucratic experts, scholars, and journalists.

Studies of foreign policy culture offer an alternative for tracking paradigms used in discerning political change. This large body of literature shows how enduring patterns of thought, symbols, and values affect policy deliberations and inform perception of the future. Although direct empirical links between prevalent intellectual modes and foreign policy practitioners are hard to demonstrate, they are necessarily pervasive. One scholar used the image from Indian cosmology to describe how fundamental beliefs affect policymakers: "The table at which policymakers sit is like the platform . . . on which the world stands: under it is a pyramid of arbitrary assumptions, untested and indeed untestable hypothesis and imprecise measures" (Staniland 1991, 275–276). While unquestionably true, this definition is too broad to capture the paradigmatic assumptions that underlie a given forecasting episode.

To go beyond these limits requires a more dialectically oriented psychological, sociological, and ethnographic approach. Ralph Pettman (1975), an authority on epistemology of foreign policy, argued that in identifying the paradigms that determine how practitioners conceive of foreign realities, the entire community of discourse on a given issue should be studied. More recently, Giandomenico Majone (1989, 161–164), in his *Evidence, Argument and Persuasion in the Policy Process* formalized this proposition. Majone defined the *discursive community* as all those who share an active interest in a certain policy domain; scholars, public intellectuals, political actors, lay experts, journalist, and others, because such a community is jointed loosely and its members have different professional, ideological, and intellectual commitments, and the focus of inquiry should involve the *entire discourse* rather than *select* participants.

The use of the output of a discursive community for understanding how forecasting occurs makes it possible to combine the features of the more traditional approaches to decision making with elements of political culture and the epistemology of collective concept-use. Unfortunately, like many sociological constructs, a discursive community is a somewhat loose set of assumptions and concepts. The complexity and opacity of the discursive process pose a considerable analytical problem. In particular, the influence wielded by academics and intellectuals is seldom direct or measurable. To quote one scholar, "[I]deas are not a consumer good shipped from intellectual warehouses . . . to be retailed in executive branches or Capitol Hill" (J.A. Smith 1993, 49). Tanter and Ullman (1972, 3) asserted more bluntly that policymakers "have seldom given much heed to the writings of theorists." Yet other observers noted that the "thinking professions" have a major, albeit indirect and diffuse impact on policy; they create a "climate of ideas," define the situation, and mold the perspectives of the policymakers. Over time, these ideas come to amount to an "almost rigid, congealed mass of conventional wisdom" (Etzioni-Halevy 1985, 26). Given their pervasiveness, "academic pens leave a mark . . . policymakers basic understanding of their world seldom differs fundamentally from social scientists" (Shafer 1988, 12).

An analysis of the discourse process of the foreign policy community is especially useful in discussing American perceptions of the Middle East, which have been heavily shaped by academic-intellectual paradigms. Indeed, this book is based on the assumption that a dialectical relation exists between such paradigms and the way in which collective concepts inform politicians, bureaucrats, and intelligence officials. To restate the Kuhnian proposition, the paradigm or paradigms developed in the relevant branches of social knowledge influence the epistemology of foreign policy practitioners who are in charge of predicting and managing political change. In turn, political reality will influence the structuring and restructuring of these paradigms. This interaction is essentially inseparable; however, for analytical purposes, elements of this process can be isolated.

First, this study discusses the series of paradigms that have evolved in the discourse on political change in the Middle East. The widely popular developmental model dominated the field in the first decades after World War II. Alternatively called modernization theory, it postulated that Muslim societies in the region are ultimately destined to secularize, westernize, and develop a market economy. The failure of the third world to follow the prescriptive path of the West, as well as the war in Vietnam, discredited the tenets of developmentalism and popularized a neo-Marxist critique of modernization theory. Known as dependency, or *dependencia*, the new paradigm predicted that the Middle East would reject what was described as the Western-imposed colonial and imperialist model of development in favor of a secular-socialist one. However, the fundamentalist revolution in Iran and the growth of Islamic fundamentalism and terrorism had undermined the dependency paradigm and plunged the Middle East studies into a paradigmatic crisis.

In the struggle to explain the failure of the Arab countries to follow the global wave of democratization that came in the wake of the collapse of the Soviet Union, two rival epistemic communities emerged. The first comprised scholars in the Middle East Association Studies (MESA) who, often influenced by the work of Edward Said, have pinned the blame on the ongoing Arab-Israeli struggle and American support for Israel. The second, closely associated with the neoconservative movement, postulated that, unwilling to democratize, the Arab rulers utilized the Middle East conflict as an alternative source of legitimacy. Not incidentally, neoconservatives advocated an American campaign of democratization as a way of solving the conflict and stabilizing the region.

Second, this book analyzes how these paradigms affected American policy toward Iraq. Since the discursive approach presupposes the cross-fertilization between practitioners and the dominant paradigm of the day, it was only natural that the initial contacts between the United States and Iraq were underpinned by assumptions embedded in developmentalism. The leading hypothesis in Washington was that Saddam Hussein could be moderated and Iraq could be brought into the "community of nations" in exchange for economic and diplomatic concession. However, Hussein's unpredictable behavior, culminating in the invasion of Kuwait in 1990, shattered this belief. A search for alternative approaches was launched by the Clinton administration, in the midst of growing anxieties over a lethal combination of Islamic terrorism and its state sponsors. Amid Clinton's halting efforts to contain Iraq, the neoconservatives, though still an intellectual minority in the field of Middle East studies, were making a growing argument for regime change in Iraq.

Third, this work demonstrates how, in the wake of the September 11, the MESA community was disgraced because of its vehement denials of a mega-terrorist attack, thus elevating the standing of its epistemic rival. Adopted by President George W. Bush, the regime change option was applied first to Afghanistan and then Iraq. However, as the planned democratization envisaged by Operation Iraqi Freedom turned into sectarian violence, the neoconservatives, along with the Bush administration, found themselves on the defensive.

The organization of this book reflects the above research strategy. Chapter 1 provides a theoretical discussion of the evolution of the paradigms through which the United States perceived the developments in the Middle East. Chapters 2–5 use a *chronological-thematical* approach to the analysis of American policy toward Iraq. Chapter 2 details the failed effort of the Reagan and Bush Senior administrations to modify the foreign policy behavior of Iraq. Chapter 3 analyzes how the Clinton administration, facing a growing Islamist terrorist threat, struggled to contain what it labeled as the rogue Iraqi regime. Chapter 4 discusses the paradigmatic change triggered by September 11 and its effect on the younger Bush administration's decision to institute a regime change in Iraq in order to forestall an emerging threat of WMD (Weapons of Mass destruction) and international terrorism. Chapter 5 analyzes the politics of the intelligence debate prior to Operation Iraqi Freedom.

Chapter 6 offers a rigorous comparison of the assumptions that underpinned the decision to invade Iraq, including the presence of WMD and the prospects for an Iraqi democracy to the postwar reality. Chapter 7 provides a systematic analysis of the predictive predicament posed by Iraq at the paradigmatic, policy, and intelligence levels and offers some insights into how these predicaments apply to other problems in American foreign policy.

1

Paradigmatic Views of Political Change in the Middle East: Arab Exceptionalism and the International Order

Starting with Aristotle and Plato, the search for principles that underlie political change has been a staple of Western philosophy. This quest has been made particularly perplexing because of the seemingly inexplicable nature of political change. One scholar wrote that "ideologies stand for centuries and then one day the temples are empty." Socrates speculated that changes in legitimacy formulas precede political change, setting off a long quest for uncovering the way in which communal norms crystallize into a collective belief system and a corresponding political structure, only to be eroded by further changes (Selilktar 1986).

However, analyzing legitimacy has been problematic, prompting Samuel Huntington (1993, 46), a leading authority on political change, to note that legitimacy is "a mushy concept that political scientists do well to avoid." As another scholar put it, the task is comparable to "a surgical probing for that which is unseen, but nevertheless crucial for survival" (quoted in Bialer 1986, 418).

Much of the insight into the way in which legitimacy norms evolve in the collective belief system was derived from anthropological studies. Linton (1945) postulated that in order to survive, a group legitimizes parts of its perceptual-ideational beliefs into an all-encompassing worldview. Such a collective belief system forms the parameters of social order in a given society at a given period of time. The discursive perspective holds that norms of legitimacy are internalized by group members and translated into actions through repetitive roles. In due course, these roles crystallize into structures—institutions and processes—that shape and bind the collective through an endless stream of politics.

Douglas (1992, 43, 133–134) posited that the three dimensions that require a normative consensus are rules for gaining membership and territory, principles for establishing an authority system, and rules for distributing wealth. These principles or *validity claims* are used to build the three axes of the collective belief system. The first axis is horizontal and compromises the principles of group boundary criteria for granting membership and acquiring territory known as group *membership/territory* legitimacy. The second axis is vertical and denotes the principles upon which the authority system rests, defined as *authority system* legitimacy. The third axis is diagonal and articulates the principles of *distributive justice* that bind group membership and authority system together.

Weberian sociology holds that membership/territorial legitimacy has evolved from the *Gemeinschaft* community in which validity claims were based on kinship into *Gesellschaft* association that ties members through "feeling of interdependence" and a secular "community of faith." The end product of this process is nationalism, which puts the loyalty to the nation-state above primordial attachments.

Authority system legitimacy comprises a set of validity claims that justify the creation of a system of controls over a group residing in a defined territory. Since controls involve an exercise of power, validity claims help to ensure members' compliance. Max Weber identified three pure validity claims: (1) rational grounds—a belief in the legality of rule; (2) traditional grounds—based on the sanctity of traditions and the legitimacy of those who exercise authority according to certain traditional tenets; and (3) charismatic ground—resting on the commitment to a certain individual and the order revealed to him. Numinous legitimacy, based on claims of divine origin, spanned the traditional and charismatic categories, leading many to prefer the *numinous-traditional* label. Weber's taxonomy has generated an enormous critical literature, not the least because of the ambiguity surrounding rational legitimacy. To those who hold that rational legitimacy should translate into popular sovereignty, the democratic process of electing representatives is the only legitimate form for setting up an authority system. The latter has been often referred to as *civic*-based validity claims.

Distributive justice is part of a larger domain of social justice, defined as a series of principles for assigning particular things to particular individuals (Galston 1980, 5). Distributive justice is concerned with the more limited question of "who distributes to whom, in virtue of what criterial characteristic, by what procedures, with what distributive outcomes." To satisfy the requirements of social justice, distributive schemes have been based on a number of validity claims. Three pure validity claims can be identified: (1) ascriptive-traditional claims that underpin traditional economics; (2) utilitarian-productive claims that underline market economies; and (3) egalitarian principles that inform communist economies.

Much as the notion that political change is driven by changing validity claims in one or more of the axes of the collective belief system is theoretically compelling, there are no easy ways to track the dynamics of the societal discourse that generates such change. What is more, study of political reality is shaped by a set of distinctive meta-assumptions, creating distinctive paradigms to which observers, whether knowingly or not subscribe to.

Methodology of Political Change: The Paradigmatic Views of Political Reality

Central to all investigation of social life is the idea that it involves a philosophy of science and a corresponding theory of human nature. First, there is the *ontological* question that divides those who consider the "reality" under investigation to be external to an individual and therefore objective and those who view it as a subjective product of one's mind. Second, there is the *epistemological* dispute between positivists who maintain that it is possible to obtain knowledge which is "hard" and capable of being transferred into tangible "true" and "false" findings and antipositivists who suggest that knowledge is "softer, more subjective and even transcendent." Third, the debate about *human nature* has created a dichotomy between the secular notion that humans are conditioned in a mechanistic way by their environment and the religious concept of a divinely informed human will (Burrell and Morgan 1985, 1–3).

Reflecting the behavioral revaluation in American social sciences, scholars in the 1950s showed a clear preference for a highly positivist and nomothetic view of political change. Pioneered by Talcott Parsons (1951) and his student David Easton (1953, 1965), the system analysis of change used the mechanistic-deterministic properties of Newtonian physics to describe a closed and orderly process of change that could be measured in linear terms. Karl Deutsch (1963), an early follower of Parson, postulated that the deterministic properties of the system would make it easy to predict change by tracking a series of empirical indices. Almond and Verba (1965), another leading Parsonian, noted in his presidential address to the American Political Science Association that such exactitude was "exhilarating." These and other experts pointed out that their methodology makes prediction of the future entirely possible. As the eminent philosopher Karl Popper (1963, 3) put it, "[J]ust as astronomy can predict eclipse, it will be possible for sociology to predict revolutions."

The discovery of the alleged laws of political change could not have come at a more opportune moment for social scientists. As the cold war took hold, there was an increasing sense in Washington that political change in third world countries may breed instability and provide an opening for the Soviet Union. The Truman administration enlisted a large number of academics to both study and guide political change in this region. Inspired by such seminal figures as Max Milikan and Walt W. Rostow, this collective effort generated the developmental paradigm, also known as modernization theory.

The Developmental View of Change: Linear Progression toward the West

Three meta-assumptions were at the core of the developmental paradigm. Ontologically, the assumption was that political reality could be broken up into discrete parts amenable to statistical treatment. The companion epistemic assumption was that political beliefs form a fairly autonomous realm of attitudes shaped by meaningful forms of social experience such as education, income, or occupation. As for human nature, it involved postulated rationality derived from the secular humanistic view that human beings are imbued with a "natural rationality" that is deterministic. Such rationality was said to contrast sharply with religious beliefs that were labeled as "irrational." To conform to epistemic realism, social science literature either expunged reference to a supernatural reality or treated it as a pathological aberration.

Given these assumptions, it was easy for developmentalists to postulate that societies move from "primitive" (underdeveloped) stages to more "advanced" forms patterned on the secularized, democratic, and industrialized Western nation-state. The Parsonian-Eastonian system theory greatly facilitated this view. The West was considered to be a positive agent of change, with new skills and values diffusing into less developing areas. A study by the authoritative Committee on Comparative Development of the Social Research Council prognosticated that this type of change was political, would be incremental, and orderly (Binder et al. 1971).

Since the problem of nation building was high on the developmental agenda, scholars tackled the issue of membership/territory first. By and large, tribalism and other ethnic and ethnoreligious sentiments were consigned to a residual category of traditional societies. Deutsch (1953, 1963) asserted that there is a direct correlation between levels of socioeconomic development and a decline in primordial forms of attachment. To measure the alleged progress in nation building, Deutsch devised a series of quantitative indices such as levels of literacy, rates of industrialization, and volume of international communication.

Developmentalists were also greatly interested in the norms that undergird changes in the authority system of different societies. During the heydays of behaviorism, modernization theory held that societies are bound to delegitimize traditional-numinous norms and embrace rational-civic ones. Leading liberal theologians added their prestigious support to this prognosis. Harvard's Harvey Cox (1965, 63) argued that modern man is becoming pragmatic and profane and wastes no time thinking about the "ultimate or religious questions." By the time Stark and Glock (1968) published their influential book on the subject, the notion that numinous-religious legitimacy, especially of the fundamentalist variety, was "primitive" and doomed to pass from history was widely accepted, leading to the "God is dead" postulate. According to one observer, fundamentalists were treated as a "bizarre" spectacle and "denizens of the zoo" (Warren 1979).

Fired by nomothetic zeal, modernization theorists tuned these ideas into a linear law of transition. In their famous study, Almond and Verba (1965) purported to show that societies go through stages of parochial, subject, and civic cultures. Starting from the parochial base where attitudes toward the political realm are suffused with numinous and ethnoreligious norms, individuals were said to move on to a subject level that legitimizes the authority system through secular, albeit authoritarian norms. At the last stage of this linear progression, individuals were expected to develop civic participatory norms, an attitudinal structure prevalent in Western democracies. To demonstrate the validity of the linear transition law, modernization theorists quoted the work of the Dutch political scientist Arend Lijphart (1968) on the emergence of consociational democracy in the Netherlands. The much-celebrated consociational model purported to show that societies deeply divided along lines of ethnicity and religion could legitimize an authority system based on secular rationalistic norms.

Developmentalists were equally sure that norms of distributive justice are subject to a linear trajectory of change. Rostow (1964), the author of the developmental "bible," *The States of Economic Growth*, argued that as societies develop economically, they reject the validity claims based on ascription in favor of market-based meritocracy. Such a change was said to occur at the "takeoff" stage, triggering a transformation into a market economy based on the American model. From this perspective, markets offered the best antidote to the high levels of inequality present in traditional societies. In making this prediction, Rostow and his colleagues borrowed heavily from the pioneering work of Sergei Kuznet (1955) who demonstrated that, as the level of economic development rises, inequality declines.

As noted earlier, by reaching out to the academic community, the Truman administration hoped to develop a blueprint for blocking the third world's slide into the Soviet orbit. Developmentalism was a projection of American postwar optimism that political change could be managed and molded into a "desirable," that is, Western direction. However, by the mid-1960s, it became quite clear that none of the early assumptions worked: tribal and ethnic strife, often driven by religious differences, was tearing postcolonial societies apart, and brutal dictatorship sprouted where democracy was expected to flourish. More to the point, far from disappearing, economic inequality was seen as a major factor driving communist insurgencies around the globe. In the words of one discouraged observer, it became obvious that American effort will not create "a lot of little Americas around the world" (Campbell 1971, 181).

Delegitimized by the facts on the ground, developmentalism faced a serious challenge from the neo-Marxist *dependencia* (dependency) paradigm.

The Dependency View of Change: Linear Progression toward a Socialist Utopia

The dependency paradigm was developed by a number of mostly Latin American scholars who sought to challenge modernization and the American foreign policy that powered it. A mixture of Marxist and neo-Marxist concepts, *dependencia* was grounded in ontological nominalism, which is a subjective approach to social sciences and antipositivist epistemology that rejected the view that human behavior can be understood through empirical research on individual attitudes and intentions. Methodologically ideographic, the dependency paradigm followed the Marxist notion of subjective states of "false consciousness" that were said to be imposed on people by capitalism and its global manifestations—imperialism and colonialism.

Dependency scholars frequently denounced developmentalists as "butterfly collectors" who set up laws, categories, and other forms of classification. Paul Feyerabend (1975), the author of an elaborate neo-Marxist critique of positivism, urged a rebellion against "method" and "liberation" from constraints of empirically based social inquiry. As one of the radical scholars noted, "a moralist needs no evidence other than his senses to judge something right or wrong, and [needs] no elaborate scientific calculus to ascertain what the proper course of action should be" (quoted in Kadushin 1974, 163). In what was certainly an opportune coincidence, the French critical school of Michele Foucault, Jack Derrida, and Jack Lacan pioneered the highly influential postmodernist approach that celebrated subjectivity and relativism in lieu of epistemic positivism and "objective truth."

Unlike their behavioral counterparts who advocated value-free research, *dependencistas* emphasized the role of scholar as both the interpreter and shaper of social reality. To succeed in the latter mission, they followed the writings of the Italian Marxist Antonio Gramsci who urged scholars to be "agents of struggle" for change. According to the Gramscian formula, academics should offer a radical critique of society and social advocacy to change the discursive practices of their society and promote alternative values and norms. Thus, in an effort to change the ruling paradigm, critical inquiry is aimed at raising the "true consciousness of people"; "once they appreciate how oppressed they are, they can act to transform the world" (Gaba 1990, 24).

Using these subjective tools, radical scholars challenged the evolutionary trajectory of modernization theory. Rather than embracing the model of liberal democracy as a source of progress worthy of emulation, they regarded it as the root of third world "peripheral" position and economic backwardness. *Dependencistas* noted that terms such as "backward" and "peripheral" described a third world that was not simply a rung or two below the West on the evolutionary ladder, but a location to which developing countries were permanently condemned by Western capitalism and colonialism.

Using the same logic, the dependency paradigm postulated a very different course for each of the three axes of the collective belief system construct. As for membership/territory legitimacy, radical scholars criticized the notion that primordial allegiances are the hallmark of traditional societies. In their view, tribal and ethnic strife was manufactured by Western colonial powers in a bid to divide and rule (Galtung 1971). In the words of one scholar, it was the colonial "administrative penetration" that inflamed primordial sentiments in formerly peaceful and cohesive societies (Newbury 1983). Influential neo-Marxist world theorists such as Immanuel Wallerstein (1997) and Richard Falk (1976) predicted that once capitalism and colonialism were eliminated, people would legitimize inclusive norms of membership leading to a one-world alliance.

As for authority system legitimacy, dependency scholars agreed that numinous-traditional validity claims are destined to fade from history.

However, they emphatically rejected the forecast that such "outmoded" sentiments would be replaced by a Western-style civic society and a matching democratic system. Neo-Marxists described the apparatus of democracy—elections, political parties, and legislature—as mere "formalism," or worse, an elite mechanism to hold the masses in check. They argued that in the future, such formalism would be replaced with processes that reflect the deeper human need for "conscious formation" and "institutions and processes that serve people" (Cardoso and Faletto 1979, xxix; Evans 1979, 48; Galtung 1976).

While casting doubts on democratic formalism, neo-Marxist observers extolled the virtues of "substantive democracy," a euphemism for a society guided by egalitarian principles of distributive justice. Thus, third world countries were believed to shed their dependency status and reach a socialist "golden age." Cuba was often mentioned as a possible model, followed by China or even Vietnam (Cardos and Faletto 1979; Fagen 1978, 299; Packenham 1992, 30). Samir Amin (1982), an Egyptian neo-Marxist economist, claimed that the Middle East economies would similarly embrace a pure form of socialism.

Initially, neo-Marxist scholarship was limited to the fringes of American social sciences. However, within less than two decades, the dependency paradigm had managed to permeate mainstream thinking on Latin America and other underdeveloped regions. Mainstream scholars took to writing that "the concept of development is now widely scorned," adding that "many doubt that the Western path is a desirable path" (Brown 1985; Packenham 1992, 238; Payne 1984, 1). Faced with a massive vote of no confidence, the founding fathers of the behavioral revolution crumbled. In an extraordinary about-face, Easton (1969) spoke about a "post behavioral revolution" and urged his colleagues to focus on "contemporary needs" rather than methodological sophistication.

The call to political advocacy fell on the receptive ears of a younger generation of scholars in humanities and social sciences. The expansion of universities in the 1960s and early 1970s created positions for a large number of New Left activist faculty. These academics formed the basis of the so-called New Class, whom Lipset (1979, 67) defined as "socially liberal or radical, highly critical intelligentsia." This cohort was swelled by scholars and public intellectuals who found employment in the increasing number of leftist think tanks such as the radical Institute for Policy Studies established in 1963 and its many affiliates.

The younger scholars exhibited a deep commitment to egalitarian norms and a matching disdain for American capitalism and liberal democracy. Although not every member of the New Class went so far as to proclaim, in the words of Fidel Castro, that "capitalist nations would pass into the trashcan of history," predictions about the coming crisis of legitimacy in capitalist societies were common. Much of this prognosis was influenced by the enormously popular work of Jurgen Habermas (1975), a German neo-Marxist philosopher, who stipulated that once capitalism runs out of "payoffs," people were bound to embrace socialism. Robert Heilbroner, a prominent economist and a vice president of the American Economic Association declared that socialism was the "collective expression for mankind" (quoted in Taubman 1974). The leading liberal economist John Kenneth Galbraith (1967, 332) asserted that socialist planning holds significant advantages over laissez-faire economy. Bogdan Denitch (1979, 8), a noted socialist sociologist, felt confident enough to proclaim that the "general optimism [about capitalism] is replaced by an increasingly fashionable pessimism."

The spread of neo-Marxism provoked some tepid response from modernization theorists. Almond (1990, 13–19; 1996), a frequent target of the radical critique, protested against "ideological propagandists" in scholarly garb. Some International Relations (IR) experts complained that dependency has more in common with Marxism than international relations theory (Holsti 1978). However, the notion that egalitarian norms are more legitimate than other forms of wealth distribution was virtually unbeatable in the increasingly leftist academy. Galbraith and other prominent social thinkers stipulated that future political change would bring a convergence of capitalism and communism. The convergence theory became so popular that Olaf Helmer (1986), the inventor of the Delphi technique and a top authority on forecasting, declared that by the early 1990s, the Soviet Union would incorporate some features of market economy while the United States would adopt many socialist policies.

Political Change in the Middle East: Developmental and Dependency Visions of the Future in the Region

The emergence of the United States as superpower transformed Middle East studies from a European-style inquiry known as orientalism to a multidisciplinary field where traditional historians mixed with behaviorally oriented social scientists. When the Middle East Studies Association (MESA) was established in 1966, it presided over a network of departments and centers, many in elite universities that attracted considerable financial support from government and private foundations.

Reflecting the developmental optimism, leading MESA authorities were able to report that the Middle East was moving from a traditional society toward a modern one as measured by rates of literacy, urbanization, and industrialization (Lerner 1958). A top expert used the metaphor of "shattered glass" to describe the alleged break with traditional legitimacy; he asserted that the Arab professional class was articulating new rational-legitimacy claims (Halpern 1963). A 1963 conference sponsored by the American University Filed Staff concluded that the "secularization process" in the Middle East "was fundamental" and irreversible (Silvert 1964, 103). In his book on Arab search for legitimacy, Michael Hudson (1977, 17), the director of the influential Georgetown Center for Contemporary Arab Studies, found a growing "irrelevance of Islamic standards and criteria."

Those looking for evidence that the region was well on the path toward a Western-style liberal democracy most often touted the example of Lebanon. In a conference on "Lebanese Democracy," Leonard Binder (1966, ix) complained that "few people credited Lebanese political achievements as the purposeful accomplishment of a mature society." Lijphart (1968) gave his seal of approval, writing that in spite of its deep divisions, Lebanon was moving toward a consociational democracy.

If Lebanon was a prime academic exhibit, Iran's developmental trajectory was crucial for American foreign policy in the Gulf. After the CIA helped to quash a challenge from the nationalist Prime Minister Mohammed Mossadeq in 1953, consecutive administrations tried to help the shah to modernize his county. Acting upon advice of Washington experts, the shah launched the White Revolution, an ambitious land reform, speeded up industrialization and civic reforms, including an effort to equalize the status of women. This process of westernization and secularization was deemed so successful that a leading expert on Iran predicted that the influence of the ulema, the Islamic clergy, was dwindling to the point of irrelevance (Keddie 1972). Looking at such an impressive array of objective indices of modernization, academic experts estimated that Iran would join the club of fully developed countries by the end of the twentieth century (Amirie and Twitchell 1978; Lenczowksi 1978; Looney 1977).

Amid general optimism, questions about the legitimacy discourse of Islamic societies in Iran and elsewhere in the region went largely ignored. Weber himself expressed doubt whether "oriental societies" could secularize enough to sustain rational legitimacy claims without going through a Reformation-like process that purged numinous and other "irrational" elements from the European collective belief system. Indeed, a handful of Muslim "Weberians" such as Taha Hussein and Malik Bennabi urged a similar reformation in order to secularize and modernize Muslim countries.

For those conversant enough with the internal Muslim discourse, the reception of Hussein and Bennabi's advocacy for a Muslim Reformation was not encouraging. Sayed Qutab, a major Islamist theoretician, attacked would-be secularizers and warned that the westernization project would turn Muslims into a *Jahil* society, described in the Koran as faithless and ignorant of divine guidance (Safi 1994, 155–156, 167–168). In a similar vein, the Iranian intellectual Jalal Al-e Ahmad accused his countrymen of "Westoxication," a form of corrupt and debased Western identity. Anxiety about modernization and westernization prompted Ayatollah Ruhallah Khomeni, then a largely unknown Iranian cleric, to foment a fundamentalist movement along the lines pioneered by the Muslim Brotherhood in Egypt. Analyzing such trends, Bernard Lewis (1976), published a prescient essay "The Return of Islam," which rejected the fashionable modernization theory. Lewis wrote that religion was emerging as the primary form of Arab legitimacy and predicted the rise of Islamic extremism. In 1978, in an effort to warn the Carter administration, which wanted to replace the shah with a liberal government, Lewis translated parts of

Veelyaat al Fakiq: Hokumat e-Islam, Khomeini's programmatic book on the virtues of Islamic theocracy.

While Lewis' reservations went virtually unnoticed, Middle East dependency-oriented watchers made important inroads against the developmental creed. Leading the way was the Institute for Policy Studies which in 1971 funded the Middle East Research and Information Project (MERIP) and the Transnational Institute (TNI) under the Chilean communist Orlando Letelier. In 1975 MERIP created a storm with a survey of Middle East studies entitled "Middle East Studies in the United States." The report accused leading MESA professors, including Leonard Binder, of practicing academic "imperialism" and using their scholarship "to subjugate" the people of the Middle East (Johnson and Tucker 1975). MERIP and TNI's organ *Race and Class* mocked the notion that countries in the region were well on their way toward a market economy. Evoking the "false consciousness" argument, they claimed that Western colonialism and multinational companies thwarted the foundation of a "genuine democracy," based on egalitarian distributive justice system. As Fred Halliday (1979), a neo-Marxist scholar and TNI fellow asserted, Iran, far from being a showcase for American developmentalism, was striving to become an India or even a Yugoslavia of the Middle East.

Radical scholars were particularly encouraged by the work of Ali Shariati, a leading Iranian philosopher, who developed a novel synthesis between Islam and socialism. Shariati postulated that political change in the Middle East would entail a return to a genuine Islamic identity and an embrace of an egalitarian economy based on the Koran. The highly influential Shariati inspired a whole generation of Iranian activists such as Abolhasan Bani Sader who joined forces with the growing fundamentalist movement of Ayatollah Khomeini, to advocate the so-called Islamic-socialist Third Way (Seliktar 2000, 61).

The civil war in Lebanon and the 1979 fundamentalist revolution in Iran discredited the developmental paradigm and disgraced its intellectual architects. A special issue of *Race and Class* (1979) accused many "orientalists," including Binder, of being in the service of "imperialism." One contributor chastised James Bill and Marvin Zonis, two top Middle East experts, of failing to analyze the "issue of dependency" in Iran and "for hedging their predictions" on the shah (Schaar 1979). Thomas Ricks (1980, 267–268), a Georgetown professor active in the anti-shah movement in the United States, noted that the "Iranian revolution challenges the 'objective' and 'value-free' theories of social science" and asserted that future scholarship should be considered" either in the service of the Iranian struggle for national independence or in the service of U.S. interventionist policies and the Pahlavi monarchy."

However, it was Edward Said's *Orientalism* (1978) that cemented the view that Western Middle Eastern scholarship was an intellectual construct aimed at legitimizing imperialism and colonialism. The book, which achieved iconic status in the United States and elsewhere, drew from a number of sources. Said acknowledged his intellectual debt to Noam Chomsky who had offered a scathing denunciation of American scholarship in "service of the war in Vietnam" in his *American Power and the New Mandarin*. Said also mentioned Foucault's postmodernism and Amin's critique of capitalism and imperialism in the Middle East as fundamental to his thinking.

Said's forceful critique of "orientalism" was accompanied by an equally powerful claim, supported by the Iranian fiasco, that Western scholars fundamentally misperceived the cultural realities of the region. Said (1981) expanded on these themes in another academic bestseller, *Covering Islam,* which amounted to a wholesale denunciation of the founding generation of MESA experts as "policy hacks" working for Washington. Coming atop the leftward shift in academia, the Said theory inspired a new generation of scholars and helped to radically change the field of Middle East studies.

THE RECONSTRUCTED MESA AND ITS CRITICS

Said's assertion that native observers have a "privileged" view of reality went hand in hand with the increase in the number of graduate students and scholars of Middle East origin in the United States. In 1971, MESA rolls carried about 20 percent of scholars from the Middle East; by the early 1990s, approximately half of its members hailed from the region (Aswad 1993). This trend was very much in line with the epistemics of critical scholarship that extolled "privileged" understanding of reality born out of "indigenous experience." Indeed, Said (1993, xxvii) welcomed this new "nativist" generation as an antidote to "cultural Western domination" and promised that a reinvigorated MESA would provide a more realistic view of the Middle East and Islam.

Acting upon the Gramscian imperative, MESA became highly activist and politicized, with the Israeli-Palestinian conflict leading the agenda. A 1990 survey of Middle Eastern programs found that as much as 73 percent of the courses emphasized the Arab-Israeli conflict (De Atkine 1994). Taking up the Palestinian cause was a natural extension of Said's notion that European anti-Arab prejudice and colonial interests drove the creation of the state of Israel. Said himself joined the Palestinian National Council; Rashid Khalidi and Hisham Sharabi were heavily involved in promoting the cause of the Palestinian Liberation Organization (Khoury 1999; Said 1994; Sharabi 1988).

The centrality of the Palestinian oppression in the MESA model of scholarship and its wholesale attack on the "orientalist," that is, alternative points of view, mobilized critics such as Bernard Lewis, Binder, Fouad Ajami, and Daniel Pipes. In an early exchange, Lewis (1982), whom Said depicted as the quintessential orientalist, denounced Said for providing a deeply flawed history of the field and for turning an important problem into "political polemic and personal abuse." Daniel Pipes, the head of the Middle East Forum and its newly established journal *Middle East Quarterly (MEQ)* took a lead in criticizing MESA standards. A review article in the *MEQ* concluded that politicization, apologetics, and intense preoccupation with the Palestinian issue rendered MESA scholars irrelevant in the national discourse on the Middle East. According to its author, "[I]ndigenization has changed MESA from an American organization interested in the Middle East to a Middle Eastern organization meeting in the Untied States"; it provided a platform for scholars who were "loyal to their country" not to their scholarship (De Atkine 1994, 9–10).

Martin Kramer (2001, 20–31, 44–60, 117), a scholar at the Moshe Dayan Center for Middle East and African Studies at Tel Aviv University drew on these and other themes to produce a comprehensive critique of MESA in his *The Ivory Towers on Sand: The Failure of Middle East Studies in America.* Kramer charged that, reflecting Said's writings, much of MESA scholarship tended to be short on empirical research and long on polemics. He noted that the influx of Arab money, which underwrote many new Middle East centers in the 1980s, shaped their research agenda and colored their findings. Kramer concluded that "Middle East studies under the post-orientalists had become a remote enclave of esoteric and irrelevant endeavor resting on an ever-narrowing base of moral support."

Published shortly after September 11, the book, in the words of one observer "rattled teacups at faculty clubs," and produced a storm of publicity well beyond the academy (Gause III 2002, 164). While MESA advocates dismissed the book as a "politically motivated polemic," Kramer pressed his charge that, in spite of their "privileged" understanding, the younger generation of experts did even less well than the older orientalists (Lochman 2004, 264). Worse, the failure to predict the September attack was driven by a willful denial of the dangers of Islamic fundamentalism and the rush to "obscure Islam." In follow-up articles, Kramer (2002a, 2002b), described the MESA community as closed, "self-referential, not accountable to anyone" and "impervious" to outsider advice. Its "group think" mentality, bolstered by a skewed peer review system "enslaved" scholars to a "dogmatic adherence to the academic fashion of the day." Pipes (2003a) added that MESA was apologetic and intolerant, adversarial to American interests, and abusive in its treatment of dissenting scholars.

Much of the acrimony between MESA and its critics was related to the so-called issue of Arab exceptionalism and the treatment of Islamic terrorism.

Arab Exceptionalism: Clashing Views on the Source of Authoritarianism in the Middle East

After decades of setbacks, the wave of democratic reforms in South America, Africa, and eventually Eastern Europe seemed to have vindicated the original assumption of the developmental paradigm. A new wave of political science theorizing postulated that this so-called Third Wave democratization was driven by ideas spread by nascent civil society in the newly democratizing countries (Heo and Tan 2001; Huntington 1993, 1996; Ledeen 1996; Shain 1994; Wantchekon 2004).

Translated into the language of legitimacy, democratic norms were said to be introduced into the collective discourse, where they delegitimized the validity claims of the authoritarian authority system. In the words of one observer, the "discursive venue" is the most important one, because this is the arena "where domination is undermined" (Shapiro 2003). Many academic observers utilized the newly fashionable contagion model to explain how political change occurs. Accordingly, ideas spread in a contagion-like manner: after reaching a tipping point they become pervasive enough to challenge the old norms and lead to new political structures and processes. By mid-1990s, the normally fractious field of political science was almost unanimous that civil society is critical to the process of legitimizing democratic norms.

With democracy spreading around the world, there was a great deal of expectation that the contagion model would change the Middle East as well. The Social Science Research Council of New York launched an ambitious program "Retreating States and Expanding Societies" in 1987. After its initial financial stumble, the Ford Foundation stepped in by funding it and aptly renamed it "Civil Society in the Middle East" program under the direction of August Richard Norton, a former professor of Middle East studies at West Point. Norton and his team argued that secular Arab regimes suffered from an acute and persistent crisis of legitimacy and cautiously predicted that sooner rather than later the burgeoning forces of Arab civil society would sweep them away (Norton 1993; Norton and Wright 1994–95; Sivan 1990). Many in the MESA community had similar expectations. However, the spreading Islamic revival forced these and other observers to engage in a broader debate about the compatibility of Islam and democracy.

Leading MESA scholars such as John Esposito (1992, 7), John Voll (1994), Richard W. Bulliet (1993, 1994), and Yvonne Haddad (1991) maintained that Islamism is a legitimate political expression quite compatible with democracy. They pleaded for a "more sophisticated" and less ethnocentric understanding of Islamic politics. The notion that democracy should not be "boxed" into the narrow confines of a Western parliamentary system was not new. During the cold war, the dominant revisionist school of Sovietology found many "democratic equivalents" in the Soviet system of governance. It was now the turn of Middle East experts to urge Americans to "transcend their narrow, ethnocentric conceptualization of democracy" to envisage an "Islamic democracy that may create effective systems of popular participation, though unlike the Westminster model or the American system" (Voll and Esposito 1994, 11). Bulliet added that Western definition of democracy was part of a "hegemonic discourse of Western cultural imperialism" and urged to view democracy "within world term in which there is a dialogue of discourse and not simply a Western hegemonic discourse" (quoted in Kramer 2001, 50).

For those who were not totally assured that Islamism was a functional equivalent of civic democracy, MESA scholars were ready to unveil the theory of Islamic Reformation. In this view, after a poor start in Iran, Islamism was moving into the direction of a separation of religion and state. To back this theory, MESA adopted the Iranian intellectual Abdoulkarim Soroushi who emerged as a leading critic of the restrictive theocracy in his country. Mohammed Khatami, a moderate Iranian president elected by a large majority, was viewed for a short period as an Islamic "Martin Luther." When Khatami failed to deliver, the hopes for an enlightened interpretation of Islam were vested in a Syrian engineer Muhammad Shahrur who produced a lengthy treatise on the rational reading of Islam. In the opinion of one scholar who showcased Shahrur at a MESA conference, the writings of Shahrur and other Islamic liberals signaled a change as profound in the Muslim world "as the Protestant Reformation was to Christendom" (Eickelman 1988, 82; 1993).

While holding out for a better future, these and other like-minded students of the Middle East cautioned that the Arab-Israeli conflict was a huge impediment to democratic change in the Middle East. Said (1978, 1979) inspired this line of reasoning by contending that the colonial implantation of a Jewish state thwarted the natural political processes in the region. Joel Beinin (1988), a Stanford historian and a ranking MESA leader, argued that Israel was a "garrison state" characterized by an economy geared toward military production and a society riveted by social and economic tension. In Beinin's view, such a configuration promoted a "more belligerent stand toward the Arab world."

For Said, Beinin and other MESA academics, the implication of this equation was clear; without first solving the Arab-Israeli conflict, there could be no meaningful democratization of the region. Over time, this assumption congealed into the epistemic understanding that the way to democracy in the Middle East "passes through Jerusalem." To recall, Kuhn's definition of a scientific paradigm entails the existence of *an epistemic community* that agrees on a cause-and-effect structure of explanation of natural phenomena. In humanities and social science, such a "generally accepted understanding about cause-and-effect linkage of set of phenomena considered important to society," is derived from "information scientific and nonscientific" that is considered "authoritative by the interested parties" (Haass 1991, 65).

Standing in the way of MESA efforts to "authoritatively" relate the Middle East conflict to the democratic deficit in the region was a body of anthropological studies of Arab and Muslim culture and its discursive practices. Much of it was influenced by Raphael Patai (1983, 23, 73–75, 156), a figure reviled in MESA circles. Patai emphasized the "irrational" elements in Arab culture, including the disconnect between language and reality, extremes of emotion, and the stronghold of familism and tribal mores of honor, and shame on the collective discourse. Fouad Ajami (1981) described this flight from reality as the "Arab predicament," a point made by other commentators as well. One scholar explained that the rulers in the region who need to present their failures as successes, have relied on linguistic manipulations that create a "disconnect" from reality (Pryce-Jones 1989, 375). A group of prodemocracy Arab intellectuals in Beirut offered a scathing critique of what they defined as an "assassination of reason" and the "corruption of the Arab discourse" (al-Jabri 1982; Ghalyoun 1985) Pipes (1996, 1997b) called attention to the powerful role of conspiracy theory and paranoia in shaping political debate in the Middle East, an argument given clinical weight in a book about the pathologies of political paranoia (Robins and Post 1997, 53).

Building on this and other sources, some scholars argued that Middle East societies were predisposed to legitimize a patrimonial or neopatrimonial "sultanist" authority system. They explained that such societies are dominated by a premodern form of loyalty to family, tribe, and other "nonrational" forms of allegiance. In other words, "neopatriarchal patronage displaces legality, renders public institutions superfluous and takes away the individual's claim to autonomous rights" (Bratton and Van De Valle, 1994, 458; Moghadam 1991, 205; Sharabi 1988, 4).

These and other observers noted that while some of the regimes in the region were moderately authoritative, others developed into virulent totalitarian states with fascist overtones. Drawing on a large volume of newly available research on "generic fascism," a number of experts pointed out that the secular Ba'ath Party of Syria and Iraq as conceived by Michel Aflaq and Salah al-Bitar combined both Nazi and communist elements. The religious variant of fascism, first articulated by the Palestinian leader Haj Amin al Huseini, was said to be adopted by Ayatollah Khomeini in Iran (Donaldson 1996, 142; Lewis 1996; Safi 1994, 146–148; Sharon 1990).

According to this view, secular and religious fascist states in the Middle East shared many characteristics, including the concept of an absolute leader (*Fuehrerprinzip*), centralization of power, suppression of civil discourse, and heavy reliance on security forces (*mukhabarat*). By ruthlessly suppressing opposition, the regime could create a veneer of legitimacy and superficial stability. To generate mobilizatory legitimacy, Arab and Islamic fascism has ritualized war as a supreme social value, encouraged the cult of death, and a profound hatred of the "other," most notably Jews. Commonly depicted as "lice" or "vermin," Jews were said to be a "corrupt monstrosity" poised to engulf the globe. United States, often depicted as the "Great Satan," has been another frequent target used to mobilize the population. Amir Taheri (2004a, 17; 2004b), a major proponent of the fascist theory, noted that the use of violent language and imagery in the public discourse was borrowed from the Nazi propaganda chief Joseph Gobbles (Frisch 2002).

Analyzing this persistent legitimacy deficit, MESA critics settled on an alternative cause-and-effect explanation of the relation between the Arab-Israeli conflict and democracy. In what became the basis of a rival epistemic community, they asserted that the conflict has been used by Arab dictators to prop up their illegitimate and coercive rule. In other words, the absence of democracy in the region had turned the conflict into a festering sore. As Ajami put it, "the narcotic of anti-Zionism" was used to keep the masses quiescent (quoted in O'Rourke 2004, 106). Kanan Makiya (1993, 253–254; al-Khalil 1989, xviii), an Iraqi dissident, went further; he attacked Said and other MESA activists for being "spinner[s] of grand theories...diverting responsibility" from dictators such as Saddam Hussein onto the Israel-Palestinian conflict.

The new claim that the way to democracy and peace in the Middle East "passes through Baghdad" was making some impact on the foreign policy discourse in Washington. The notion that the United States should take on authoritarian regimes was particularly popular in the neoconservative intellectuals circle that had pushed for a confrontation with the Soviet Union during the Reagan presidency. MESA academics acknowledged as much. An article published in *Middle East Policy*, a journal sympathetic to MESA, discussed the two epistemic communities, each promoting a "common causal model and set of policy prescriptions." However, in the author's view, MESA academics were pursuing "objective truth" and "American national interests" whereas their rivals, labeled "policy entrepreneurs," represented "special interests" of "unconditional support for Israel and American military hegemony" (Khan 1997).

Under normal circumstances, these exchanges would have been limited to a relatively small circle of scholars. However, Arab exceptionalism was more than an academic problem for American foreign policy and the international order that emerged after the end of the cold war. Indeed, the two issues linked to the region—Islamist terrorism and the phenomenon of the rogue state—replaced the Soviet Union as the major topic of foreign policy discourse.

Islamist Revival: Peaceful Coexistence or Clash of Civilizations?

For all their criticism of orientalism, the radical generation of MESA experts was taken aback by the Islamist revival. Said (1981, 52–53; 1985, 3), who failed to predict the fundamentalist upheaval in Iran, expressed disappointment with the "horrific aftermath" of the revolution, but stuck to his line that the West was to blame for all the ills of the region. Invoking a variant of "false consciousness," Said claimed that, after being demonized by orientalists, Muslims acted the part "decreed for them" by the West.

In spite of the growth of Islamic terrorism in the 1980s, much of it directed by Teheran through its Lebanese proxy Hezbollah, MESA scholars were reluctant to discuss the subject. Esposito (1990) explained that "new forms of orientalism flourish today" at the hands of those who "equate revivalism, fundamentalism, or the Islamic movement with violent revolution."

To prevent creating negative stereotypes and inflaming passions, Esposito counseled against undue emphasis on Middle East terrorism. Such appeals were well heeded. Hermann F. Eilts (1990, 27), the chairman of the International Relations Department at Boston University and a former ambassador to Egypt and Saudi Arabia, blamed the Judea-Christian perspective for a "widespread misunderstanding" of Islamic fundamentalism and its depiction as a "new Crusade" against the West. The prestigious Fundamentalist Project at the University of Chicago, which, among others, covered fundamentalism in Iran and Lebanon, had no "terrorism" entry in its index. The book referred to Hezbollah as a species of "Shiite activism" (Marty and Appelby 1991, 403–456).

In his widely read *The Islamic Threat: Myth or Reality?* Esposito (1992, 166) set out to prove that Islamic revival posed no threat to the West and that terrorism was on the decline because it was "counterproductive." Bulliet (1993) speculated that the Palestinian Hamas, which pioneered suicide bombing in Israel, decided that violence was "too risky" a strategy. For MESA academics, minimizing the potential of Islamic violence was essential to the larger task of squaring fundamentalist Islam with the tenets of democracy and peaceful coexistence. This task was made all the more urgent because of the inroads made by the "clash of civilizations" theory offered by MESA critics.

Lewis, who was virtually alone in 1976 in warning about an impending Islamic revival, went one step further in 1990. In an essay published in *Atlantic Monthly,* Lewis (1990, 53, 59; 1993), by then the undisputed dean of orientalists, wrote about the "roots of Arab rage" and predicted the spread of militant Islam. Lewis asserted that the "cultural like crusade" of the Islamists would result in a "clash of civilizations," where America "is symbolic of Western civilizations." Pipes (1983), who had previously drawn attention to the fact that oil money in Iran and Saudi Arabia was fueling the expansion of militant Islam, claimed that Islamism would replace communism as the next challenge to American and Western interest in the world.

Building on Lewis' assertion, Samuel Huntington (1993; 1996, 217) popularized the theme of the coming "clash of civilizations" in his famous *Foreign Affair*s article and a subsequent book. Huntington rejected the notion advocated by Espostio and other MESA scholars that Islamist terrorism represents "a small, extreme minority." He argued that the virtual absence of "Muslim criticism of Islamic terrorism" was evidence that the Islamist "quasi war" waged by the extremists had broad popular support and thus involved a "whole civilization." Pipes (1995b) contended that, far from being a marginal phenomenon, a substantial hard core Islamist movement was seeking to challenge the West. Kramer (1997, 16) pointed out that Islamism represented "relentless and often ruthless pursuit of power," and accused MESA experts of "whitewashing Islam under the guise of diversity." Instead of patience and co-optation, these critics urged the West to confront Islamist extremists (Rodman 1994).

To complicate matters, the dispute over Islamic terrorism was closely related to the issue of state-sponsored terrorism and proliferation of weapons of mass destruction in the Middle East. Generating as much acrimony, the debate about the linkage between domestic legitimacy, international behavior of states, and the post–cold war order spilled into the field of international relations.

THE RISE OF THE ROGUE STATE AND THE INTERNATIONAL ORDER: FOREIGN POLICY IMPLICATIONS

The discourse on the linkage between domestic structure and the international behavior of states have a long philosophical pedigree dating back to Immanuel Kant. In his 1796 essay *Project for a Perpetual Peace*, Kant postulated that republican systems would not fight each other, thus assuring a peaceful international order. Woodrow Wilson used the so-called Kantian democratic peace to formulate his influential brand of international idealism. However, the ascendancy of realism in the United States made the domestic character of the regime all but obsolete. Realists and neorealists have argued that it is the power calculus of state actors that generates wars or sustains peace. The spread of nuclear weapons added another element to the realist critique of the democratic peace. As the consequences of using nuclear weapons were assumed to deter nuclear players from engaging in conflict, Mutual Assured Destruction (MAD) made the nature of the domestic system irrelevant to international peace maintenance.

Because realism and neorealism dominated mainstream IR, defense of Kantian democratic peace came from the periphery of social science. In the 1960s, a Wisconsin University criminologist published a statistical paper corroborating the hypothesis that democracies do not fight each other. In 1983 Michael Doyle (1983) popularized this thesis in two articles that received modest attention. Rudolph J. Rummel, (1991, chapter 23) made a strong case for what he called "the freedom principle," namely that "violence does not occur between free societies." However, it was the collapse of the Soviet Union and Third Wave democratization that inspired a growing number of scholars to probe the linkage between democracy and peaceful international behavior. By some accounts, by the mid-1990s, there were more than a hundred studies devoted to the subject.

Despite its popularity, the democratic peace made few converts among leading IR realists who were quick to offer a rebuttal. John J. Mearsheimer (1990a, 6–8, 52, 1990b, 35–36) described it as a "shallow construct" and reiterated that "distribution and character of military power" were the causes of wars. He predicted an increase in conflict in Europe if communism collapsed, concluding that "the West has an interest in the existence of a powerful Soviet Union." Mearsheimer's faith in the capacity of post–cold war Europe to maintain peace was low enough to contend that "we will soon miss the Cold War."

In line with the logic of MAD-induced peace, Mearsheimer advocated a modest increase in nuclear proliferation. Kenneth Waltz (1990) was another leading proponent of MAD-anchored peace. Waltz, who in 1979 famously predicted that the cold war would last well into the twenty-first century, now argued that in order to assure the continuity of nuclear deterrence, the strict ban on proliferation should be modified or even lifted.

Mearsheimer's high-profile attack on the "Kantians" prompted some harsh criticism from other IR experts. Stanley Hoffmann (1990, 192) called Mearsheimer's theory "mediocre" and "arrogant." Bruce M. Russett (1990–91, 217, 219) stated that, like realism, democratic peace "is a venerable theoretical position, dating back to Immanuel Kant" and though not "as absolute as a law of physics," as a rule, democracies "will not fight against each other." Russett accused Mearsheimer of "peddling" a bad academic theory and noted that structural realism "which is hardly capable of explaining the past" was not fit to predict the future.

Though the Kantian-realist exchange, like other academic debates, has proved inconclusive, the democratic peace attracted a following among political practitioners. In his 1994 State of the Union Address, President Bill Clinton noted that "the best strategy to ensure our security and to build a durable peace is to support the advance of democracy" because "democracies don't go to war with each other." Margaret Thatcher (1995, 527) argued that "even the most cynical practitioner of realpolitik" would have to agree that the nature of the regime matters, especially as "democracies by and large do not make war" on each other.

Among critics of realism were those who doubted the universality of MAD-based deterrence. While it was generally accepted that the United States and the Soviet Union were rational enough to be mutually deterred, there were questions about the third world would-be proliferators. Yehezkel Dror (1971, 7, 25), an Israeli political scientist and futurologist, was the first to argue that "crazy states," his definition of a number of dictatorships in the Middle East, may not possess the rationality required for deterrability.

Foreign policy anthropologists highlighted another problematic dimension of deterrability. They drew on Weber's distinction between *zweckrational* actions undertaken on the basis of adequateness of means and ends and *wertrational* actions based on belief in ethical or symbolic values. This distinction made it possible to regard as rational, a religious crusade fought against all military odds or a suicidal campaign against a real or imaginary enemy. They warned that that this type of "cultural irrationality is deeply entrenched" in societies and thus difficult for outsiders to decipher (Hall 1977, 219).

Both anthropologists and rational choice theorists noted that risk taking was another factor difficult to measure, as propensity for risk taking varies across cultures. Though Arrow's dictum stipulates that the larger the stakes of the outcome, the more risk-averse actors become, these and other experts warned that to distinguish between high risk taking and lapses in rationality is not easy. What is more, highly centralized totalitarian systems increase the propensity for risk taking. With few systemic restraints on the dictator operating in an environment highly susceptible to deception and self-deception, where "sending and receiving misleading messages becomes the norm," bureaucratic irrationality can set in (Anderson 1986, 323; Daniel and Herbig 1981; Mitchell and Thompson 1986). Indeed, Herbert Simon, a leading expert in organizational rationality, introduced the concept of "radical irrationality" to describe the last stages of Hitler's Third Reich.

Confronted with such observations, realist scholars were forced to admit that cold war based deterrence may not carry into the third world. Mearsheimer (1992, 235) conceded that "widespread nuclear proliferation is laden with dangers for the Third World" and that "it is possible that some Third World leaders might not fully appreciate the destructiveness of nuclear weapons." But the degree to which third world countries deviated from the requisite rationality remained highly contentious. A special symposium convened to deal with rationality and deterrence in the post–cold war period by the Center for International Studies at Princeton University ended in disarray. So much so, that the organizers sadly concluded that the field "was mired in debate and controversy" (Kholi et al. 1995, 1).

Unencumbered by academic hair-splitting, political leaders were united in the view that WMD in the hands of third world totalitarian regime was a bad prospect. As Thatcher (1995, 527) noted, her worries stemmed not so much from North Korea's nuclear capability but rather from the fact that such capability was in the hands of a hard-to-predict dictatorship. In making a distinction between rational and "irrational" states, Thatcher and other leaders were clearly indicating that the domestic character of the regime does matter. Indeed, as proliferation increased in the post–cold war period, interest in what became known as "rogue states" had picked up considerably (Chan and Williams 1994).

In the Middle East, the confluence of rogue states, Islamic terrorism, and WMD was attracting a lion's share of the new scrutiny. Ostensibly focused on Saddam Hussein's Iraq, at its core, the discourse has been driven by the paradigm assumptions generated by the two rival epistemic communities.

2

Paradigms of Change and American Foreign Policy toward Iraq in the 1980s: Moderating a Totalitarian Regime and the Road to the Gulf War

For most of the cold war period, American policies toward the Gulf were part of the larger strategy of superpower relations that is beyond the scope of this work. Starting with President Truman, American administrations used Iran and Saudi Arabia, the Twin Pillars of the Gulf, to contain Soviet ambitions and forestall any threats to oil shipments from the region.

Jimmy Carter's arrival in the White House in 1977 threw American policy in the Gulf into turmoil. Propelled by the president's humanistic vision of international relations and beholden to the McGovernite wing of the Democratic Party, the new administration vowed to replace the realpolitik of Nixon-Kissinger era with New Internationalism, a blend of Wilsonian idealism and dependency-driven quest for global equity. Carter proclaimed himself cured of the "inordinate fear of communism" and promised to work with Moscow to achieve justice, equity, and human rights. His secretary of state Cyrus Vance noted that both Carter and the Soviet Premier Leonid Brezhnev shared "similar dreams and aspiration." To demonstrate that the fear of Soviet aggression in the Gulf was a thing of the past, the new team offered to negotiate a demilitarization of the Indian Ocean, a step long advocated by George McGovern and Ted Kennedy. More important, Carter promised to curb the CIA, which he described as a "national disgrace" and a symbol of superpower competition (Seliktar 2000, 52–54). Vice President Walter Mondale, whom Carter asked to reform the CIA, was a member of the Church Committee and close to activists associated with the Institute for Policy Studies and its numerous spin-offs. Many of the second- and third-tier Carter appointees such as David Aaron, Anthony Lake, and Leslie H. Gelb came from these ranks. Lake and Gelb were close to Morton Halperin from the Center for National Security Studies (CNSS), the lead author of *The Lawless State* (1976), a wholesale indictment of the CIA. Halperin's plea for an open and accountable intelligence service was incorporated into a comprehensive package of reforms proposed by the administration. Although Congress rejected some of the more radical demands, Stansfield Turner, Carter's director of central intelligence (DCI), moved against human intelligence, which was seen as "gung-ho" and corrupt, and replaced it with the "clean" technical intelligence collection. Turner eliminated approximately eight hundred covert operation positions and ordered the rest of the Agency's Directorate of Operations (DO) to uphold high moral standards when hiring foreign contacts. According to a cable sent to CIA station chiefs, "the recruitment of individuals for the purpose of espionage should be a morally uplifting experience." As Turner (1991) later explained, the "purge of the K.G.B types" was carried out to uproot the "outdated view" that the Agency should go to "extremes" in order to spy (Paseman 2004, 76; Seliktar 2000, 52–53).

Carter's New Internationalism, which was shared by many prominent Democrats in Congress, aimed to reduce American commitment abroad. The administration wanted to withdraw its troops from South Korea in protest against human rights violation there, and hoped to negotiate an agreement with the Moscow on demilitarizing the Indian Ocean. Even the bedrock of American influence in the Gulf, the "Twin Pillars" policy did not escape scrutiny. Carter pressured the shah to improve his human rights record and announced a curb on the sale of American weapons to Iran.

Indeed, limiting military transfers to right-wing allies was at the core of the Institute of Policy Studies (IPS)-related Military and Disbarments Project (MDP) headed by Michael T. Klare. MDP, in conjunction with the leftist lobby in Congress, Member of Congress for Peace through Law, was instrumental in the Presidential Directive (PD-13) that pledged to limit American military exports to promote global peace. Carter explained that he was particularly concerned by "our nation's role as the world's leading arms salesman," adding that America should be the world's "moral beacon and breadbasket, not gun shop" (Stoessinger 1985, 278; Vance 1983, 319). The president's initiatives received rave reviews from New Internationalists who felt that after decades of realpolitik, the administration was moving the United States to the "right side of history."

Nothing in its foreign policy vision prepared the administration for the crumbling of the shah's regime. After a frantic effort to install a moderate government in Teheran, Washington watched helplessly the arrival of Ayatollah Rukhalah Khomeini on February 1, 1979. Whatever hopes the Carter team had for cooperating with the new leaders, were dashed when, on November 4, a group of Khomeini followers seized the American embassy in Teheran, and turned the diplomats into hostages for the subsequent 444 days. The equally unexpected Soviet invasion of Afghanistan on December 24, 1979 drew the curtain on the president's quest to lead the world into an era of peace and goodwill. Worse, it left the administration with the urgent task of addressing the new geopolitical reality in the Gulf. As Washington would soon discover, restoring the balance in the Gulf was a tall order that would bedevil the Carter administration and beyond.

THE IRANIAN REVOLUTION AND THE NEW GEOPOLITICS IN THE GULF

The debacle in Iran undermined the influence of the New Internationalists who pushed hard for the removal of the shah and vindicated Zbigniew Brzezinski, Carter's national security adviser, who had warned all along against destabilizing Iran. Brzezinski was so worried about the imbalance in the Gulf that he raised the possibility of a tilt toward Iraq during an inter-agency meeting in January 1979. Although Iraq, one of the most radical regimes in the Middle East, was a staunch ally of the Soviet Union, there was hope that, with the right package of incentives, Baghdad, which already had extensive ties with France, could be weaned away from Moscow.

The prospect of moderating Iraq with a view to turning it into a new "Twin Pillar" divided security experts in the administration. Richard Haass, a member of International Security Affairs (ISA) in the Department of Defense, seemed to back Brzezinski but Paul D. Wolfowitz, a deputy assistant secretary of defense for regional planning and Howard Teicher, a junior analyst, argued that Iraq was the real danger in the region. In a top secret memorandum, "Capabilities for Limited Contingencies in the Persian Gulf" Wolfowitz wrote that "Iraq has become military pre-eminent…and may in the future use her military force against such states as Kuwait or Saudi Arabia." Wolfowitz, who submitted the memo to the Defense Secretary Harold Brown, urged an increased American military presence in the region to warn Iraq. Acting outside the administration, Richard Perle, a high-ranking neoconservative, maintained that there were "echoes of the 1930s" in the Middle East and argued that the United States might have to contend with a hostile Iran and Iraq (Friedman 1993, 23; Gordon and Trainor 1995, 6–7; Mann 2004, 79–62; Shimko 1993, 289; Teicher and Teicher 1993, 63–65).

For an administration that refused to make a show of force to shore up the shah, military presence in the Gulf was not an acceptable option. Brown rejected Wolfowitz's recommendations and Brzezinski was authorized to pursue the path of moderating Iraq. According to accounts that Brzezinski vehemently denied, King Hussein of Jordan mediated a meeting between the national security adviser and the Iraqi President Saddam Hussein. An alternative account held that the Iraqi leader met in Amman with three high-ranking CIA operatives to discuss efforts to curb the spread of Khomenism. In April 1980, Brzezinski gave a green light to the new policy of rapprochement with Iraq, stating that "we see no fundamental incompatibility of interests between the United States and Iraq and…do not feel that American-Iraqi relations need to be frozen in antagonism" (Aburish 1985, 70; Ahmad 1991, 201; Rubin 1982, 117; Teicher and Teicher 1993, 62–63; Timmerman 1991, 76–77). The radical twist that the Iranian revolution was taking vindicated those who counseled a thaw with Iraq, In addition to the refusal of Teheran to release the hostages, there were signs that Khomeini was fast becoming an "Islamist Trotsky." Iran's Ministry of Intelligence and

Security (MOIS) and the Pasdaran (Revolutionary Guards) were put in charge of training terrorists, including suicide bombers; one of them, Ali Reza Asghari, became the "founding father" of the Lebanese Hezbollah (Stern 2007). Within a year of taking power, the regime was well on its way to spreading fundamentalism abroad. Teheran hoped to foment a series of revolutions by mobilizing the Shiite population in neighboring states, including attempted coups in Kuwait and Bahrain and an attack on the Grand Mosque in Mecca during the annual pilgrimage in November 1979.

Much of Iranian hostility was directed toward Iraq, whose Shiite population, estimated at about 60 percent, was historically oppressed by the Sunni minority. After repeated efforts, Hezbollah managed to blow up the Iraqi embassy in Beirut in December 1980. Iranian forces were also implicated in attacks inside Iraq, including an attempt to assassinate Iraq's Deputy Prime Minister Tariq Aziz in April 1980. Iraq's retaliation against its own Shiites, including the execution, in 1980, of the leading Ayatollah Muhammad Baqir al-Sadr and a bloody purge of members of the Shiite Dawa Party, aggravated the tension. Ayatollah Khomeini personalized the crusade by openly calling for the removal of Saddam Hussein whom he described as the "fascist butcher," "a mentally ill tyrant," a "gangster from Takrit," a "nincompoop," or the "puppet of Satan," epithets that were designed to elicit a strong response in the honor-bound culture of the Middle East (Taheri 2004b).

While Saddam reciprocated by calling the Ayatollah a "lunatic," and a "frenzied charlatan and imposter," from an Iraqi perspective, the animosity went well beyond the personal. The 1975 Algiers Agreement between the two countries limited Iraq's claim to the disputed Shatt al Arab waterway and Baghdad harbored even more ancient historical claims to the oil-rich Khuzestan (Arabistan), home to a large Arab population . Iraq had sheltered the Khuzestan Liberation Movement since the 1960s and apparently activated it in early 1980. The U.S administration was fed hopes of getting back at Khomeini by prominent Iranian exiles. The former prime minister Shahpur Bakhtiar and the former chief of staff General Ghulam Ali Oweisi told Iraqi officials that the chaos in Iran and the virtual disintegration of its military would make regaining Khuzestan easy. Iraq's own intelligence services estimated that, given the level of anarchy under Khomeini, Khuzestan could be taken in three weeks (Hiro 1991, 38; Kimche 1991, 202; Marr 2004, 183; Miller and Mylroie 1990, 309; Pollack 2004, 183).

The Arab states, notably, Saudi Arabia, Jordan, and Egypt, increasingly alarmed by Khomeini's aggressive efforts to push fundamentalism, were conflicted. Apprehensive about a conflagration in the Gulf, King Fahad warned against a war only to be told by Saddam Hussein that he wanted to go to Teheran to "pull Khomeini by the beard" (Simpson 2006, 174). King Hussein and President Hosni Mubarak were hopeful that enmity toward Iran would unite the Arab camp, badly fragmented by Egypt's separate peace treaty with Israel in 1979. The Iraqi leader vindicated this hope when, in February 1980, he made a major pitch for a new Pan-Arab charter and the healing of the split over Israel.

Acting upon these various imperatives, Iraq launched an attack on Iran on September 22, 1980. In an effort to highlight the Pan-Arab importance of the war, Saddam Hussein revoked the memory of the battle of Qadaisya in 637 CE in which Arab Muslims defeated the Persian Zoroastrians. According to a later account by General Wafiq Samarri, a senior Iraqi intelligence official, the Iraqi military hoped to duplicate Israel's strategy during the Six Day War. Yet in spite of Iraq's tactical advantages, the popular rebellion in Khuzestan did not materialize and the Iranian army did not disintegrate as expected. On the contrary, the attack garnered Khomeini some legitimacy among the Farsi-speaking majority while giving the regime a license to increase its bloody suppression of the opposition. By mid-1981, all hopes for a quick Iraqi victory vanished (Aburish 2000, 195; Hiro 1991, 44; Wright 1980–81).

The Iran-Iraq War: Washington's High-Wire Balancing Act

Facing the prospect of losing the election in the fall of 1980, President Carter vowed to embrace traditional realism. In a confession born out of what some critics called "crushed naïveté," the president admitted his past mistakes and declared that American forces would protect the stability of the Gulf. In a show of strength, Carter ordered a squadron of F-15s fighters to be sent to Saudi Arabia, but the gesture backfired when it was announced that the planes were not armed (Bush and Scowcroft 1998, 323). In the elections that followed, Ronald Reagan, who called for a replacement of what he considered the bankrupt New Left international philosophy, defeated the beleaguered Carter. In his inauguration speech in January 1981, the new president promised a crusade against the Soviet Union and world communism.

In spite of the fact that the Reagan foreign policy team included Perle, Wolfowitz, and Teicher, there was no change in American Gulf policy. Washington declared itself to be neutral in the conflict between Iran and Iraq, but according to the capital's rumor mill, many in the administration were not displeased with the prospect of a costly struggle between Iran and Iraq. Invoking Truman's quip about a lot of Russians and Germans killing each other, one insider noted that "although I did not order it [the war], it did not displease me" (Algosaibi 1993, 10; quoted in Friedman 1993, 15). Certainly, both combatants presented real dangers to American interests in the region. In due course, Iran went beyond its verbal assault as the "Great Satan;" its surrogate Hezbollah bombed the American embassy in Beirut and the marine barracks in 1983, resulting in the loss of lives of hundreds of Americas.

Iraqi behavior was potentially even more worrisome. American intelligence knew that since mid-1970s, Saddam Hussein, then second-in-command, had embarked on an ambitious plan to acquire nuclear technology from France. Hussein struck up a personal friendship with Jacques Chirac who came to Baghdad to negotiate the nuclear reactor deal. In a follow-up visit to Paris in

1976, Hussein allegedly cemented the friendship by helping finance *the Rassemblement pour la Republique*, a new party that Chirac had launched. The CIA had also evidence that German firms were helping Baghdad to build chemical plants with a dual capacity potential and that Iraqis had purchased biological agents (Aburish 1985, 4–13; Freedman and Karsh 1993, 38; Guitta 2005; Sciolino 1991, 144–149). Last but not least, the Iraqi regime assiduously cultivated the Palestinian Liberation Organization (PLO) and a host of more radical terrorist organizations, including the Abu Nidal group, which was engaged in spectacular acts of terrorism against Israeli and, on occasion, American targets. Dealings with terrorist groups were handled at the highest level by Saddam's personal office, earning Iraq a place in the State Department list of countries that supported terrorism (Coughlin 2002, 142).

Iraq's nuclear ambition was especially worrisome to Israel, which for a number of years had complained to American and French authorities about the Osiraq nuclear reactor near Baghdad. With no help forthcoming from the West, in early 1981, the Likud government of Menachem Begin held a number of meetings to consider bombing the facility. Subsequent accounts revealed that the cabinet concluded that Saddam Hussein was too unpredictable and thus undeterrable, an opinion shared by Amazia Baram, an Iraq expert from Haifa University who apparently advised Israeli intelligence. In a psychological profile of the dictator, Baram (1980) found Saddam Hussein to be a high risk taker prone to miscalculations. Over strong objection from the Labor Party, the Osiraq facility was destroyed on June 7, 1981 (Claire 2004; Miller, Miller, and Zetouni 2002, 151; Shamir 1994, 125–126; Tamir 1988, 205; Weizman 1981, 109–110).

Following harsh international demands to punish Israel, the Reagan cabinet met within hours of the raid, but the discussion demonstrated the deep split between the pro-Iraqi and the pro-Iranian factions in the administration. Perle and Wolfowitz reiterated the view that in spite of its revolutionary ardor, Iran was less of a danger than a nuclear armed Iraq. Yet Secretary of Defense Casper Weinberger overruled his junior aides and pressed for sanction against Israel by delaying the delivery of four F-16s fighters. Jeanne Kirkpatrick, the U.S. ambassador to the United Nations who developed a rapport with her Iraqi counterpart Nizar Hamdoon, backed Weinberger. To demonstrate that the Ayatollah was taking his crusade seriously, Hamdoon distributed Iranian maps showing plans to liberate Jerusalem, a move that made a strong impression on the American delegation (Friedman 1993, 4–5; Karsh and Rautsi 1991, 153; Mantius 1995, 54–54; Teicher and Teicher 1993, 141–142).

By early 1982, Washington's hopes for a prolonged stalemate in the Iran-Iraq war were replaced by a growing alarm over Baghdad's losses. Even without Hamdoon's diplomatic gimmick, the message that Saddam Hussein was instrumental in blocking the spread of Khomeinism was clear. Early in the year, President Hosni Mubarak of Egypt told Deputy Secretary of State Walter Stoessel that if Iraq lost the war, the Middle East would be "dangerously destabilized." In February 1982, the Reagan administration decided to tilt toward Baghdad and notified Congress that Iraq was removed from the list of countries sponsoring terrorism. In March, William Casey, Reagan's Director of Intelligence, went on a secret mission to Baghdad to assess the battlefield situation, thus opening the way for limited military aid. In July, Assistant Secretary of State Nicholas Veliotes disclosed that the United States would share satellite intelligence with Iraq (Mantius 1995, 238). In August, Saddam Hussein received Congressman Steven Solarz, an outspoken supporter of Israel, for a rare interview. According to Solarz, Hussein told him that the existence of a secure Israeli state was necessary for regional peace. The Iraqi leader pursued this "charm offensive" during the September Arab League summit in Fez, where he tacitly accepted the two-state solution to the Arab-Israeli conflict, a major shift from Iraq's position as the premier rejectionist state.

By 1983 the American modest tilt toward Iraq was acquiring momentum. In a conversation with King Fahd, Hussein voiced alarm about the military situation, adding that he wanted "to disengage" (Simpson 2006, 174). A National Security Council report concluded that the Iraqi military would collapse without American help. In November 1983, Donald Rumsfeld, Reagan's special envoy, arrived in Baghdad for a number of meetings in which Iraqi leaders urged the United States to stop sale of arms to Iran. The new policy, which also urged reestablishment of diplomatic relation, was strongly supported by the "Arabists" in the State Department: Richard Murphy, the assistant secretly of state for Near East and South East Asia, William Eagleburger, the head of U.S. interest section in Baghdad, Ambassador Richard Fairbanks, and Richard Armitage, assistant secretary for international security affairs in the Department of Defense. Senator Bill Bradley, Solarz, and other congressional Democrats came aboard as well.

The Iraqi tilt was a major diplomatic coup for Saddam Hussein. Diplomatic relations between the two countries were restored in November 1984, and the United States launched Operation Staunch, an effort to deny arms to Iran. Iraq was given satellite intelligence on the movement of Iranian troops and some restrictions on selling American dual technology items were lifted. The administration also opened a line of credit through the Commodity Credit Corporation (CCC) that ultimately reached one billion dollars annually (Jentleson 1994, 57; Miller and Mylroie 1990, 145; Teicher and Teicher 1992, 277; Timmerman 1991, 130–131; 141).

For many of the Iraq supporters in the administration, the deal was part of a larger policy maneuver aimed at undermining the Soviet position in the Gulf. However, other officials pointed out that Moscow had used the rapprochement between Washington and Baghdad to strengthen its alliance with Teheran. In 1985, Graham Fuller, national intelligence officer for the Near East and South East Asia, and vice chairman of the National Intelligence Council raised the specter of a Soviet grab of Iran, a long-standing American concern. Fuller and the former CIA chief William Colby argued that in case of an Iranian defeat, the ensuing internal turmoil would invite Soviet interference, a move that Moscow had allegedly contemplated during the turmoil of the fundamentalist revolution (Sciolino 1991). Reagan's National Security Adviser Robert McFarlane and Robert Gates, deputy director for intelligence (DDI) supported the Fuller scenario. In a 1985 memorandum Gates wrote that "Moscow was gaining a foothold in Iran" and the Khomeini government was on the verge of collapse. McFarlane considered a Soviet–dominated Iran a catalyst for a World War III. When in 1986 the Israelis had offered to mediate an arms deal with Iran in exchange for a return of a number of Americans kidnapped by Hezbollah in Lebanon, Casey had authorized a highly secret operation (Gelb 1991; Kimche 1991, 208; Parmet 1997, 304; Persico 1990, 444).

The numerous accounts of what subsequently became the Iran-Contra affairs have thrown some light on the reasons behind the Iran tilt. There is little doubt that Casey hoped to rescue William Buckley, the CIA's chief in Lebanon, and other Americans kidnapped by Hezbollah. According to David Kimche (1991, 209– 215), an Israeli official involved in the Iran deal, both Israel and Casey fell prey to the notion that the arms sale could advantage the moderate faction in Teheran against the hard-liners. At the same time, it is equally plausible that Casey, a master international manipulator, was engaged in his own efforts to fine-tune the Gulf conflict (Cooley 1991, 119). Ultimately, the complex maneuver backfired badly. The KGB, which knew about the operation, tried to blackmail Reagan to destroy his rapprochement with Gorbachev and the hard-line Iranian faction leaked it to the press. In November 1986, a Lebanese newspaper *al Shira* published the details, creating a scandal that tarnished the Reagan administration (Seliktar 2004, 135).

Initially, American policy toward the Iran-Iraq war received little attention from scholars and lay observers alike. The liberal *Foreign Affairs*, a publication of the Council on Foreign Relations and an acknowledged leader in the foreign policy discourse, carried a few articles cautioning neutrality (Van Hollen 1981, 1078; Wright 1979–80). The Carnegie Foundation's *Foreign Policy* was more enthusiastic about moderating Iraq, noting that it was a new "West opportunity" (Dawisha 1980–81). However, *Orbis*, published by the conservative Foreign Policy Research Institute in Philadelphia, warned against a tilt toward a "narrow based regime with a bad human right record" (Sicherman 1981, 715).

Iranian gains in the war created some public alarm. Sounding a note of concern, a number of Middle East observers pointed out that an Iranian invasion of Iraq and the toppling of Saddam Hussein would have far-reaching consequences for Gulf stability. They drew attention to the fact that virtually all American allies in the region predicted that the fall of Iraq would enable Khomeini to spread his revolution (Tanner 1982; Taubman 1982).

The anxiety about the "Iranian Trotsky" apparently led to a more positive evaluation of the Iraqi leader. One scholar wrote that Saddam Hussein was trying to move out of the Soviet orbit pursuing a more independent, that is, a pro-Western path (Kashkett 1982). Another concluded that the

Iraqi president was a "rational, calculating cool-headed leader" who was prepared to take risks only when the "dangers of not taking the risk are greater than taking them." He added that Hussein was a "pragmatist" with whom the West could do business (Mansfield 1982, 65). Virtually all observers found that the Iraqi invasion of Iran was justified by repeated Iranian provocations. Khomeini's move to establish, on November 12, 1982, the Supreme Assembly for the Islamic Revolution in Iraq (SAIRI), a group dedicated to increasing the power of the Shiites, deepened the anxiety over the spread of fundamentalism in the region.

As the notion that Iraq can be brought into the "family of nations" was born out of strategic necessity, there was little independent incentive to assess whether Saddam Hussein could be moderated. Under normal circumstance, the intelligence community would have undertaken an in-depth analysis of Iraq and its leader. However, by the early 1880s American intelligence operations in the Middle East were in shambles. The Carter-Turner reform, which both eliminated operational staff and imposed severe limits on recruitment of foreign agents, had in the words of a senior CIA official a "devastating impact" on the Agency (Clarridge with Diehl 1997, 164–165). In a rare public criticism of a friendly service, Count de Marenches, the head of French General Directorate for External Security (GDES), noted that Turner had a "most corrosive influence" on the CIA, calling the Agency's new operational procedures "an open, running sore" (de Marenches and Andelman 1992, 249–295). The bombing of the American embassy in Beirut in 1983 that killed Robert Ames, CIA's chief in the Middle East, and other operatives, wiped out the remaining intelligence assets in the region. According to Casey, the analytical side of Middle East intelligence was not much better because of the "low caliber" of analysts and their poor language skills; Casey attributed it to the fact that the CIA, having lost its elite luster, was forced to recruit among "state universities, Catholic colleges," and other non-Ivy League establishments (Leebaert 2002, 570–573).

With little ability to penetrate a highly secretive society, the Reagan administration had a view of Iraq that was informed by a hodgepodge of academic opinions and tidbits proffered by its Arab allies.

Moderating a Totalitarian Regime: The View from Washington and Baghdad

Even by the standards of the Middle East, Iraq's history was extremely bloody: both the royal family and the communist-leaning government of Brigadier Abdul Karim Kassem had been swept away by violent upheavals. The turmoil continued after the Ba'ath party came to power in 1963, but by the early 1970s, a group of officers from Tikrit led by Ahmad Hassan al-Bakr had managed to solidify its rule. When Saddam Hussein took over the presidency in 1979, a number of official hagiographers declared him to be both a military leader and a philosopher-statesman (Iskander 1980, 20–181; Matar 1981, 108).

The new leader rounded out his political vision in a number of speeches and writings. He described himself as a Pan-Arabist and an ardent nationalist determined to restore the lost glory of Iraq robbed by Western imperialism. He promised to build a large army and an indigenous arms industry to cut dependence on foreign suppliers "who do not necessary agree with . . . our aims." In order to realize these goals, Hussein wanted to establish a strong economy based on the "socialist experiment" of "controlling the means of production" (Hussein 1979, 72; Iskander 1980, 225). Hussein moved fast to create an image of Iraq as a benign, efficient, and progressive state. Much was made of Iraq's educational system, comprehensive health care, and the highly visible role of women, as embodied in the General Federation of Iraqi Women. Phebe Marr (1985, 241–245, 311), a professor at the National Security University and a ranking American authority on modern Iraq, reflected these themes in her work. Marr gave Hussein high marks for turning Iraq into an egalitarian welfare state and for effort to diversify the economy. She argued that the war with Iran had softened Saddam's outlook and prompted him to embrace moderate Arab states. Although Marr felt that Saddam had made a mistake in attacking Iran, she concluded that, overall, "Iraqis . . . could face the future with a reasonable degree of confidence" MESA scholars were even more complimentary, contrasting Hussein's progressive regime with the old-style, inequitable societies in the Middle East. However, some critics felt that "the image that Iraq projected" was an exaggeration pushed along lines "similar to the one celebrated by leftist Western intellectual writing about the Soviet Union" (Aburish 2000, 160–162).

The intelligence services of Arab countries bolstered the moderation theory in a stream of upbeat reports directed at Washington. The CIA's station chief in Amman who worked closely with the Jordanian General Intelligence Directorate (GID) became an unwitting conduit for King Hussein's pro-Iraqi advocacy (Friedman 1993, 26). The French, German, and Italian intelligence agencies, whose governments did significant business with the regime in Baghdad, were equally upbeat.

Even the normally wary Israelis developed a small pro-Iraqi lobby. Prodded by President Mubarak, some Israeli officials, including Labor's Shimon Peres and his Iraqi-born colleague Moshe Shahal, met with Tariq Aziz, Nizar Hamdoon, and other Iraqi officials. One promising avenue of cooperation hinged on a plan to build an oil pipeline from Iraq to the Jordanian port of Aqaba to replace the one that Syria, which sided with Iran, had shut down. The projected route along the Israeli border would have anchored Iraq more firmly in the Western camp, a fact that elicited the support of George Shultz, Reagan's secretary of state. Israel was also encouraged by the fact that Iraq had supported her Christian allies in Lebanon who were fighting the Iranian-Syrian-backed Shiite forces. However, the pipeline project fizzled out and the Israeli "Iraqi option" declined consequently (Axelgard 1988, 114; Karsh and Rautsi 1991, 269–270; Teicher and Teicher 1993, 276; Yaniv 1993).

Ironically, the totalitarian character of the regime made it possible for Saddam Hussein to present himself as a moderate leader ready to rejoin the "family of nations." The reality, which first became known after the Gulf War in 1991, was very different. To recall, theories of political change indicate that totalitarian regimes use coercion in lieu of consensual legitimacy to create a façade of stability and popular support. Hussein, who founded the security infrastructure for the Ba'ath party, perfected the system by producing a pyramid-like security structure, with an ever-increasing number of "elite" and special forces in the army and the security apparatus. By early 1980s, the Iraqi security apparatus alone employed more than 200,000 people. To intimidate the population, internal security used 107 kinds of tortures, including rape rooms. Advisers from the KGB, the East German Stasi, and Cuba provided security training and updated torture methods (Aburish 2000, 126; Coughlin 2002, 197; Makiya 1993, 288–289; Yahia and Wendl 1997, 251, 58–60). General Tommy Franks (2004, 337) would later comment that Hussein reproduced Hitler's concentric security structure with a "good measure of Soviet KGB thrown in."

In another indicator of increased totalitarianism, Saddam Hussein gradually turned the policy bodies of the Ba'ath party—the Revolutionary Command Council (the Politburo) and the Regional Command Council, along with the handpicked parliament, the National Assembly created in March 1981—into props of a highly personalized, "sultanist"-patrimonial regime. Although not understood at the time, Iraq was actually run by an intricate network of Saddam's family (the maternal wing of Khairallah Tulfah and the paternal wing of the al-Majids), kinsmen from his birthplace Tikrit, and trusted tribal chiefs from the Al-Bu Nassir tribal group. To conceal the numerous clansmen in his regime, Hussein banned the use of the al-Takriti surname. One observer called this "personal and private networks of trust," the most literal form of Middle Eastern patrimonialism and "the very antithesis of the principle of power and authority of the formal and rational structure" of a state (Tripp 2000, 122).

In fashioning this highly personalized style, Hussein sought to combine Nazism and Stalinism with elements of Middle East culture. According to some testimonies, Hussein was an avid student of Hitler and Stalin; *Mien Kampf* and a small library of Stalin's books were high on his reading list (Aburish 2000, 177; Bhatia and McGrory, 2000, 50). The Iraqi president borrowed a page from both dictators by fashioning an unrivaled cult of personality. His chief propagandist Aziz Mohammed Jassen was charged with creating a vision of a wise and adored leader surrounded by children and peasants. Jassen also ghost-wrote many of Hussein's books, which became the most popular form of literature in Iraq (Aburish 2000, 92).

Saddam Hussein's cult of personality reached stratospheric proportion during the war with Iran. Close observers noted that Hussein, who was known as a hardworking and efficient technocrat, began to neglect decision making, preferring instead long televised appearances and organized forums of mass adulation. Hussein's personality cult was also reflected in grandiose construction projects, including the giant Victory Arch with fists cast from Saddam's own hands. Baram (1991, 110–111) would subsequently comment that such extravagant displays indicated a progressive pathology, an impression strengthened by Hussein's incessant preoccupation with the glory of Babylon and his identification with King Nebuchadnezzar who liberated Jerusalem.

The highly concentrated power amplified Hussein's secretive and arbitrary decision-making habits, a fact known and feared by his inner circles. Kimche (1991, 201), who had a good knowledge of the Iraqi regime, commented that there were "few parallels for such an arrangement in modern history." Critics were liquidated and their families were harassed, robbing the small inner circle of any feedbacks. Saddam Hussein's interference in the conduct of the war, including the constant reshuffling of the high command and arrests and killing of senior officers was a major hindrance. On occasion, the Iraqi leader was known to take matters into his hands by executing offending ministers or officers. In one infamous incident, the dictator murdered his health minister Riad Ibrahim during a cabinet meeting. By all accounts, Hussein bore a large share of responsibility for the poor performance of the Iraqi army (Hamza 2000, 174–175).

Ironically, the massive security system did little to help Hussein's sense of personal safely. In 1983 Barzan al-Takriti, Saddam's half brother and the chief of intelligence, detailed a large number of assassination attempts on the dictator. Hussein responded by increasing the use of doubles, constant movement between presidential palaces and safe houses, and frequent unannounced changes of schedule. In 1984, the regime created a special private security unit within the General Security Directorate under Hussein Kamal, Saddam's son-in-law. In the same year, Kamal uncovered a military plot, which triggered a purge in the armed forces and scores of executions (Aburish 2000, 231–233; Mackey 2002, 253; Miller and Mylroie 1990, 117; Ritter 1999, 76–77).

Personal and systemic pathologies aside, the most troubling aspect of the Iraqi regime was its crash program of unconventional weapons and continuous sponsorship of terrorism. Two weeks after the Osiraq raid, Iraq established the Military Industrial Organization (MIO) to purchase new equipment and material. The reconstituted nuclear program headed by Jafr Diah Jafr went into production in 1982; within a few years, it would employ about 8000 scientists and technicians and came close to producing bomb-grade uranium before the invasion of Kuwait. French, Italian, and the East European firms were among the major suppliers. Hussein Kamal received instruction from the KGB on deception and concealment of the nuclear program (Bhatia and McGrory 2002; 142–149; Cockburn and Cockburn 2002, 90; Ritter 1999, 75; Schoenfeld 2003). The International Atomic Energy Agency (IAEA) whose inspection system was penetrated by Iraqi agents did not register any objections. When the Israeli expert Shai Feldman (1982) questioned the efficiency of the IAEA, its external affairs director Christopher Herzig (1983) sternly rebuked him.

Iraq launched the less technologically challenging production of chemical weapons with the help of West German firms in late 1981. Under the cover of State Establishment for Pesticides Production (SEPP), the large Samara facility was credited with manufacturing the gas used to repeal the Iranian human wave attacks in 1983 as well as in the 1984 battle in the Majnoon Marshes and the Fao Peninsula offensives in 1986. On Hussein's direct order, Abdoul Nassir al-Hindawi made a classified study of biological agents for battle use in 1983. By 1987 Iraq was experimenting with a variety of biological agents where Dr. Rihab Taha, nicknamed Dr. Germ, made her mark (Ritter 1999, 86–87; Timmerman 1991, 134–135). Khidir Hamza (2000, 188–199), a former nuclear scientist, claimed that chemical and biological experiments were performed on political prisoners in the Salman Pak training facility and that Iraqi Shiites were trucked to trenches that simulated battle conditions for similar purpose. The massive WMD program was fed by a sophisticated purchasing Iraqi network directed by Husein Kamal. A Cambridge University researcher subsequently compiled a list of 207 firms from 21 countries, including 86 West German, 18 British, 16 French, 12 Italian as well as Swiss, Dutch, Belgian, in addition to the massive help from the Soviet block (Everest 2004, 103; Sciolino 1991, 144–149).

Closely related was the effort to develop a missile delivery system, which was under partial control of Hussein Kamal and his Special Institute for Technical Industry (SOTI). Starting in 1984, more than a hundred engineers were sent to Brazil to train in ballistic technology and form, upon return, the Research and Development Group (RDG) in SOTI. Among other tasks, the RDG was charged with producing delivery systems for chemical and biological weapons. Around the same time, Baghdad offered Argentina a top secret contract to build a factory for producing a missile codenamed Condor that could reach Teheran. Not to be outdone, in 1983, Adnan Khairallah, Saddam Hussein's cousin and the defense minister, formed the Scientific Research and Technical Development Organization (SRDTO) to produce conventional weapons. Khairallah's program reached staggering proportions during the Iran-Iraq war. France, the second larger supplier of arms to Iraq after the Soviet Union, sold around $25 billion worth of equipment throughout the 1980s (Freedman and Karsh 1993, 38; Guitta 2005; Keegan 2004, 108; Ritter 1999, 84; Timmerman 1991, 150).

Iraq's blossoming WMD program attracted some public attention in the United States. On March 30, 1984, the *New York Times* revealed that a German consortium was helping Iraq with chemical weapons. The case received more publicity in Germany where Karl Kolb, the company head, was a well-known figure (Timmerman 1991, 146–147, 189). The same year, two researchers, Joseph D. Douglass and Neil C. Livingstone (1987), published a short monograph, calling attention to Iraq's chemical and biological capability, which they dubbed "the poor man's atomic bomb." Another expert warned about this "silent spread" in a *Foreign Policy* article (Spector 1985). In January 1986, ABC News alleged that Iraq was developing a line of biological agents (Clarridge with Diehl 1997, 176; Jentleson 1994, 195–196).

Though Iraq was taken off the State Department terrorist list, Saddam Hussein had continued to sponsor terrorist groups. Contravening its professed moderation, the Hussein regime developed a high-level terrorist infrastructure. Scott Ritter (1999, 120–121), a weapons inspector, would subsequently find top secret documents indicating the existence of a special terrorist school under the Directorate M-21 of the *Mukhabarat*, which was also linked to Directorate-4, *Mukhabarat's* covert operations unit. The president's personal office was deeply involved in liaison with many of the terrorist groups in the region. Yasser Arafat, the head of the Palestinians Liberation Organization, was given considerable financial help and a private plane to travel in the region. Iraqi military intelligence even created a new terrorist unit named 15 May under Mohammed Rashid and Abu Ibrahim (Hussein Mohammad al-Omari), a former operative in the Palestinian Front for National Liberation. Al Omari, who specialized in blowing up planes, also worked for Muammar Qaddafi, the Libyan dictator and another sponsor of terrorism. Baghdad directed the group and provided it with explosives and false passports sent through diplomatic pouches (Dobson and Payne 1986, 166–168; Emerson 1991).

According to some accounts, Saddam Hussein ordered Abu Nidal, the head of a highly lethal Palestinian group headquartered in Baghdad, to assassinate the Israeli ambassador, Shlomo Argov in London on June 3, 1982. The botched attempt was allegedly masterminded by Nawal Rosan, a colonel in Iraqi intelligence services, using a sleeper cell in London run by Abu Nidal's nephew. The attack, which was initially attributed to Arafat's PLO, triggered Israel's invasion of Lebanon. Outside Israel, there were some speculations that Hussein had tried to create a diversion in Lebanon because of his dire situation on the Iranian front. Indeed, in June the Revolutionary Command Council had announced Iraq's willingness to end the war and deploy its forces to Lebanon, but Ayatollah Khomeini had rebuffed the offer (Darwish with Alexander 1991, 65; Hiro 1991, 63; Karsh and Rautsi 1991, 165; Pollack 2004, 199).

Iraq was also involved in the 1985 Abu Nidal operation that killed scores of passengers at the El-AL ticket counters in the Rome and Vienna. More brazenly, following the hijacking of the Italian cruiser Achille Lauro in October of the same year, Baghdad refused to give up Muhammad Zaidan (Abu Abbas) who masterminded the operation (Clarridge with Diehl 1997, 319; Emerson 1991). When the first Palestinian Intifada broke out in 1987, Iraq made an initial $50 million donation to the Palestinians, followed up by large cash transfers (Walker and Gowers 2003, 298).

In spite of such gross violations of the moderation theory, by the late 1980s, Washington was hopeful that Saddam Hussein would be ready to join the "family of nations."

ROAD TESTING THE MODERATION THEORY: PERCEPTIONS AND MISPERCEPTIONS IN WASHINGTON AND BAGHDAD

The Iran-Contra fiasco had not only discredited the pro-Iran faction in the U.S. administration but also terminated the careers of its architects, many of who found themselves in legal trouble. The Senate hearings in 1987 undermined whatever little appetite for calibrating the Iraq-Iran war the beleaguered White House still had. The scandal played into the hands of Casper Weinberger and the growing pro-Iraqi lobby in the State Department.

A subtle but important factor helped to consolidate the dominance of the State Department's "Iraqists." As some in the pro-Iranian faction were American Jews connected to Israel, it vindicated those who described themselves as champions of "true" American interests. Among them was April Glaspie, the then head of the Northern Arabian division in the State Department. Joseph Wilson, Glaspie's charge d'affaires when she was appointed U.S. ambassador to Iraq, was also partial to the idea of deepening the relation with Saddam Hussein. With the reputation of Graham Fuller besmirched by his Iran advocacy, Tom Twitten, the chief of the Near East division in the DO, found it easier to circulate reports about alleged Iraqi moderation, backed up the Jordanian and Egyptian intelligence. On March 3, 1988, the State Department published the memorandum "Iraq's Foreign Policy Deeper into the Mainstream," which held a "bullish view of Saddam Hussein." It was followed up by a CIA conference on May 19, 1988 to discuss ways to bring Iraq into the "family of nations" (Jentleson 1994, 54; Kaplan 1992, 58; Teicher and Teicher 1993, 380–381).

A powerful professional lobby created in Washington by the Iraqi government and supported by Saudi Arabia and other Arab states pushed hard the moderation theory. Marshall Willey, a former American ambassador to Oman, set up the U.S.-Iraq Business Forum, which soon listed Bechtel, Continental Grain, General Motors, Mobil Oil, and others leading corporations among its members. Ambassador Richard M. Fairbanks, who had retired from the State Department in 1985, joined the public relation firm of Paul, Hasting, Janofsky & Walker as a paid Iraqi lobbyist. Said Aburish (2000, 212–220), an Iraqi military procurements official turned public relations expert, described how the regime paraded Tariq Aziz, Nazir Hamdoon, and other English-speaking "moderate faces" before the American media. Hamdoon, with the help of Congressman Solarz, imitated an outreach to the Jewish community in the United States (Henderson 1991, 184; Timmerman 1991, 220).

Borrowing a page from the Soviet Union, the Iraqi regime tried to impact the foreign policy discourse by approaching leading think tanks and academics. The Iraqi embassy in Washington invited a number of scholars to Iraq where they received "the red carpet treatment" (Kimche 1991, 232; Yaniv 1993). The strategy proved highly successful. A book published by the liberal Brookings Institution, described Saddam Hussein as a firm but enlightened leader and a "voice of moderation" in the war with Iran. As for his often violent public rhetoric, the author attributed it to the political culture in the Middle East and asserted that there is "wide gap" between this rhetoric and Hussein's pragmatic policies (Helms 1984, 171; 206). The Center for Strategic and International Studies (CSIS) was equally optimistic about Saddam Hussein's newly found moderation; it urged "a broader political understanding" with Baghdad, facilitated by a healthy flow of "commodities and technology" (Axelgard 1986b, 17).

With so many academics joining the Iraqi bandwagon, MESA scholars felt fully vindicated. Among them was Michael Hudson (1987, 1, 5, 19), who had long argued that the portrayal of Iraq (and other Arab countries) as "negative, violent, duplicitous, xenophobic, morally suspect," or "terrorist" was part of the Western "orientalist construct." Hudson accused Israel of using the Jewish lobby to cast "a shadow" over American foreign policy in the Middle East and asserted that that the Reagan administration virtually handed over its policy to the Israelis. Other Middle East specialists touted the "new Iraq" as prima facie evidence against "the conceptual orthodoxy which 'explains'...decision making in the region exclusively by reference to the leaders caprices, whims and other idiosyncrasies" (Korany 1986, xiii).

The handful of human rights activists who tried to alert the West to Saddam Hussein's brutality were virtually ignored. The dissident Kanan Makiya (1993, 17), known as the "Iraqi Solzhenitsyn," recalled the great difficulties in finding a publisher for his *Republic of Fear* completed in 1986 under the name of Samir al-Khalil (1989). In the same year, the small Committee against Repression and Democratic Right in Iraq (CARDRI) based in London published a report on Saddam Hussein's "terror and savagery." Other human rights groups publicized information about *Qasr al-Nihayyah,* the Palace of the End, a torture center in Baghdad, but generated little publicity (Bulloch and Morris, 1991, 30; Hazelton 1994). Jerry Falwell, the then head of Moral Majority, and other evangelical leaders warned against Iraq and its sponsorships of terrorism, but their pro-Israeli agenda and marginal status in the foreign policy discourse made them less than effective (Simon 1984, 53–68). Even the respected military expert General Bernard E. Trainor (1987), who speculated that the military might try and remove Saddam Hussein because of his dictatorial style, could not prevail against the moderation theory.

Indeed, Saddam Hussein's rising reputation obscured the fact that, behind the façade of modernity and efficiently, the regime was growing dangerously dysfunctional. At the systemic level, the "sultanistic" network set up by the Iraqi dictator was destroying the modicum of Weberian rationality necessary for an authority system to function. The British historian and journalist David Pryce-Jones (1989, 351) was one of the very few to make this point contemporaneously, but even he could not fathom the depth of systemic pathology. At the core of the problem was the fierce competition among the three Beijat clans most closely associated with Saddam Hussein: (1) the Tulfahs, the relatives of his mother, (2) the Ibrahim al Muhammads to whom his three half brothers belonged, Barzan, Wathban and Sawabi, and (3) the al-Majids, cousins from the paternal side of his family. The struggle for power and the spoils of the highly corrupt system pitted the family members against one another, disrupting all institutionalized decision making (Cordesman and Hashim 1997, 21–22).

Adding to the strain was the equally dysfunctional family life of the dictator and his son and designated successor, Uday. According to numerous accounts published after the war, both father and son were engaged in brutal sexual exploits, drugs, and heavy drinking. By all accounts, Uday, the oldest son of Saddam and his first wife Sadija, was a sociopath given to extreme violence. Among his numerous transgressions, Uday attacked and wounded Saddam's half brother Wathban and beat to death his father's trusted bodyguard Kamel Hanna Jejjo during a reception for the wife of the Egyptian president Susanne Mubarak in 1988. Uday accused Jejjo of procuring women for his father. One of them, Samira Shahbandar, became Hussein's second wife and mother of his young son. Adnan Kairallah Tulfah, Sadija's brother and the defense minister also viewed the marriage as a personal affront and a threat. Kairrallah, who was already feuding with Hussein Kamal al Majid, Saddam's son-in-law over lucrative procurement bribes, made his displeasure known. Less than a year later, in 1989, it was announced that he had died in a helicopter crash (Aburish 2000, 262–265; Bhatia and McGrory 2002, 193–195; Hamza 2000, 171–173, 179; Henderson 1991, 80–81; Sasson 2003, 266; Timmerman 1991, 344–345; Yahia and Wendl 1997, 282). By mid-1980s, Hussein's megalomania and cult of personality skyrocketed. In addition to his obsessive monument building, Saddam embarked on a campaign to embellish his modest, probably illegal origins. He declared himself to be the son of King Ghazi through a secret but legal liaison with his mother Subha Tulfa; this would have made him both a descendant of the Kuraisha tribe of the prophet Muhammad and Sa'ad ibn Abu Wagas who brought Islam to Iran. Although such claims could have been part of the wartime propaganda, many insiders emphasized that Hussein believed his own narrative.

More significant, the mixture of royal and Islamic lineage apparently symbolized the dictator's resolve to develop a new synthesis between Ba'ath's secularism and Islamism in the Middle East. Saddam's longtime biographer Fu'ad Matar argued that "the ground is being prepared for something novel" in the Middle East, a notion that was given credence by the announcement that Michel Aflaq, the creator of the Ba'ath movement, converted to Islam before his death in 1989 (quoted in Bengio 1998, 192–193).

If the synthesis between secular socialism and Islamic revivalism was one indication of Hussein's apparent effort to position himself as the undisputed hegemon in the Middle East, the increased use of anti-Semitism by the regime was another. Hussein ordered the reprinting of a large number of the virulent anti-Semitic tract written by his uncle, *Three Whom God Should Not Have Created; Persians, Jews, and Flies.* Numerous references to a Jewish "world cabal" found their way into official propaganda, along with assurances that Iraq would take on Israel and its Western allies.

The end of the war with Iran in 1988 evidently exacerbated the pathologies of the regime. With no restraints on his personal rule, the military bore the brunt of Saddam's displeasure and paranoia. Scores of senior military commanders were executed in a Stalin-style cycle of purges; the very senior ones, including General Maher Abdul Rashid, were declared to be victims of "accidents" (Aburish 2004, 200; Timmerman 1991, 343). More bizarre, the dictator required his loyalists and members of security service to kill a persona from their own tribe as well someone from another tribe. According to Prince Bandar, longtime Saudi ambassador in Washington, Hussein told him that this constituted the best method to assure loyalty, since only the regime could protect them from a blood feud (Woodward 2006, 88).

However, the tribal system of governance set up by Hussein aggravated his security. The little understood khams tradition whereby a five-generation family unit requires every male to avenge the death of the person at the core of the circle, prompted tribal groups to launch numerous assassination attempts against Hussein to avenge the death of relatives. These attacks were followed by bloody retribution and more acts of revenge. There were also a number of coup attempts by the military. According to rumors, the Iraq Army Day scheduled for January 6, 1989, was canceled because of a possible coup (Henderson 1991, 85; Ritter 1999, 76–77).

Virtually none of these developments was included in the Iraq assessment undertaken by the incoming administration of George H.W. Bush in 1989. As Reagan's vice president, Bush shared many of the premises of the moderation theory and was familiar with the both the CIA and State Department reports (Henderson 1991, 180–181). What is more, the moderation theory received a substantial boost from the so-called exhaustion thesis, which stipulated that Iraq was too "war weary" to engage in aggressive behavior. The CIA's Iraq National Intelligence Estimate (NIE) of 1989 bolstered this belief by stating that Saddam Hussein would concentrate on rebuilding his devastated economy and society. Although Richard Kerr, deputy CIA director, would later describe the NIE as "sloppy," the document was noncontroversial. With no policy debate, President Bush signed in October the secret National Security Directive 26 that formalized the policy of "limited engagement toward Iraq" (Gordon and Trainor 1995, 9–10; Jentleson 1994, 99; Mackey 2002, 343; Richelson 2001, 245). Sharing the Bush administration consensus on Iraqi moderation were a number of new academic converts. The highly respectable military expert Anthony H. Cordesman (1987, 6) argued that a "right kind of tilt" toward Iraq was critical because of the much greater threat that Iran posed. Laurie Mylroie (1987; 1988, 341; 1989), one of the scholars who visited Iraq, emphasized the regime's unprecedented stability under Ba'ath and warned against "appeasing the ayatollahs." She and Daniel Pipes, another academic visitor, coauthored an article in *The New Republic* urging an American tilt toward Iraq (Mylroie and Pipes 1987). A new book in the SCIS Iraq series, sponsored by Robert G. Neumann, the director for Middle East Studies, bore the hopeful title *A New Iraq*? Its author found evidence of a "maturing Iraqi foreign policy" and a hope for internal democratization. (Axelgard 1988, 38, 85; 1989). These and other advocates of Iraqi moderation pointed to a number of democratic reforms that Saddam Hussein had announced in 1988. Among others, he had promised a new constitution, political pluralism, freedom of expression, and elections to a newly reconstituted National Assembly.

Challenging the Iraqi consensus was the nearly marginalized group of neoconservatives and the pro-Israel Washington Institute for Near East Policy. In 1988, Zalmay Khalilzad, a State Department policy planning analyst, warned the Bush foreign policy transition team about the growing threat from Iraq. Frank Gafny who resigned from the Pentagon's Missile Technology Control Regime over licensing of exports to Iraq, and Stephen Bryen, the head of the Defense Technology Security Administration in Reagan's Department of Defense, called attention to Iraq's growing military ambitions. Bryen, who moved to the Jewish Institute for National Security Affairs (JINSA), a strong pro-Israel advocacy group, warned that Saddam Hussein was preparing to use his arsenal to achieve dominance in the Middle East (Carus 1989; Gordon and Trainor 1995, 9; Timmerman 1991, 265– 267).

Iraq's treatment of its Kurdish population had also raised questions about Saddam Hussein's resolve to moderate. Word about the Anfal campaign against the Kurds that included mass expulsions, the murder of about 100,000 Kurdish noncombatants, and the use of chemical weapons, notably the gassing of around 5,000 people in Halabjah in March 1988 filtered out, attracting congressional attention. The Republican Senator Jessie Helms and his Democratic colleague Claiborne Pell on the Foreign Relations Committee introduced the Prevention of Genocide Act in the fall of 1988 which sought to impose sanctions on Iraq (Darwish with Alexander 1991, 79–81; Gunter 1992, 43–44, 88; Henderson 1991, 260; Roth 1993).

Although in hindsight these warnings were prescient, Iraq's detractors faced an uphill battle in Washington. The State Department's ambassador-at-large Richard Kennedy called Bryen's complaints "poppycock" (Timmerman 1991, 267). The fact that the Jewish Institute for National Security Affairs (JINSA) and the Washington Institute for Near East Policy, a think tank with ties to American Israel Public Affairs Committee (AIPAC, the powerful Israel lobby in Washington, played an active role, made it easy to dismiss the warnings as "Israeli propaganda." A study of the Army War College found evidence about Iraq's use of gas "inconclusive" (Pelletiere, Johnson II, and Rosenberg 1990). Stephen C. Pelletiere, the lead author of the report and CIA's chief Iraq analyst during the Iraq-Iran war, argued that it was Iran and not Iraq that might have launched the chemical attack.

Additional factors worked to minimize the forebodings about Saddam Hussein. Lawmakers from grain-producing states that exported agricultural commodities under the CCC program were eager to portray the Iraqi dictator in the best light. Indeed, in a rare display of bipartisan unity, Senator Robert Dole, a Republican from Kansas and Representative Dan Rostenkowski, a Democrat from Illinois, formed a coalition with like-minded colleagues to oppose the Helms-Pell bill. The influential Iraq lobby, under Marshall Wiley from the U.S. Business Forum, worked incessantly to defeat the proposed legislation (Timmerman 1991, 307).

Temperamentally, the Bush administration was strongly inclined to pursue a cautious policy of integrating Iraq into the "community of nations." The Bush foreign policy team, headed by cautious realists such as Secretary of State James A. Baker and National Security Adviser Brent Scowcroft, was already overwhelmed by the disintegration of the Soviet bloc on their watch. Changing the policy toward Iraq to accommodate the warnings of the neoconservatives would have been inconceivable. As Joseph Wilson (2004, 81) subsequently admitted, the belief that the "regime was incorrigible and irredeemable" "left us no tools" to work with.

Still, by the fall of 1989 the notion that Saddam Hussein was moderating his stance was increasingly difficult to sustain. In August there was a mysterious explosion in the top secret al-Qaqa facility where fuel propellants were produced, raising suspicions about Iraq's nuclear program. In September, the Defense Intelligence Agency (DIA) and the CIA showed the Iraqi conventional weapon program to be far larger than previously thought. On December 5, Iraq launched the al-Abid, its first long-range missile, part of the ambitious missile program under Lieutenant General Amer al-Saidi. With the more cautious Adnan al- Kahirrallah eliminated, Hussein Kamal's MITI (Ministry of International Trade and Industry) made little secret of it long-term plans to establish Iraq as a major producer of both conventional and unconventional hardware. Indeed, Baghdad announced that it was planning a large military equipment fair to be held soon (Timmerman 1990, 117; 1991, 354–355).

For those who watched Iraqi finances, Saddam Hussein's spending plans raised additional red flags. It was known that the war left Baghdad with a foreign debt of approximately $70 to $80 billion. The servicing of the debt, coupled with regular expenditures, was estimated to exceed the income from Iraq's OPEC (Organization of Petroleum Exporting Countries)-mandated annual production quota of 2.6 million barrels of oil. To make matters worse, in addition to the huge military outlays, Hussein, sensing popular unrest, decided to offer the population a lavish "peace dividend" in the form of massive quantities of imported consumer goods (Hiro 1991, 269; Miller and Mylroie 1990, 118).

Baghdad's spending priorities stalled attempts at restructuring the foreign debt and frustrated Hussein who increased his verbal assault against the West. The collapse of communism in Eastern Europe apparently added to his stridency, which, by the beginning of 1990, was difficult to ignore. A February 15 Voice of America (VOA) editorial, commenting on the killing of the Rumanian dictator Nicola Ceausescu and calling for democratization of Iraq, brought a sharp rebuke from Baghdad. Two days later, Iraq announced that it would establish an "all Arab squadron" in Jordan as a first step toward "military unity" in the Middle East. On February 19, during a meeting of the Arab Cooperation Council (ACC) in Baghdad, Saddam Hussein surprised the participants by demanding the departure of American ships from the Gulf. He was even more aggressive during a February 23–24 Council meeting in Amman. In a speech that was described as "incredible," he insulted President Mubarak by calling him a "boot licker" and attacked other "timid" Arab leaders. He demanded a moratorium on $40 billion that Iraq owed the Arab states and $30 billion in new loans. He also wanted OPEC to cut production in order to increase the price of oil. Most ominously, the Iraqi leader threatened the United States and Israel, at one point declaiming his intention to "liberate Jerusalem" (Cooley 1991, 185; Darwish and Alexander 1991, 244–246; Jentleson 1994, 149; Timmerman 1991, 371–373). Saddam Hussein's personal involvement in the execution, on March 15, of the British journalist Farzad Bazoft who was arrested while investigating the explosion in al Qaqa, reflected even more harshly on the dictator. Reviving his old image as the "Butcher of Baghdad," Hussein mocked the British Prime Minister Margaret Thatcher who, along with thousands of others, appealed to spare Bazoft's life. As the Iraqi information minister put it, "Thatcher wanted him alive," but "we sent him home in a box" (Darwish with Alexander 1991, 249; Timmerman 1991, 376). Just as the international indignation over Bazoft was dying down, Saddam Hussein stirred up a new storm during a military ceremony on April 2, in which he announced that Iraq had acquired binary chemical weapons that could "burn up half of Israel," if provoked.

While threats against Israel captured most of the attention, Baghdad was also engaged in an increasingly shrill vilification of OPEC. On May 3, Tariq Aziz, Iraq's foreign minister, announced that OPEC's "overproduction" of oil, which kept the price per barrel low, posed a national security threat to Iraq. On May 30, Saddam Hussein told a closed session of the Arab summit meeting that a one-dollar drop would cost Iraq a billion dollars a year. He also accused Kuwait of overproduction and of illegal pumping of oil from the disputed section of the Rumailah field, adding that Iraq demanded $27 million in compensation. As earlier, he ended his speech with a fiery pledge to liberate Jerusalem (Darwish with Alexander 1991, 253–254; Henderson 1991, 221).

Hussein's belligerent rhetoric was matched by continuous display of Iraq's military power. In January Baghdad announced that its million-strong army would not be demobilized. It was also revealed that Iraq had made preparation to move five SCUD-type missile launches to Western Iraq for possible use against Israel (Baram 2002, 253). In March Iraqi planes capable of taking high-resolution photography arrived in Jordan as part of the "all Arab squadron" (Baram 2002; Ritter 1999, 98). More secret but equally compelling were the crash efforts to produce unconventional weapons. American and Israeli intelligence learned that a new uranium enrichment plant had been unveiled in Tarmiya in February. On March 28, British custom officials seized a shipment of nuclear triggers to Iraq. Six days earlier, a Canadian ballistic expert Gerald Bull, working for Iraq on the supergun project, had been assassinated in Brussels. According to speculations, the killing had been carried out by the Israeli Mossad to prevent the development of a weapon designed to deliver long-range conventional and unconventional payloads (Freedman and Karsh 1993, 33–34).

Saddam's behavior alarmed Israel, which publicized classified information about Iraq's advanced nuclear program. The government of Yitzhak Shamir also warned that stationing Iraqi aircraft in Jordan was a breach of its "red lines" and would entail retaliation. When the Iraqi leader responded on April 18 that the "war would not end until Israel is eliminated," the Israelis pressed the Bush administration to change its moderation theory. AIPAC increased pressure on the White House to impose sanctions on Iraq. The Washington Institute for Near East Policy began to work on a report listing the Iraqi arsenal and the Simon Wiesenthal Center, a Holocaust research institute, commissioned a report on Iraq's chemical weapons programs (Cooley 1991, 185; Eisenstadt 1990; Ritter 1999, 98; Timmerman 1990).

However, even the specter of a "new Auschwitz" in Israel raised by the Wiesenthal Center analysis, did little to alter the position of the administration. Baker, whose dislike of Israel was well known, and the Arabists in the State Department had stuck to the moderation policy. John Kelly, the assistant secretary of state for Near East and South Asian Affairs, who on a previous occasion had lauded Hussein as a "voice of moderation," complained to the secretary about "democracy pushers" in the VOA. On February 28, Ambassador Glaspie sent a letter to Hussein apologizing for the VOA incident (Darwish with Alexander 1991, 252; Timmerman 1991, 371). An April 16 meeting in the White House to assess the relations with Iraq in view of Saddam Hussein's puzzling behavior revealed some anxiety but produced no change in policy. During an April 26 hearing of the House Foreign Relations Committee, Kelly testified that United States hoped to "attempt to develop gradually a mutually beneficial relationship with Iraq" (quoted in Jentleson 1994, 160).

Bolstering the administration's stand was the Iraq lobby, which by the early 1990s could count on many former American ambassadors in the Middle East, the National Association of Arab Americans, and a growing number of lawmakers. In March, the Association paid for a trip of Senator Wyche Fowler, a Georgia Democrat, who praised the Iraqi regime even as international protest over the Bazoft case was mounting. In April, a large bipartisan congressional delegation led by Dole and Alan Simpson, a Republican from Wyoming, met with Saddam Hussein in Mosul. The dictator, who was honeymooning there with his third wife Nidal al Hamdani, was reassured by Simpson that the "problem lies with Western media, and not the American government" (Kaplan 1992; quoted in Mantius 1995, 148, 160).

Ironically, it was a domestic scandal that finally forced the administration to change course. Triggered by charges of embezzlement against Christopher Drougal, the manager of the Atlanta branch of the Italian bank Banca Nazionale Lavoro (BNL) that dispensed American CCC credits to Iraq, the affair focused media attention on the larger question of American's role in arming Iraq. Coming on top of the seizure of the nuclear triggers, the public scrutiny forced the administration to signal its unease with Baghdad. Ambassador Glaspie was instructed to meet with Saddam Hussein to convey American concerns over Iraq's unconventional weapons and its continuous support for terrorism. The Commerce Department took unilateral action to limit trade with Iraq and the Department of Defense wanted to limit the transfer of technology. Facing a mounting opposition from other parts of the bureaucracy and a public outcry, the State Department dispatched a National Security Council (NSC) official, Richard Haass, and Kelley to inform Hussein that the United States was suspending the $500 million commodity program (Freedman and Karsh 1993, 157–164; Gordon and Trainor 1995, 13).

American displeasure increased Hussein's acts of belligerence, which by June included more threats against Kuwait and a refusal to extradite Abu Abbas. On June 27, Glaspie met with Nazir Hamdoon, by then a deputy foreign minister, to inform him that Iraq may be put back on the list of countries sponsoring terrorism, a move that would have resulted in the suspension of 85 percent of licensed American exports (Jentleson 1994, 165–166). As if to signal his defiance, in a July 17 speech, Saddam Hussein threatened action against Kuwait in spite of the fact that during a July 10–11 meeting, Arab members of OPEC had agreed to reduce pumping until the oil reference price of 18 dollars was restored. On July 19 Hussein ordered large-scale army maneuvers in the south of Iraq.

A day later, the Israeli Defense Minister Moshe Arens, accompanied by the chiefs of the Mossad and Aman met with his American counterparts, Richard Cheney, and CIA Director William Webster (Baker 1995, 263; Mann 2004, 182–183). The Israeli delegation warned that Saddam Hussein was developing nuclear technology and that he posed a threat to Kuwait and Saudi Arabia. As if to confirm the Israeli warning, on July 21, the National Intelligence Officer for Warning, Charles E. Allen notified the White House that Republican Guard troops had begun arriving in Basra and were massing on the Kuwaiti border.

The prospect of an Iraqi action against Kuwait revived the split in Bush's foreign policy team. Wolfowitz, with the support of Cheney, argued that the dictator could be only deterred by a show of American troops in the region. However, the small "deterrence faction" was overruled by Baker and Scowcroft who felt that a personal appeal to Hussein was in order. On July 25 Glaspie met with the Iraqi leader to assure him that "we have no opinion on the Arab-Arab conflict, like your border dispute with Kuwait." Soon after Glaspie left for a scheduled vacation, creating the impression that relations between the two countries were on an even keel (Henderson 1991, 227; Gordon and Trainor 1995, 17).

With few independent intelligence sources in Iraq, President Bush, a former CIA director, turned for advice to Arab leaders, including King Fahd, King Hussein, and President Mubarak. In repeated phone conversations they assured him that Hussein was "bluffing" and would never invade another Arab country. American diplomats who served in the region supported this view; one of them argued that the troop maneuvers were an Iraqi version of "coercive diplomacy" (Woodward 1991, 257). The well-informed Egyptian journalist and a political insider Mohamed Heikal (1992, 156) revealed that, though taken aback by Saddam's erratic and bullying behavior, Arab leaders believed that their round-the-clock diplomacy would resolve the conflict.

To further the deception, the dictator told King Hussein that he would not invade Kuwait. Prince Bandar, then King Fahd's envoy to Baghdad, recalled that Hussein had given the Saudi king his personal word of honor to the same effect. Fahd asked Bandar to convey this assurance to the American and British governments and approved his departure for a vacation to China on July 31 (Simpson 2006, 191–194). The extent to which the Arabs misread Hussein was perhaps best demonstrated by the fact that, when the Iraqi army started crossing the border on August 2, the Kuwaiti government was caught off guard along with everyone else. Richard Perle, a critic of the CIA, would later note that the Agency became so dependent on Arab intelligence services that it adopted, along with the rest of the administration, the Arab perspective (Frum and Perle 2003, 206).

Indeed, Bush himself confessed that hours before the invasion, he had "found it hard to believe that Saddam would invade," hoping that "it was just maneuvers to bring heavy pressure on Kuwait" (Bush and Scowcroft 1998, 303). Hussein's decision to occupy another Arab country was just the first in a series of surprises in store for the administration. Washington's efforts to compel Iraq to leave Kuwait posed a larger question mark about Saddam's rationality.

The Invasion of Kuwait and the Gulf War: Deciphering the "Real" Saddam Hussein

The initial response of the Bush foreign policy team was firm but flexible, with primary attention given to what Secretary Baker (1995, 303) described as "coercive diplomacy." According to this scenario, the American show of military force in the Gulf, its burgeoning coalition, featuring a number of Arab countries, and Saudi Arabia's unprecedented decision to station American troops, would be enough to persuade Saddam Hussein to withdraw from Kuwait. Amazia Baram (2002), who polled prominent Arab intellectuals in the fall of 1990, was told by most of them that Saddam would back down in the face of the ultimatum of the Allied forces, a belief that was shared by senior Iraqi commanders who were debriefed after the war.

Much the same message was delivered by the various Arab emissaries who traveled to Baghdad; they assured Bush that a "face saving" formula could be found. Yasser Arafat, who met with Hussein a number of times in August and September, King Hussein, and President Mubarak were also among the optimists (Salinger and Laurent 1991, 126). However, Yevgeny Primakov (1991), a former KGB official in Iraq who met Hussein was less upbeat. During a White House meeting on October 19, Primakov responded to Bush's query as to whether Hussein was a "realist," by noting that "honor and dignity" were extremely important to the Iraqi ruler, implying that he may fight rather than compromise.

Hussein's state of mind was also important in the context of the larger discourse on the merits of using sanctions as opposed to military action to liberate Kuwait. Influential sections of the liberal foreign policy community and many in the Democratic Party felt that sanctions should be tried as a first step in forcing Iraq out of Kuwait. They were joined by the libertarian Cato Institute, which tended to oppose any war on the grounds that it enlarges the power of the federal government. Patrick Buchanan, speaking on behalf of the isolationist faction of the Republican Party, similarly endorsed sanctions while arguing that a war would serve only Israeli interests.

However, neoconservatives took a dim view of Western capacity to dislodge the dictator through peaceful means (Decter 1990; Perle 1990a, 1990b). They, along with Republican hardliners, were in favor of military intervention to remove the Iraqis from Kuwait. Although not publicized at the time, King Fahd and Prince Bandar were also anxious to see Hussein punished. The Prince felt that "what happened in Kuwait" was "so unique, so blatant, so arrogant, so violent, and so deceiving" that Hussein could never be trusted again. To Bandar, Hussein's miscalculations were compounded by the "dangers of autocracy" where "you have individuals making decisions through emotions, rather than thinking through institutions" (Simpson 2006, 177, 191).

Congressional hearings on Bush's request to authorize a military action against Iraq at the end of November reflected the same sharp disagreements between those who felt that Saddam Hussein was "rational" enough to respond to economic disincentives and the more pessimistic observers. Unfortunately, predictive psychobiography pioneered by Gertrud Kurth's profile of Hitler for the Office of Strategic Services (OSS), and subsequently used by the CIA fell short of producing solid forecasting results (Rosenbaum 1998, 242). Still, Jerrold Post (1990), a foremost authority on leaders' psychology and a former CIA profiler, implied that Hussein was both too "messianic" and a high-stake international gambler to be dissuaded by sanctions. Although not a "madman," in Post's view, Saddam was highly dangerous because of a mixture of "messianic ambitions, absence of consciousness, unrestrained aggression and a paranoid outlook." Baram repeated his 1980 assertion that Hussein was a high-stakes security gambler caught up in "spirals of elation and risk taking" (quoted in Miller and Morad 2002). Another scholar who joined this burgeoning discussion argued that such high-stakes gambling was equivalent to irrationality (Steinberg 1990).

As surmised by the pessimists, the January 12, 1991 congressional vote authorizing a war and the half a million American and coalition troops amassed in the region did little to change Saddam Hussein's mind. When, in a last ditch attempt to avert the war, Baker (1995, 441) met Tariq Aziz in Geneva on January 19, the Iraqi foreign minister informed him that "we accept war." Back in Baghdad, Hussein was forecasting a convincing Iraqi victory in what he described as the "mother of all battles." According to reports from occupied Kuwait, Iraqi confidence was so high that troops did not interrupt their widespread looting, and efforts to transport parts of Kuwaiti infrastructure to Iraq continued unabated. When the allied forces launched a large-scale air offensive on January 16, followed by a ground attack, there was very little coordinated resistance. Senior Iraqi war prisoners told their debriefers that Saddam Hussein should have been in a position to understand that the Iraqi army stood no chance on the battlefield.

To compound the psychological mystery, as soon the cease-fire was signed on February 28, Saddam Hussein proclaimed Iraq to be victorious in the "mother of all battles." Hussein ability to survive in spite of a devastating defeat forced the administration to defend its decision not to depose the Iraqi dictator. Still, Bush, Secretary of State Baker, and Scowcroft readily admitted that, as the president put it: "[E]verybody felt that Saddam Hussein could not stay in office" [after his loss] (Baker 1995, 273; Bush and Scowcroft 1998, 489–490; quoted in Mylroie 2003, 81; Schweitzer and Schweitzer 2004, 534).

With Saddam Hussein firmly entrenched in Baghdad, the intense scrutiny of the regime and its leader transformed the marginal field of Iraq studies into a flourishing discipline. The mass of documents seized during the war threw some light on the elusive regime. Much of the new data indicated that, far from moderating, Hussein had presided over an increasingly brutal and corrupt national enterprise. After reviewing some of the thousands of documents, one scholar wrote that "now we can piece together" a story of "state terror and degradation of Iraqi politics" (Frelick 1992, 15). Elaine Sciolino (1991, 11, 14), the intelligence correspondent for the *New York Times* noted that "Saddam was an outlaw who built an outlaw state." She argued that "Iraq under Saddam had become a world unto itself, a world of untruth and illusion," adding that the Iraqi strongman "deployed techniques from such masters of illusion as Hitler and Stalin." Mylroie (1991, 6), who had discarded her earlier pro-Iraq advocacy, asserted that Saddam's regime was "totally repudiated" by the population. Not incidentally, these and other studies were close to Makiya's portrayal of the regime in his *Republic of Fear* (Darwish with Alexander 1991; Freedman and Karsh 1993; Henderson 1991; Karsh and Rautsi 1991; Rizvi 1991).

Much of the postwar commentary dealt with the personality of the Iraqi strongman. Using the newly available data, Post rounded out his initial portrayal of Saddam as a leader "whose flawed perception of reality" was "acerbated by isolation and sycophants." Post held Saddam to be narcissistic and paranoid, a characteristic apparently exacerbated by the frequent assassination attempts on his life. In an update of his 1980 study, Baram (1991) drew attention to Hussein's increasing need to mythologize his rule and his place in world history.

But other observers depicted Hussein as a fairly rational leader who miscalculated his moves because of the overwhelming economic difficulties faced by his country. According to this line of reasoning, Saddam turned against Kuwait only after failing to restructure his international debt (Bulloch and Morris 1991, 87– 90; Kimche 1991, 229). Another variant of the miscalculation theory depicted the Iraqi dictator as counting on the Vietnam syndrome to keep the United States from intervening in Kuwait. Hussein allegedly told Ambassador Glaspie that American society would not bear "tens of thousands of casualties" and ordered a special research unit to monitor public opinion in the United States (Heikal 1992, 335; Nelson 1990). Hussein was particularly encouraged by the congressional hearings where respected figures such as Edward Luttwak, a leading authority on military strategy, and high-ranking military officials such as the former chairman of the Joint Chiefs of Staff Admiral William J. Crowe, testified that a ground war would produce 6000—36000 American casualties (Erdman 1999; Hilsman 1992, 87; Kann 1991).

Leftist scholars took the miscalculation theory one step further by arguing that the United States tricked Iraq into invading Kuwait. Edward Said (1991a; 1991b, 3) charged that President Bush, who had a "Captain Ahab"-like obsession with Saddam Hussein, was behind the scheme to manipulate Iraq. This notion was bolstered by a forged memorandum that detailed a November 1989 agreement between Kuwait officials and William Webster to destabilize the economy of Iraq and do away with Saddam Hussein (Finnie 1992, 174; Salinger and Laurent 1991, 234–241). Eric Alterman (1991) from the leftist World Policy Institute argued that Saddam Hussein was a bogey created by the United States to shift attention from the real international dangers such as "weakening productivity, a deteriorating environment, and collapsing infrastructure." Phyllis Bennis (1991, 113), an Iraq expert in the Institute for Policy Studies, explained that the Gulf War was created by Washington as a "new public relation" exercise to "validate its international hegemony."

Some IR experts though were chastened by Hussein's behavior. The much-respected Stanford professor Alexander L. George (1993, 79), who devoted much of his career to applied uses for IR theory, lamented that "high-level policy makers and other foreign policy specialists were genuinely surprised that coercive diplomacy failed to persuade Saddam to withdraw his forces from Kuwait." George, who was commissioned by the U.S Institute for Peace to find ways of "bridging the gap between theory and practice in foreign policy" called for more research on deterrence and containment of rogue states. In the arcane language of academic debates, this might have been an admission that IR theory, heavily infused with cold war realities, was not adequate to cope with third world countries and their rulers.

However, the retooling of IR to fit the new developments was a huge task. As already noted, the contentious debate on Hussein's rationality was a proxy for the more vexing issue of his deterrability. Not since the profiling of Hitler by the OSS was so much riding on predictive psychology. The advanced stage of Iraq's nuclear program, which came as a total surprise to the CIA, alerted proliferation watchers to the dangers of what would subsequently become known as the Second Nuclear Age, and stressed the urgency of the task of deterring third world proliferators. With all the reservations about MAD, the underlying assumption was that Soviet leaders were rational and that the Politburo provided some built-in roadblocks to personal adventurism of a Stalin or a Khrushchev.

Iraq's attack on Kuwait seemingly validated the neoconservative argument that, given Hussein's shaky rationality and his highly personalized regime, such assumptions could not be taken for granted in the Iraqi case. In fact, Makiya (1993, 271) described the "burning desire to dig up all this Iraqi reasonableness" as a ploy of liberal observers to shield Hussein from international censure. Wolfowitz (1990–91) felt vindicated enough to argue that Saddam Hussein was "an international thug" who slaughtered his own people and was a major menace to the region, a view that was echoed by Pipes (1991).

While neoconservatives stopped short of publicly criticizing the decision not to invade Iraq, Cheney, Wolfowitz, and other hardliners pressed for a new approach to meet the challenges posed by Saddam Hussein. However, shortly after, Bush lost the 1992 election, leaving the incoming foreign policy team of Bill Clinton to fashion a new Iraq policy.

3

Containing a Rogue State: The Iraq Policy of the Clinton Administration

When George W.H. Bush lost the 1992 election to Bill Clinton, many commentators blamed it on his preoccupation with foreign policy. With the collapse of the Soviet Union and the Gulf War behind, there was a feeling that the New International order, a term coined by Bush, would make it easier to concentrate on domestic affairs. Still, the foreign policy team that President Clinton drafted from among the New Internationalists of the Carter era saw an opportunity to adjust America's international vision to post–cold war realities. By merging the moral-universalistic creed of the McGovern faction of the Democratic Party with economic liberalism, Liberal Internationalism was officially adopted by the administration.

Warren Christopher, the new secretary of state, was a prominent McGovernite in the Carter administration and Anthony Lake, the national security adviser, was a leading figure in the network of centers and lobbies spawned by the radical Institute for Policy Studies. In the mid-1970s, Lake served as a consultant at the Center for International Policy (CIP), a far left think tank, where he defended the genocidal policies of Khmer Rouge; he also cooperated with Morton Halperin, the head of the Center for National Security Studies (CNSS) in the anti-intelligence initiatives that lead to the publication of *The Lawless State,* a wholesale indictment of the CIA and a precursor to the Church committee (Heilbrunn 1997; Seliktar 2000, 42–50; Timmerman 1997). Les Aspin, another veteran of the anti-CIA campaign, became secretary of defense and Strobe Talbott (1990) who once had castigated Bush for turning Saddam Hussein into a "personification of evil" was named deputy secretary of state.

A number of second and third tier appointees rounded out the Liberal Internationalist contingent. Because of a determined congressional opposition, Morton Halperin was forced into a number of positions that required no Senate confirmation; among others, he was senior director for democracy at the National Security Council. Jeremy Rosner and Will Marshall from the Institute for Policy Studies-linked Progressive Policy Institute joined the White House as Clinton's foreign policy speechwriters (Christopher 1998, 19).

Repeating the pattern of the Carter administration, the new team wasted little time in pressing its vision of Liberal Internationalism on the inexperienced president. Ahead of the elections, Carter urged his party to pursue globalism and "meaningful peace" within the "international community" (Ramphal 1992, 8).

From a Military Superpower to a Moral Superpower: The Intellectual Basis of Clinton's Liberal Internationalism

In the view of many Liberal Internationalists, the collapse of communism put an end to the perennial debates between realists and moralists. Although few went so far as to argue that "international relations are undergoing a irreversible transformation toward global interdependence" and "good will," there was hope that the United States could help to create what Lake called "a word where tolerance, freedom and democracy prevail" (quoted in Haslam 2002, 243). Paul Kennedy, the author of an influential book on American decline was especially enthusiastic. Although his prediction did not come through, Kennedy was still concerned by the cost of empire; he argued that in the absence of Soviet obstructionism, international institutions such as the United Nations could achieve their true potential of global liberal institutionalism (Haslam 2002, 241).

Rejecting Bush's "imperial" vision of American power, the intellectual architects of Liberal Internationalism advocated the idea of "soft power," a notion first articulated by Joseph S. Nye (1990, 31), a Harvard political scientist and an assistant secretary of defense in the Clinton administration. Unlike direct power, "soft power" was said to be subtle, based on "sticks and carrots" administrated through a reinvigorated network of global institutions. Charles William Maynes (1989), the longtime editor of *Foreign Policy,* was another early advocate of such assertive multilateralism. Nye, Maynes, and others produced a long list of "soft nostrum" policies: international dialogue, an elevated role for nongovernmental organizations (NGOs) and other nonstate actors, and a new push to address "root causes" of international problems such as disparities of wealth and power. In addition to avoiding the appearance of "imperial" power, multilateralism was seen as the antidote to what Kennedy called "imperial overreach" (Mann 2004, 100–101).

Although Liberal Internationalism became the official foreign policy creed in Washington, it provoked strong criticism on the left and the right. Taken aback by the collapse of the Soviet Union, the hardcore left soon regrouped under the banner of antiglobalization. According to Noam Chomsky, Richard Falk, Michael Parenti, Gabriel Kolko, and Eqbal Ahmad, "soft power" multilateralism was a smoke screen for an American design to convert the world into a global capitalist economy ruled by multinational corporations. Ahmad (2000, xii, 152), a onetime director of the Transnational Institute, urged progressive forces to "confront" the new capitalist and imperialistic American empire. In a keynote speech at the Middle East Institute in 1993, Falk warned that globalization would not only deepen the divisions between rich and poor but also spread the American culture "shaped by the commercialization of violence...and official corruption" (quoted in De Atkine 1994, 8). Parenti (1995, 1–13) described Clinton's policy as "imperialism 101." In spite of the fact that *Foreign Policy* annual Globalization Index showed a steady increase in income equality, antiglobalization advocates were not persuaded. Ahmad (2000, 122) accused the Word Bank and the Intentional Monetary Fund of exaggerating the "success" of capitalist economies in Asia and Kolko (1997) continued to warn about an impeding global economic crisis.

If the market character of Clinton's Liberal Internationalism irked the leftist critics, a coalition of isolationist right-wingers and libertarians was riled by its global reach. Patrick J. Buchanan, a onetime speech writer for Reagan, emerged as the leader of this group. Buchanan (1999, 362–363) who previously opposed the Gulf War as a "Jewish intervention," developed a passionate critique of Liberal Internationalism in his book *A Republic, not an Empire.* He called Washington's new vision "messianic globalony" and argued that the neo-Wilsonian concept of a "global community" was utopian and fatally flawed (Buchanan 1999). Buchanan's critique was strongly supported by the libertarian Cato Institute and the Randolph Bourne Institute, a Libertarian Party project opposed to American intervention abroad (Carpenter 1994; Hadar 1996). Buchanan and other isolationists approved and quoted the work of the political scientist Eric Nordlinger (1995, 6) who advocated a "new reconfiguration" in American foreign policy in which the traditional doves and hawks would be replaced with the American eagle, a metaphor for isolationism. In the words of Buchanan (1999, 390) the eagle "is powerful...remotely perched and thus eminently well-protected." By and large, the isolationists, such as the radical left, charged American Jews with acting on behalf of Israel and with penetrating Washington, where they reached "posts that are extremely sensitive for US policies" (Cockburn and Silverstein 1996, 134–135).

The emergence of an isolationist right wing had split the Republican Party, leaving the neoconservative faction scrambling to establish an autonomous base of power. Even before Clinton reached the White House, the neoconservatives suffered a serious public relation setback when the draft of the 1992 Defense Planning Guidance, a top secret document was leaked to the press. Written by Zalmay Khalilzad, Paul Wolfowitz's assistant, and Lewis "Scooter" Libby on behalf of Cheney's Defense Department, the Guidance postulated a world order backed by American hegemonic power. The document put little faith in the United Nations and other international organizations, and called for "ad hoc" coalitions based on American interests. Moreover, the Guidance argued that while deterrence and containment would be retained, strategic preemption should be contemplated with regard to certain adversaries. The ensuing furor was so severe that the normally understated Wolfowitz (2003) would later describe it as "hysterical" and the neoconservative writer Michael Ledeen (1996, 144) noted that "it was assailed as if it had come from *Mein Kampf*."

In an effort to undo the damage, a group of neoconservative thinkers associated with *The Weekly Standard* founded by William Kristol, fleshed out a more positive international vision. Kristol, Wolfowitz, and Robert Kagan, among others, urged the United States to become a "benevolent hegemon," but criticized Clinton's trap of "multilateralism" and the "haphazard" and "experimental use of force," as manifested in the failed intervention in Somalia in 1993. In their view, "benevolent hegemony" firmly linked to American national interest would bring moral clarity to American foreign policy while spreading democracy, market economy, and respect for liberty around the globe (Kristol and Kagan 1996a, 1996b; Wolfowitz 1994a).

In spite of the double assault on Clinton's Liberal Internationalism, the formula developed by Carter's disciples resonated well with the American public in the midst of the longest economic expansion on record. Coupled with a relatively easy transition of many Eastern Europe countries into market democracies, the new vision seemed to vindicate the expectation that assertive multilateralism would bring peace and prosperity to all. Even the bloody conflict in Yugoslavia did not erode the faith in internationalism. In spite of a belated and somewhat grudging involvement, the United States and its NATO allies managed to stabilize the situation in the Balkans.

If the settlement of the Balkan conflict was the high point for Washington, the continuous problems with fundamentalist terrorism and Iraq seemed immune to the "soft policy" prescriptions offered by Nye and other Liberal Internationalists. Benjamin Barber (1995, 51), the author of a widely discussed book *Jihad vs. McWorld* noted that for "soft power" to work, it has to be rooted in "the universalism of a country's culture and its ability to establish a set of favorable rules and institutions that govern areas of international activity." Even those who disagreed with the Lewis-Huntington prediction of a "clash of civilizations" found it difficult to envision that such benign international norms could be easily developed in the Middle East. Indeed, it was the double problem of Islamic terrorism and a belligerent Iraq that posed the most severe test for President Clinton's international philosophy.

SHADOWBOXING: THE CLINTON ADMINISTRATION AND THE EMERGENCE OF GLOBAL ISLAMIC TERRORISM

By the time Clinton arrived in the White House, the United States had been coping with attacks of Arab and Muslim terrorists for more than 20 years. The Congress mandated the State Department to compile an annual list of terrorist organizations and countries sponsoring terrorism, but the low number of American casualties created little incentive to act. With the exception of Reagan's bombing of Libya, a state sponsor of terrorism, military retaliation had few advocates. The Clinton White House was especially adverse to public discussion of Islamic terrorism. Madeline Albright (2006, 8), then Clinton's ambassador to the United Nations, admitted that "we did all we could to distance ourselves from [Huntington's] theory of an interreligious clash of civilizations."

Using muscular antiterrorist policy was even more of a problem for the Clinton team of Liberal Internationalists. When, in February 1993, the Word Trade Center was bombed by a number of Arab nationals, the administration treated it as an isolated criminal act. Although the Clinton appointed-CIA director, James Woolsey, the FBI agent in charge of the investigation, James Fox, and Laurie Mylroie, among others, indicated the possibility of a larger network in operation, it was not until 1996, when Ramzi Yousef who masterminded the attack was captured, that a link to Osama bin Laden's al Qaeda organization was established. Mylroie (2000, 87, 109), then an Iraq expert in the American Enterprise Institute, a center of neoconservative thinking, was even less successful in persuading the administration that one of the 1993 conspirators was related to the Iraqi intelligence services. In 1994 an official from the CIA's Counterterrorism Center (CTC) described Mylroie's charges as "grandstanding" (Miniter 2003, 34; Reeve 2002, 247; Weiss 2003, 81).

As an outsider, Mylroie stood little chance of being acknowledged by the intelligence community. What is more, the state-sponsored model of terrorism collided with the new theory of a freestanding terrorist organization. In 1995, a National Intelligence Estimate reported that a "new breed" of Islamic terrorism had emerged, one that had no "state sponsor," was "loosely organized" and "had an extreme penchant for violence." The commission investigating the 9/11 attack would later note that the intelligence community was slow to "recognize the emergence of this type of terrorism" (Kean and Hamilton 2004, 426).

The "Lone Range terrorist," as some critics dubbed it, ignored a complex reality unfolding in Sudan, a country on the periphery of American intelligence interests. In 1989 the democratically elected Prime Minister Sadiq al Mahdi was deposed in a coup engineered by General Omar al Bashir, and a fundamentalist cleric Hassan al-Turabi became the speaker of the parliament. Encouraged by the success of Ayatollah Khomeini, al-Turabi established the National Islamic Front (NIF) to foment fundamentalist revolution in Arab North Africa and in Muslim black Africa. General al Bashir and al-Turabi had developed good relations with Saddam Hussein, who agreed to supply Sudan with both chemical and conventional weapons to quell a Christian and animist rebellion in the South. According to reports published in the *Guardian*, Baghdad sent ten planeloads of weapons to Khartoum before the Gulf War (Pugh 1990).

On October 1, 1990 al-Turabi led a large delegation of fundamentalist leaders to Jordan where they met with representatives of Saddam Hussein. A CIA report that was published more than a decade later claimed that the group included officials from the Syrian and Egyptian Muslim Brotherhood and envoys of Osama bin Laden. According to some sources, it was al-Turabi, the primary go-between for the Iraqis on the one side and the Advise and Reformation Committee, a precursor to al Qaeda, on the other, who decided in 1991 to create a permanent institution for the "terrorist brotherhood." About 50 terrorist delegations participated in the biannual Popular Islamic People's Conference; the Popular International Organization (PIO) served as its "parliament." Al-Turabi also invited would-be Muslim terrorists to set up training camps in his country, luring, among others, Osama bin Laden who established a number of "farms," that is, compounds that included training facilities (Bodansky 1999, 235; Hayes 2004, 62–64; Miniter 2003, 112; Robinson 2001, 136; Sageman 2004, 35–49).

Sudan's ambitious efforts to bring fundamentalism to Africa deepened its ties with Iraq. The impoverished country apparently received financial aid from Baghdad and, in return, agreed to house some of the chemical stocks that Iraq was ordered to destroy after the Gulf war. According to a report in *Jane's Intelligence Review*, the Yarmuk Military Manufacturing Facility complex, south of Khartoum, served as a storage site. There was also evidence that Iraqi engineers helped to build the pharmaceutical plant al Shifa, which had a dual capacity use. Some sources indicated that Emad al Ami, the father of the Iraqi VX program attended the opening ceremony of the facility in 1996 (Croddy 2002; Smyth 1998; Stern 2003, 255–256).

Iraq's interest in Sudan extended to its terrorist capability. General Wafiq Samarri, a onetime head of Iraqi military intelligence, disclosed that after the Gulf War Saddam Hussein had established a special committee to plan acts of terrorism against the United States (Mylroie 2004b, 231). After Iraqi intelligence failed to assassinate President Bush during his 1993 visit to Kuwait, Hussein decided to seek a higher degree of deniability by contracting with al Qaeda. Between 1992 and 1995, a deputy head of the Iraqi Intelligence Service (IIS) Faruq Hijazi met a number of times with bin Laden's second in command, the Egyptian fundamentalist Ayman al Zawahiri. Since 1992, senior al Qaeda officials, including al Zawahiri, had been traveling to Iraq where they had been entertained by intelligence personal in safe houses around Baghdad. Members of the Syrian Muslim Brotherhood who escaped to Iraq and joined al Qaeda established contacts with the Iraqi vice president Taha Yasin Ramadan (Hayes 2004, 33; 2003a, 2003b). A captured Iraqi intelligence document contained a 1992 list of Mukhabarat's contacts with Islamic terrorists that included Osama bin Laden (Woolsey 2004).

The turning point in the budding cooperation between Iraq and al Qaeda came in 1993 when Khartoum planned a top secret operation to dislodge Americans from Somalia. Al-Turabi wanted to turn Somalia into "another Vietnam," making the struggle against American forces in Mogadishu a focal point of his 1993 Islamic conference. A number of al Qaeda and Somali Islamists under sheik Hassan Dahir Aweyer joined forces with the Iraqi Saiqah commando and the Somali warlord Muhammad Aidid in a fight that ended with the downing of American helicopters. Al-Turabi, who viewed Africa as a scene of crucial turf war with the United States, was also instrumental in persuading bin Laden to plan a series of spectacular attacks on American facilities there. Convinced that the CIA in Kenya and Tanzania was leading the struggle against the NIF, bin Laden began to plan an attack on the American embassies in Kampala and Dar al Salam in 1993 (Bodansky 1999, 74–75).

Encouraged by the triumph in Somalia, the relation between Iraq and al Qaeda reached a new dimension. Michael Scheuer (2002, 124–125, 184), writing as "Anonymous," a CIA official in charge of tracking bin Laden, disclosed that Iraq provided training for al Qaeda members in Salman Pak, a terrorist training facility south of Baghdad where terrorists from the PLO and Hamas and Islamic Jihad had also trained. Other recruits were sent to camps run by the Iraqi-sponsored anti-Iranian Mujahedin el-Khalq (MEK) which provided training for the Taliban fighters. Khadir Hamza (2000, 257), a Iraqi nuclear scientist who defected to the West, claimed that bin Laden's men were allowed to train in the Abu Khalid farm, the main PLO facility in Iraq.

Training aside, bin Laden was interested in acquiring chemical, biological, radiological, and nuclear weapons. Scheuer (2002, 124–125, 184) revealed that the production of chemical weapons was approved by the INF and supervised by Colonel Abd-al-Basit Hamza. Starting in 1994, up to 60 Iraqi experts under Dr. Khalil Ibrahim Muharuchah helped, on a rotating basis, with the program that included al Shifa. Over time, the contacted were upgraded. In 1992 al Zawahiri traveled to Baghdad, where he allegedly met with Ramadan and Hussein's two sons, Uday and Qusay (McInerney and Vallely 2004, 108; Parmelee 1992; Shanker 2004).

A number of press reports in the early 1990s expressed concern over the growing terrorist hub in Sudan (Greenberger 1992; Parmelee 1992). Following a report from Khartoum about plans to assassinate Tony Lake, in 1993 the State Department put Sudan on the list of states sponsoring terrorism. However, the role of bin Laden was not well understood at the time: the CIA assumed that the Saudi multimillionaire served as the paymaster of the terrorist operations, a view that was adopted by the State Department as well. Indeed, as late as January 1996, the CIA described bin Laden as a "financier" (Tenet 2007, 102).

Fighting back the charges, Hassan al-Turabi gave an interview to Western journalists to deny that Muslims have a right to wage a military jihad, and accused the Western media of fomenting negative stereotypes. Al-Turabi emphasized that Sudan had no intention of destabilizing secular Arab countries, but praised Saddam Hussein for "gradually" returning his society to Islam (Hedges 1994).

Al-Turabi's denials notwithstanding, by 1995 the CIA and the FBI had begun to suspect that bin Laden might be a major operative rather than a "Gucci" terror financier. Starting early in the year, the CIA received a stream of cables from Khartoum corroborating the rumors that Iraq was helping Sudan and bin Laden to develop explosives and chemical weapons. According to these sources, the premier Iraqi bomb maker Brigadier Salim al Ahmed visited one of bin Laden's farms in the company of the Director of Iraqi Intelligence Mani abd al Rashid al Tikriti. Sudan's opposition group, the National Democratic Alliance, wrote to Human Right Watch complaining that the regime had used chemical weapons and that Iraqi engineers worked on the chemical munitions projects (Hayes 2002; 2004, 97; Reeve 2002, 184). In June 1995, President Hosni Mubarak was almost assassinated while on an official visit to Addis Ababa, an attack widely attributed to Sudan and al Qaeda. On November 13, 1995, a bomb exploded outside the Office of Program Managers for Saudi Arabian National Guard in Riyadh where a number of Americans were killed. The National Security Agency intercepted a communication from one of bin Laden's farms that blessed the Riyadh attack. Sixteen days later the Egyptian embassy in Islamabad was bombed, and fifteen people were killed. The series of attacks was preceded in April by an anonymous leaflet threatening strikes against U.S. and British forces, if they did not leave Saudi Arabia. Ominously, around the same time, the CIA received what was described as a credible report about bin Laden's efforts, in cooperation with Sudan and Iraq, to develop chemical weapons (Lesch 2002; Mahle 2004, 189; Miniter 2003, 97). Faced with growing evidence, the administration was forced to take steps. In January 1996, the chief of the CTC, Winston P. Wiley, acting under the directive of John Deutch, the director of intelligence, created a "virtual station" named Terrorist Financial Links (TFL) to track terrorist finances. The group, which was nicknamed "Alec station" by its first head, Michael Scheuer, soon turned its attention almost exclusively to anti–bin Laden operation. In the same month, Clinton informed Congress that bin Laden's assets in the United States would be frozen. However, the unit suffered a setback when, soon after, the State Department decided to close down its embassy in Khartoum. The move was recommended by the CIA, after its station chief there, Paul Quaglia, reported that al Qaeda was planning to target the National Security Adviser Tony Lake and had threatened the embassy personnel (Tenet 2007, 100–102).

The growing al Qaeda profile prompted the administration to demand the expulsion of bin Laden. After the outgoing ambassador to Sudan Timothy Carney met with President al Bashir and al-Turabi, on February 6, 1996, the Sudanese Foreign Minister Ali Osman Mohammed Taha told Carney that Sudan was concerned about its relations with the United States and offered to expel the al Qaeda chief. When Saudi Arabia declined to accept him, on March 3, the Minister of Defense Elfatih Erwa flew to Washington where he met with Carney, David Shinn, Director of Eastern African Affairs in the State Department, and members of the CIA's Directorate of Operations. According to Erwa, the Sudanese offered to extradite bin Laden to the United States, but the administration declined.

Following September 11, the details of the March meeting became highly controversial. Clinton's critics maintained that his foreign policy team was too timid and overwhelmed by the legal complications of a bin Laden trial (Gertz 1999; Miniter 2003, 99–104, 122–133). According to some accounts, the U.S. case against bin Laden rested on "heresay evidence"—much of it from the Sudanese opposition, a Moroccan intelligence source with credibility problems and an occasional satellite intercept—that would not stand up in court (Randal 2004, 123–124). Defenders of Clinton sought to undermine the significance of the episode, commenting that "conservative authors like Richard Miniter" relied on "false reports of a discredited Sudanese intelligence officials" (Brooks 2004, 241). George Tenet (2007, 103), then Deputy DI stated that he was not aware of "anything to substantiate" the rumors that the United States had rejected the deal.

Testimony before the 9/11 commission indicated that Samuel "Sandy" Berger, deputy national security adviser and others concluded at the time that there was no legal basis for extradition. According to Berger, the Counterintelligence and Security Groups (CSG) had a "hypothetical discussion" about indicting bin Laden during which a senior official from the Justice Department rejected the idea. Berger added that bin Laden then was still mainly perceived as a "terrorist financier." Daniel Benjamin and Steven Simon (2003, 247), experts on terrorism in Clinton's NSC, confirmed that "since he had not been indicted, the Justice Department had no ground to hold him" (Kean and Hamilton 2004, 162; Strasser 2004, 63).

Indeed, though the State Department upgraded bin Laden to "one of the most significant sponsors of Islamic extremism," in 1996, it still viewed him as financier. With stories about bin Laden's alleged great wealth in circulation, the theory of a freestanding terrorist organization was gaining more traction. As one British expert on terrorism commented, "[T]error does not have to be state sponsored" (MacLeod 1996). After departing from Sudan for Afghanistan on May 18, 1996, bin Laden set up a new chain of training camps and sought new state sponsors for his costly endeavor. Once again, bin Laden's move proved providential. Unknown to American intelligence, al Qaeda was already collaborating with Iran, mainly through the Lebanese Hezbollah. Planning to increase attacks on American forces in the Gulf, Teheran hosted a "terrorist summit" during June 21–23, 1996. Mahdi Chamran, the head of the Iranian external intelligence service, was in charge of the Committee of Three, which morphed into Hezbollah International. Osama bin Laden, Imad Mughniyah, the legendary Hezbollah terrorist, and Ahmad Saleh served as appointed members.

The move to unite the disparate terrorist groups made sense to both al-Turabi and the Iranians who in 1992 had taken over the Kubar prison in Khartoum to house a contingent of their Islamic Revolutionary Guard Corp (IRGC). Two days after the conference ended, on June 25, a massive explosion destroyed the Khobar Towers in Dahran, Saudi Arabia, killing and wounding scores of American military personnel.

The Teheran summit was followed up by a July 10–15 conferences in Konli, Pakistan, which boasted representatives from virtually all Middle East terrorist groups as well as half a dozen officers from the Iraqi security services (Jasper 2001; Posner 2003, 106–111; Robinson 2001, 188). The Konli meeting ended with a resolution pledging a "relentless war" against the West. It was followed up by an August 26, *bayan* (statement) of Osama bin

Laden, a 12-page document summarizing the main Islamist grievances against the United States, Saudi Arabia, and Israel. The *bayan* ended with a official declaration of war on the West "to be waged from the peaks of the Hindu Kush," Later in the year, bin Laden disclosed that Islamists had participated in the fighting in Somalia, a development that came as total news to the CIA, apparently because the intelligence community had ignored a top secret 1993 memorandum on the Mogadishu ambush (Robinson 2001, 207; Waller 1996; Weiss 2003, 145).

The massive scale of the Dahran attack shocked the White House, but the CIA had no firm leads on the perpetrators beyond suspicion focusing on bin Laden or Iran. The Agency had little information on both; it did not penetrate the Teheran conference and got only a secondhand account of the proceedings about four months later (Posner 2003, 106). The 2001 trial of those involved in the Khobar attack revealed that the core group was made up of Saudi al Qaeda jihadists, but the background network was never fully exposed, leaving some to speculate about an Iranian or even an Iraqi connection (Miniter 2003, 237). Still other sources alleged that senior CIA officials "played an important role" in Clinton's efforts to downplay the Iranian connection. After the Dahran bombing, the State Department quietly convened a grand jury in an effort to indict bin Laden (Risen 2006, 213; Robinson 2001, 222).

The bin Laden station was expected to provide new information, but according to critics, Scheuer, a former analyst in the Islamic Extremist Branch of the CTC, was an uninspiring choice to head the new unit. Altogether, the station was considered a "bureaucratic Siberia" by those who were on a fast track career (Mahle 2004, 192; Schoenfeld 2005, 50). The limited attention paid to the staffing of the bin Laden station was a reflection of the low assessment of terrorist threats to American national security.

The CIA's 1996 Worldwide Threat Assessment ranked only drugs and environmental hazards lower than terrorism. As with much of the CIA analysis, the increasing tight terrorist network and its global reach were viewed in isolation of broader political changes in Islam. Melissa Boyle Mahle (2004, 102) a former high-level CIA operative, bemoaned the failure to comprehend the "larger context of growing anti-Americanism and resurgent political Islam." More important, to the Liberal Internationalists in the Clinton administration and to the majority of the discursive community, a muscular intelligence agency capable of penetrating this complex subterranean structure was an anathema.

The Clinton "Reformation": Intelligence in the Service of Liberal Internationalism

As noted in chapter 2, the Carter-Turner reform weakened the CIA operational capacity and the Iran-Contra fiasco shortened the legal leash. William Webster nominated by President Reagan to "clean up" the agency, appointed a legal team to tighten the regulations for covert actions. The number of lawyers was doubled to 40 and the team moved from an annex to the CIA headquarters. The substance and symbolism of Webster decision was not lost on the Directorate of Operations; Webster was universally disliked and ridiculed for his alleged ignorance of all things foreign (Kessler 2003, 132; Posner 2003, 21). President Bush appointed Robert Gates in an effort to bolster the CIA, but the Clinton victory cut these efforts short.

Well before Clinton took the oath of office, the foreign policy community was engaged in a vigorous discourse about the future of intelligence in the post–cold war period. Leading the way was Senator Daniel Patrick Moynihan, a Democrat and a longtime critic of the Agency. Moynihan (1988, 169–174) who previously described the CIA under Casey as "out of bounds" was now attacking it for failing to predict the collapse of the Soviet Union. In a series of speeches and editorials, Moynihan argued that the Directorate of Operations should be abolished and the analytical functions of the CIA should be transferred to the State Department. The House majority leader Richard Gephardt shared some of these sentiments; in March 1993 he declared that "the world is increasingly impatient with security and clandestine activity" (Smist 1994, 323).

Many of the Liberal Internationalists who joined the Clinton team felt that the collapse of communism altered the balance between concerns for security and democracy and that a more open intelligence agency was in order (Jones 2001). Buoyed by the appointment of Morton Halperin, Marcus Ruskin the longtime director of the Institute for Policy Studies urged the dismantling of the CIA "along with the atmosphere of paranoia and conflict." Warren Christopher, an enthusiastic supporter of Moynihan, wanted to merge terrorism into a special bureau that would deal with narcotics and crime. Only a determined opposition of Republicans in Congress prevented this step (Kean and Hamilton 2004, 139).

Sensing an opening, the graduates of the Church Committee and the anti-intelligence campaign of the IPS pushed for a New Oversight policy for the CIA. Loch K. Johnson (1989, 324–325; 1992–93), a former Church committee staffer and a leading intelligence expert advocated "smart intelligence" with little covert action and plenty of openness and accountability. In his view, this was needed to balance a "secret service brought to life darkly" in a country with "strong democratic traction." Melvin A. Goodman, a one-time rival of Gates and a professor at the National War College declared that the "CIA spy service has become an anachronism" (quoted in Bamford 2004, 130). Writing in *Foreign Affairs*, Roger Hilsman (1995) a former high-ranking Intelligence and State Department official, stated that espionage provided relatively little information and should be terminated after the cold war. Another expert contended that all CIA requests for covert operations should be validated by external experts (Gries 1995). Jessica Tuchman Mathews, a former Institute for Policy Studies associate who went on to head the Carnegie Endowment, expressed hope that in the future, intelligence would be limited to matters of environmental degradation and a search for a more equitable distribution of resources (Dabelko and Dabelko 1993).

It came therefore as a surprise when the president picked R. James Woolsey, a relatively low-key intelligence expert who had worked for both the Democrats and Republicans to head the Agency (Posner 2003, 54–55). Woolsey's acceptance speech in 1993 was an eye-opener for all those who expected to hear about international goodwill and cooperation. He noted that the new world order "was a jungle filled with a bewildering variety of poisonous snakes" and promised to bolster the Agency's ability to deal with this multitude of new enemies. Among the steps the new director wanted to take were an increase in the number of Arab linguists and lowering of the barriers between operatives and analysts. He also argued against the Agency's policy of promotion based on the number of reports rather than their quality (Jehl 1993; Mahle 2004, 162; Waller 1996). However, Woolsey, described as a "compulsive truth teller," was not popular with the president whose interest in intelligence was minimal to begin with. After Woolsey rejected the White House candidate for the post of the CIA general counsel, Clinton refused to meet his intelligence chief. Woolsey speculated that his efforts to link the World Center bombing to the bin Laden network were not welcome by an administration that tried to minimize the event (Morris 2003, 74; Weiner 1995). Whatever was the status of the relations between Woolsey and the president, Woolsey would not have survived the disclosure in 1994 that the CIA had harbored for years the mole Aldrich Ames who compromised the American espionage network in the Soviet Union.

John Deutch, an undersecretary in the Department of Defense who hoped for the top job was virtually coerced by Clinton into replacing Woolsey in 1995. The new director wasted little time in making his contempt for the Agency known, stating that "compared to uniformed officers," the CIA officers were not "as competent." In his confirmation hearings, Deutch promised Congress to change the Agency so that it "will not take part in immoral or illegal intelligence activity" (Haar 1995; Kessler 2003, 145; Weiner 1995).

The intelligence scandal in Guatemala provided Deutch with the opportunity of instituting a full-scale "reformation" of the CIA. In 1992, a senior Marxist guerrilla Efrain "Bamaca" Velasques disappeared during an operation of the Guatemalan army. After an unsuccessful camping to find him, Jennifer Harbury, his American wife, approached Bianca Jagger, a leftist activist and a fierce critic of American foreign policy in the southern hemisphere. Jagger, the then lover of Robert Torricelli, a Democrat on the House Intelligence Committee asked him to look into the matter. Torricelli publicized the charges that Julio Robert Alpirez, a colonel in the Guatemalan army and an alleged CIA informant, authorized the killing of Velasquez and of Michael Divine, an American innkeeper. The story, published in the *New York Times,* energized a wide array of CIA critics, including the journalist Seymour M. Hersh, a self-appointed intelligence watchdog.

Although Clinton's own Intelligence Oversight Board found that the information about Colonel Alpirez was "unreliable and was contradicted by other evidence," the president pushed the CIA director to quell the public scandal. Deutch fired two senior officers and reprimanded seven others

(DeParle 1995; Hitz 2000; Lowry 2003, 305; Mahle 2004, 172–176). In what turned out to be even more of a humiliation for the Agency, the DI traveled to Los Angeles to meet with Maxine Waters, an outspoken African American legislator, to respond to charges that the CIA had sold crack cocaine in black neighborhoods to finance the contras in Nicaragua. The sensational accusation first appeared in the San Jose *Mercury* and spread rapidly in the African American community, Clinton's core constituency (Miller 1997).

With the tacit encouragement from the White House, Deutch, who praised Torricelli for his leadership in putting the CIA in line with "American interests and value," instituted a radical reform in the hiring practices of foreign operatives and overhauled the covert actions code. The so-called Deutch scrub involved a series of legal and personal screenings at the headquarters to prevent "unsavory elements" from getting on the CIA payroll. The "politically correct espionage" as one insider called it, discouraged any risk taking and, in effect, put a stop to most covert activities (Lowry 2003, 305; Mahle 2004, 173)

By all accounts, Deutch and his top executive assistant Nora Slatkin had a highly demoralizing impact on the Agency. Duane Clarridge (1997, 152), a senior CIA official, noted that fear pervaded both operatives and analysts, resulting in bland conclusions least likely to jeopardize promotions. The risk-averse philosophy was especially detrimental to field operatives who were encouraged to take out personal liability insurance to help cover legal fees in case of a potential problem with headquarters. Slatkin, whom many considered "clueless," generated so much anxiety that "alarm bells rang" in the hallways when she passed through and some managers appointed special assistants to "manage" Slatkin. Deutch was so despised that, after he fired the officers implicated in the Guatemala case, the Directorate of Operations "rose in defiance, ignoring for four hours Deutch's order to disperse" (Mahle 2004, 168, 177–178).

The paralysis in the Directorate of Operations headed by David Cohen, whom Deutch moved from the Directorate of Intelligence, could not have come at a worse time. Penetrating the intricate Terrorism International that had taken shape in Sudan, Lebanon, Iran, and Afghanistan would have required an aggressive covert operation. However, at the height of Deutch's tenure, there were only about 800 field operatives, and only a few of them had a Middle East background. Deutch's policy of "rotating" case officers, by which everyone was allowed to bid for the job without any restrictions based on qualifications made the situation even worse (Paseman 2004, 190–191). As a member of the 9/11 commission put it, the spread of bureaucracy and "legalism and lawyers" at every level of the policy process was "debilitating" (Lehman 2004).

Much as the Deutch "scrub" was responsible for the overall low morale of the Agency, additional factors worked to obscure the larger context of terrorism. Woolsey and other critics noted that the administration's insistence on treating terrorism as a criminal justice matter impeded the collaboration between the FBI and the CIA under the so-called wall of partition between the two agencies set up to prevent persecution of anti-Vietnam activists. The judicial approach was advocated by Jamie Gorelick, Clinton's deputy attorney general, who wrote a memo demanding a "more clearly separate" criminal probe and counterintelligence efforts. The judicial approach, which required "high evidentiary standards and arcane evidentiary rules," prompted the FBI Director Louis J. Freeh (2005, 290) to comment that we were "arming ourselves with arrest warrants ... when the enemy was arming itself with truckloads with five thousand pounds of explosives." The 9/11 commission concluded that the criminal justice methodology failed to connect the various acts of terrorism in the United States and abroad and created the impression that "the law enforcement system" was well equipped to deal with the terrorist phenomena (Hall and Locy 2004; Kean and Hamilton 2004, 106; Miniter 2003, 121; Mylroie 2000, xii; White 2001).

Perhaps equally detrimental was the methodology used by the Directorate of Intelligence (DI). According to Mahle (2004, 13, 94, 116) who described the DI as "academia on steroids," "organizational stovepipes" kept the Agency from looking at events "within an integrated matrix." For instance, the African division knew about Somali warlords but had no knowledge of Islamists there, because they were filed under a different category. Experts on Shiites "were not talking" to experts on Sunni extremism, and both failed to communicate with Asian hands. Indeed, the Directorate of Intelligence apparently misunderstood Salafism, a new variety of Sunni Islamism, and its relation to the older Moslem Brotherhood movement. Robert Baer (2003, 112–113, 122), a longtime CIA operative, alleged that the CIA had no files on the Brotherhood, even though its members were implicated in the assassination of Anwar Sadat. Not incidentally, Omar Abd al Rahman, the "Blind Sheik," who was sentenced for his role in the 1993 attack on the World Trade Center, was admitted to the United States in spite of the fact that he was a member of the group involved in Sadat's assassination.

As Karmon (2005) would subsequently show, such rigid methodology missed the terrorist coalition between revolutionaries, nationalists, and Islamists. For instance, it was not uncommon for different groups to share "real estate." Baer (2003, 218) claimed that a bin Laden detachment and a radical faction of Yasser Arafat's Fatah jointly controlled the large Palestinian refugee camp Ayn al-Hilwa in Lebanon. The growing collaboration between Iraqi Salafists and the secular regime of Saddam Hussein was another case in point. Hussein needed Sunni revivalists to counter Shiite fundamentalists and Kurdish nationalists; among other measures, they introduced a welfare system network to ease the effect of sanctions in Faluja and other Sunni strongholds. Baghdad took to hosting Islamic conferences where Izzat Ibrahim al Douri, Hussein's top aide, praised the virtues of Islamic life while intelligence officers recruited Islamic fighters. By 1996 Hussein began to appear on a televised daily prayer facing Mecca and allocated \$7.5 million to build a mega mosque in Baghdad. Although it is impossible to determine whether this was a genuine conversion or a publicity stunt, observers admitted that they missed the growth of Salafism in Iraq (Algosaibi 1993, 103; Bodansky 1999, 323; Hayes 2004, 46; Hedges 1994; Kengor 2004, 213; Lukitz 1995, 5). Only years later, the leading Iraqi expert Phebe Marr (2004, 297) would set the record straight, noting that "as the Ba'ath secular ideology declined, Saddam Hussein began aligning himself with Islam and Islamic vision."

If the methodology of the DI was to blame for a fragmented view of Islamic revival and its threat to the West, the MESA paradigm was responsible for creating the larger context through which Islamism was perceived. By mid-1990s, the epistemic community that related all Middle East ills to the Arab-Israeli conflict seemed to be gaining on Bernard Lewis, Daniel Pipes, and other critics whom Khan (1997) dismissed as "entrepreneurs." Writing on behalf of the MESA academics, Khan proudly announced that "in the struggle for sovereignty between the academy and the entrepreneurs," a "power shift" in Washington had vindicated the former.

MESA professors research was vigorously applied to demonstrate that Western perceptions of Islamic revivalism were mistaken at best and a new form of orientalism at worst, as Edward Said (1997, xvi–xix) had asserted in his revised version of *Covering Islam*. In a string of writings on the "myth or reality" of Islamic terrorism, Esposito (1995, 3, 195, 235; 1994, 19; 1990, 8) described talk about Islamic Jihad as "sensationalized" and "facile stereotyping." He categorically rejected the "clash of civilizations theory" and compared it to the "communist scare" during the cold war. In what looked like a response to Pipes's (1994) argument that an "Islamic international" is threatening the West, Esposito ridiculed the idea that an "Islamist Comintern" led by "religious Stalinists" is poised to challenge the world. Esposito blamed such negative coverage on ignorance about contemporary Islamic leaders such as Hassan al-Turabi, adding that "they are often individuals who provide fresh interpretations of Islam." Other academics agreed, pointing out that even the favorite "villain" of the West, fundamentalist Iran, was becoming moderate. Indeed, the election of Mohammad Khatami, a relative moderate, gave many observers renewed faith that Iran may become the cradle of the long-awaited Islamic reformation. At the very least, they expected an "Iranian perestroika" (Boroujerdi 1996; Hunter 1998, 1992).

To the extent that MESA scholars were ready to acknowledge the existence of "Muslim rage," they drew on the antiglobalization literature to explain its "root causes." Poverty and maldistribution of wealth in the Middle East, aggravated by the capitalist nature of globalization, were seen as major factors (Bennis 1996, 66; Esposito 1997; Karabell 1996–97; Ranstorp 1996; Wallerstein 1997). As always, the unresolved Arab-Israeli conflict was high on the blame scale. In the words of Esposito (1995, 73) "the creation of Israel in 1948" was perceived as "the boldest example of European colonialism," fueling the rage and symbolizing the "battle against imperialism" (Salame 1993).

Constructivist IR theory provided yet another explanation for the alleged inordinate preoccupation with an imaginary Islamist threat. Derived from the larger field of critical scholarship, constructivism posited that foreign policy of a given country is shaped by deep-seated identity needs and anxieties, including the view of the "other." Influenced by such notions, revisionist scholars of the cold war pushed the idea that far from menacing the West, the Soviet Union was a bogeyman created by the American industrial military complex. According to this line of reasoning, Washington turned militant Islam into a new bogeyman to fill the void. Writing in 1996, Said (2000, 48) declared that since 1991 the "U.S. defense and intelligence establishment" had sought to turn Islam into a "new common enemy," an effort aided by many "authoritative foreign policy journals," newspapers, and Bernard Lewis and his students, many of whom were Israelis.

Stephen Walt (1997, 189) a prominent Harvard professor, declared that by "portraying the contemporary world as one of restless cultural competition," we are "building up new bogeymen." Esposito (1995, 190) implied that, like the portrayal of the Soviet Union as the "evil empire," the vilification of Islam was driven by "fear and the demonization of the enemy." Parenti (1995, 92) claimed that "demonized adversaries are often accused of terrorism." Twing (1998, 20, 24–27) noted that the American foreign policy paradigm is predicated on the myth of "bad guys," which involves a tendency to demonize an adversary to the point of creating a "bogeyman."

While the MESA community stopped short of accusing all terrorist experts of Islamophobia, discussion of Islamic terrorism was not without cost. Steven Emerson (1997), who tied Osama bin Laden to the World Trade Center and the Khobar Towers attacks and predicted that there would be more World Trade Center bombings, was repeatedly attacked as a "fearmonger" and allegedly blacklisted from appearing on National Public Radio (Peretz 2002). With the threat of Islamic radicalism paradigmatically minimized and the drive for an open and democratically accountable intelligence service at peak, understanding the complex and multilayered phenomenon of Islamic terrorism proved particularly difficult. The findings of the Clinton's 1994 Presidential Commission on the Roles and Capabilities of the United States Intelligence Community chaired by Aspin and after his death in 1995, by Harold Brown, Carter's secretary of defense, was a case in point. Loch Johnson (1996b, 48–49; 54, 1996a), a protégé of Aspin who worked for the commission, argued that the report released in 1996, ushered a "new system of accountability and openness" and criticized Woolsey for his "poisonous snakes" view of international reality. Advocates of New Oversight were encouraged by the commission's recommendation that the National Intelligence Council reports should be "vetted" by an outside panel of scholars. Veteran critics of the CIA were particularly gratified by the proposal to return the Directorate of Intelligence to the Carter-era National Assessment Center. The commission's recommendations were seen as a triumph for a more open and democratic intelligence service with increased legislative control over covert actions. According to Mahle (2004, 84), the Agency was deeply dismayed by some of the recommendations, leading one critic to quip that the proposals were a "marvelous oxymoron," an "overt covert action" (Mahle 2004, 84).

Although the complex world of terrorism presented the greatest problem to the Clinton White House, the dilemma posed by the continuing challenge of Saddam Hussein to American foreign policy was only marginally less vexing.

The Travails of Containing Iraq: Testing the Limits of Liberal Internationalism

Saddam Hussein's capacity to survive a punishing defeat in the Gulf War and a widespread but poorly organized revolt by the Shiites and the Kurds came as a bitter surprise to the Bush administration. The American commander General Norman Schwarzkopf might have inadvertently contributed to this outcome by allowing the Iraqi army the use of helicopters. According to persistent rumors, Salah Omar Ali al Takriti, a high-ranking Iraqi defector acting as a double agent, persuaded Schwarzkopf that anti-Saddam plotters would need helicopters to put down forces loyal to the regime (Hamza 2000, 210). Instead, the Iraqi army used them to massacre the rebels.

The second-guessing about the wisdom of cutting short the offensive put the Bush White House on the defensive, with one military commentator calling it a "hollow victory" (Record 1993). Clinton's election strategy provided voices to the chorus of Bush's critics. Clinton accused his rival of being "soft" on Hussein and of coddling the dictator. American military sales to Iraq and the related Atlanta bank scandal dubbed "Iraqgate" featured prominently in the final month of the campaign. In fact, Iraqgate became somewhat of an obsession of the left. The liberal Arca foundation and Tom Blanton, the director of the left-leaning National Security Archives, sponsored a major investigation into what was described as the "White House illegal" arming of Iraq (Friedman 1993, xii). Although extensive investigation by Congress and the Janet Reno's Justice Department absolved the Bush administration of wrong doing, Iraqgate acquired a life of its own in the discourse on Iraq (Juster 1994).

Once elected, Clinton tried to extend the tenets of Liberal Internationalism to the Iraqi leader. In a *New York Times* interview, the president-elect hinted that if Hussein mended his ways, he would consider normalizing relations with Iraq (Harris 2005, 7). After a deluge of criticism, the new administration decided to switch Iraq to its multilateral track, a policy that was warmly welcomed by Maynes (1993–94) and other ardent multilateralists.

In fact, the scaffolding of a multilateral approach had already existed, brought on by the discovery that, before its invasion of Kuwait, Baghdad was only month away from developing a nuclear device. Some critics accused Hans Blix, the then head of the International Atomic Energy Agency (IAEA) overseeing Iraq nuclear program, of incompetence, and others charged that the agency was penetrated by Saddam Hussein's agents. With the disgraced IAEA pushed aside, in 1991 the United Nations passed Resolution 697 creating a new body, the United Nations Special Commission on Disarmament (UNSCOM) to destroy Iraq's unconventional arsenal. To assure compliance, the UN imposed punishing sanctions on Iraq, including a moratorium on selling oil, the country's chief sources of revenue. UNSCOM's intrusive inspection regime and sanction were part of a broader policy of containing Saddam Hussein and preventing him from causing more mischief in the Middle East.

Much of the theory and practice of containment was derived from American experience with the Soviet Union. Although liberals had criticized containment during the cold war as unduly harsh, the policy was subsequently praised for undermining communism (Larson 1985, 315). Bruce Jentleson (1994, 20), who served as a consultant to Al Gore during the 1992 elections and later worked in policy planning in the State Department, credited his writings with the decision to add Iraq to the containment regime imposed by the United States on Iran. On May 18, 1993, Martin Indyk, the Near East and South Asia expert on Clinton's NSC, officially announced the double containment policy. The message from the White House was clear; it considered Saddam Hussein criminal and irredeemable and hoped that containment would force a regime change in Iraq (Gause III 1994).

Bold policy announcements aside, the Clinton administration was less sure about containing the cunning and defiant dictator. Nothing in the theory of containment prepared Washington for Hussein's belligerent and confrontational attitude toward UNSCOM, Not known at the time was the fact that Saddam Hussein had established a special Concealment Committee to deceive and harass the inspectors. UNSCOM chief, Rolf Ekeus (1996) subsequently revealed that his inspectors were not optimistic about finding Hussein's hidden arsenal.

When Hussein Kamal, Saddam's son-in-law, his brother, and their wives defected to Jordan in 1995, Ekeus's pessimism was borne out. Kamal, who was in charge of much of the WMD program, disclosed that in spite of a signed declaration, Iraq still had considerable stocks of lethal weapons. The reasons for Kamal's defection generated a lot of speculation in the intelligence community but no firm conclusions. The normally knowledgeable Israeli scholar Amazia Baram (1995) attributed Kamal's decision to a power struggle within the progressively dysfunctional family. Kamal was reported to be offended by Uday's efforts to muscle in on his "territory" of weapon production. Watching Uday wounding the president's half brother Watban Ibrahim during a violent quarrel, Kamal apparently decided to flee (Yahia and Wendl 1997, 277). Others surmised that Kamal advised Saddam Hussein to come clean about the WMD and was turned upon by either the president or his sons (Bhatia and McGrory 2000, 266; Buzby 1995). Whatever the reason, Kamal's revelations forced the regime to disclose the existence of large stockpile of illicit weapons.

If the behavior of the Iraqi president and his dysfunctional family made for tabloid-type headlines, it posed a challenge to the authors of containment policy. Like all theories of international behavior, containment theory was premised on a certain mode of rational thinking embedded in the broader context of deterrence theory. Containment and economic sanctions were based on the notion that to avoid paying prohibitive costs, a "rational" leader would eventually desist from policies that went against the community of nations.

The case of Iraq triggered a new round of theorizing about the meaning of deterrence after the cold war. In the words of one scholar, the key question was whether the assumption "of a rational opponent who can be deterred from a given course of action if the costs of pushing it clearly outweigh the benefits to be gained" could be applied to rogue regimes and terrorists organizations (Payne 1996, 45). The debate split along predictable paradigmatic and ideological lines, with realists, neorealists, liberals, neoliberals, and constuctivists, all proffering different answers. Much of this arcane theorizing drew upon European history, prompting one expert to denounce the intense focus on U.S.-Russian relations in a world of novel challenges (Payne 1996, 9). Another critic denounced the habit of applying the "intellectual baggage" from the cold war to "today's... different world" (Clark 1997, 130; 1998).

At the heart of this and similar criticism was the contention that the old rules of deterrence do not apply to the Second Nuclear Age, a world populated by rogue proliferators and overshadowed by a threat of an "Islamic bomb" and a "clash of civilizations." While Second Nuclear Age theorists questioned whether the Lewis- Huntington's dark prediction will come true, they were fairly sure that the "millennial optimists," a reference to Liberal Internationalists, were wrong to put their faith in the compelling power of the international system (Gray 1999, 17–78).

Even though Iraq, Iran, and Sudan were part of the rogue gallery, the IR literature carried little reference to the problems posed by the discursive habits of Arab politics. An early study of the Egyptian president Gamal Abdel Nasser showed how his linguistic flourishes turned into symbolic entrapment; when Israel called his bluff, he was forced to take action and this triggered the Six Day War (Barnett 1998, 247). Commenting on the cultural peculiarities of the Middle East, another study noted that "what a culture finds meaningful" cannot be predicted "based on an external perspective" (Lebanon and Crocker 2000, 59). But in the absence of research on strategic thinking in the Arab world, abstract theorizing laced with European examples was routine, prompting the prominent intelligence expert Richard Betts (1997, 31) to ask whether strategic studies have a future. Betts noted that "theorizing becomes a closed system" among scholars who have no interest in empirical reality. Betts explained that such academic detachment was easy for those who did not have to "meet a payroll in the policy world" (1997, 31).

Front and center on the policy burner, the Clinton team, already humbled by the debacle in Somalia, decided to tackle the issue of failed and rogue states. Vice President Gore created the "State Failure Task Force" to investigate how states such as Somalia disintegrate. The Task Force considered hundreds of possible factors, concluding that high levels of infant mortality and high numbers of unemployed youth are the chief contributing factors (Esty et al. 1995). Critics suggested that the large amount of money spent on producing such trivial results could be better used to feed poor children (Zimmerman 1996).

Tony Lake (1994) took a more applied approach to the phenomenon of "backlash states" and the measures needed to confront them. In a high-profile *Foreign Policy* article, the national security adviser admitted that Iran and Iraq are "particularly troublesome," but expressed confidence that "selective pressures" would modify the behavior of both regimes. True to his Liberal Internationalist credentials, Lake announced that the administration would use the less inflammatory "state of concern" label.

Neoconservative critics, however, strongly doubted whether rogue states, under whatever label, could be deterred, mollified, or modified. They argued that ruthless dictatorships such as Iraq were especially difficult to deal with as the international community had little input into the insular world of its leadership and no effect on public opinion (Trevan 1999, 375). Neoconservative veterans of the Reagan and Bush administrations were quick to point out that Baghdad had a record of outwitting international controls. Paul Wolfowitz (1994b), the then dean of Johns Hopkins School of Advanced International Studies, warned about the trap of "multilateralism" and predicted that it would be hard to maintain the type of sanction regimen necessary to contain Hussein. Daniel Pipes (1995a) made much the same argument in his testimony before the Senate on March 2, 1995. Commenting on the divergent opinions, Tanter (1998, 89), the author of a comprehensive study of rogue states, stated the obvious when he wrote that there were "two schools of thought" on how to handle a rogue state such as Iraq.

The debate on containment revived interest in Hussein's rationality and, by extension, his deterrability. With a few exceptions, champions of modification through sanctions believed that the Iraqi strongman was rational, at least to the extent of being able to weigh the consequences of his deeds. Referring to Saddam's decision not to leave Kuwait, Jentleson (1994, 206) noted that "there is nothing inherently undeterrable about such a pattern of behavior." The U.S. Institute of Peace found Hussein rational enough to understand international constraints (Lund 1996). William Arkin (1996), a former IPS associate, was similarly sure that deterrence could work on Hussein. Andrew M. Bacevich (1993), a strategy expert, bemoaned American propensity for making simplistic analogies between Hitler and Hussein. Two Middle East observers found that, although an "odious dictator," Hussein could be quite pragmatic. These and other commentators assailed the "demonization of Saddam...with the hysterical support from the media" (Peck 1998, 21; Sariolghalam 1994). Gary Hart (2004, 68), a onetime Democratic presidential contender went so far as to accuse the media of spreading "lurid" misinformation about Hussein such as his killing of the health minister during a cabinet meeting.

Neoconservatives and some other Hussein watchers emphasized that the Iraqi leader was displaying growing signs of irrationality while presiding over an increasingly tyrannical and dysfunctional regime. Sensational accounts of Saddam Hussein skyrocketing cult of personality, his bizarre behavior, topped by that of his son Uday, made one author describe the situation in Baghdad as "demonic comedy." News of the brutal murder of Hussein's sons-in-law who were lured back from Jordan strengthened the view of a system as one out of control (Kirk and Raceanu 1994; Mylroie 1995–96; Roberts 1997, 54–70; Robins and Post 1997, 92–144). Seizing on such accounts, by mid-1995, neoconservatives increasingly argued that Hussein could not be contained and they called for regime change (Kristol and Kagan 1996a, 1996b).

Ironically, regime change was part of American policy toward Iraq since the end of the Gulf War. After the popular uprising failed and the military coup promised by Ali al Tikriti did not materialize, President Bush signed a "lethal finding" in May 1991. The finding authorized the CIA to use covert action to create conditions for Saddam's removal. Frank Anderson, the then chief of the Near East division in the DO, was skeptical because the Agency did not have a mechanism in place to carry out such a mission. The neoconservatives in the administration were more optimistic, pinning their hope on Ahmad Chalabi, a longtime Iraqi dissident who organized the Iraqi National Congress (INC) in 1992. Chalabi was already connected to the Rendon Group, a public relations firm used by the State Department and the CIA to publicize Saddam Hussein's brutality and advocate for a democratic Iraq (Cockburn and Cockburn 2002, 31, 165).

Going public in a *Foreign Policy* article, Chalabi (1991, 21) wrote that Iraq was perceived as "country fraught with political violence... and hard to govern," making the West opt for the stability of a dictatorship over the promise of democracy. Secretly, Chalabi proposed a plan for a "rolling" coup, part military action, part popular uprising in the autonomous Kurdish territory. The INC leader hoped to draft the pesmherga (the Kurdish independence fighters), disaffected Iraqi military units and, at a later stage, the Shiite in the south into the fighting. After his defection in 1994 General Wafiq al Samarri joined Chalabi's group and proposed a plan to assassinate Saddam Hussein during one of his rare visits to the countryside. Al Samarri's suggestion was close to a controversial Israeli plan to kill Hussein that was abandoned following a training accident in 1992 (Dan 2003; Gunter 1999b, 57–58). Iyad Alawi, a former Hussein supporter-turned dissident, was considered to be another potential candidate to rid Iraq of the dictator. With the help of Ali al Takriti, the London-based Alawi, a protégé of the British MI6, founded al-Wifaq, the Iraqi National Accord (INA). Unlike the Chalabi "rolling" coup, the INA intended to organize a palace coup led by a large group of military conspirators. Both plans took a nosedive when the dovish foreign policy team of Clinton took over. However, the assassination attempt against President Bush in 1993 and the secret information supplied by high-ranking defectors from Iraq's WMD programs convinced the administration to revive the plan (Bhatia and McGrory 2000, 236; Dan 2003; Hamza 2000, 250).

CIA operatives from the Northern Iraq Liaison Element (NILE) established their headquarters in the Kurdish town Salahudin, but Robert Baer

(2002, 234) the CIA liaison to the INF described the operation as a "Potemkin village." Baer charged that many of the NILE operatives were either alcoholics or incompetent. There were a number of additional factors that complicated the efforts to depose Saddam Hussein. The foreign policy community in Washington, including the CIA, split into Chalabi and Alawi camps. Chalabi's foes pointed out that he had been accused by the Jordanian authorities of embezzling and bankrupting the Patra bank in Amman; his supporters claimed that Jordan, under pressure from Baghdad, had "framed" him and had started a smear campaign against him (Mylroie 2003, 98–100).

Going beyond the personal, senior CIA officials had major reservations about the "rolling coup," not the least because of the fractious relations between Chalabi's Kurdish partners, Masoud Barazani's Kurdish Democratic Party (KDP) and Jalal Talabani's Patriotic Union of Kurdistan (PUK). When the disagreements between Barazani and Talabani deteriorated into a civil war, PUK appealed for help from Iran and the KDP became aligned with Saddam Hussein (Cockburn and Cockburn 2002, 175; Mackey 2002, 309–312). Dismayed by the specter of a fractious and unruly alliance, a larger metaphor for Iraq, the supporters of Alawi pushed for the less messy "silver bullet" coup against Hussein The notion that the dictator could be replaced with a more amenable military regime was especially appealing to the risk-averse Deutch and his DO David Cohen (Gunter 1999b, 57).

Emblematic of the confusion in the administration, both plans were allowed to proceed. Chalabi's "rolling coup" idea received a huge boost in 1994 when Uday raped the daughter of a relative of General Muhammad Madhlum al-Dulaymi, a member of the large Dulaymi tribe. After tribal leaders complained, Hussein arrested General al-Dulaymi and launched a campaign of brutal retribution against others. The wave of repressions pushed many Dulaymi officers as well as some of the military personnel of the Jibaries, another tribe close to Hussein, into the INC camp (Wurmser 1999, 18–19). With al Samarri serving as a liaison to Hussein opponents, the INC planned to start the offensive on March 4, 1995. Baer (2003, 175, 203, 204), stationed in Salahaudin, assumed that the administration would go along with the plan.

But the anti-INC faction in the CIA apparently informed Lake that Chalabi had shown his Iranian contacts a letter written on NSC stationery promising American support. Lake was also told about al Samarri's plan to assassinate Hussein, thus promoting an unprecedented personal intervention. The national security adviser ordered Baer and other NILE members to Washington where they were investigated by the FBI on charges of running a rogue operation and trying to assassinate Hussein in contradiction to U.S. laws. The operatives were subsequently exonerated, but, bereft of American support, the "rolling coup" collapsed. A year later, Hussein invaded the Kurdish enclave, arresting and executing hundreds of INC fighters (Gunter 1999a, 1999b, 57–58; Kessler 2003, 267; Mahle 2004, 216).

Although the Iraqi invasion was a clear violation of the post–Gulf War arrangements, the White House limited itself to another cruise missile attack. According to press reports, INC actions created "extreme anxiety" in Washington where Lake and Christopher viewed it as a second Bay of Pigs invasion, a comparison that was taken up by leftist critics (Lowry 2003, 289; Wise 1996). Under intense pressure from congressional Republicans, the administration airlifted more than 6000 INC and Kurdish fighters, but nothing was done to help the tribal rebellion inside Iraq, which was brutally crushed by the end of 1996 (Cockburn and Cockburn 2002, 248–249; Wurmser 1999, 18–19).

In his book on the affair, Baer (2002, 174) argued that far from treating it as a rogue operation, Martin Indyk approved the INC offensive. Baer and others speculated that, faced with an uncertain outcome and fearing a disintegration of Iraq, the administration got cold feet. Seizing the moment, Deutch and the Alawi faction in the CIA pushed for the INA version of regime change through a "palace coup." King Hussein, who had his own sources in the Jordanian General Intelligence Directorate, backed Alawi in a meeting with the CIA in September 1995. The INA chief received a strong endorsement from the CIA's London station, a close partner of the MI6. Gen. Mohammed Abduallah al Shawani, a senior Iraqi defector on the CIA payroll, was expected to recruit antiregime officers inside Iraq (Cockburn and Cockburn 2002, 215–218).

In January 1996, the administration authorized $6 million for the INA coup that was scheduled for the summer. In a press conference in Amman in February, Alawi announced the creation of a military council that boasted a number of senior Iraqi commanders in exile. Inside Iraq, the INA network, which al Shawani's three sons helped to run, attracted a large number of senior officers, including members of the supersecret B32 unit responsible for Saddam's safety. However, the network was penetrated and liquidated in June. Saddam put his younger son Qusay in charge of a special committee made up of the heads of the security services, which arrested thousands. Many were interrogated and tortured and hundreds were executed, including the al Shawani brothers.

The scope of the penetration raised speculations that the entire plot was a sting operation of the regime against inexperienced plotters and their hapless CIA handlers. Chalabi claimed that he had warned that the Alawi network had been compromised, but Deutch and Steve Richter, the new chief of the Near East division in charge of the operation, had paid no attention (Cockburn and Cockburn 2002, 226; Leebaert 2002, 609). Foes of Chalabi in the CIA accused the INC chief of betraying the plot in order to block his INA rival (Filkins 2006). Khadir Hamza (2000, 251) fingered Ali al Takriti as a Hussein "plant" who again managed to deceive the Americans. However, Rick Francona (2005), a CIA operative who worked with al Shawani claimed that one of the plotters had compromised the operations during a brutal interrogation.

Whatever the source of Saddam Hussein success, the events of 1995–96 had dramatically improved the dictator's position. The administration, in the middle of an election campaign, focused almost entirely on domestic events. Senator Robert Dole, Clinton's rival charged the White House with being "soft" on Iraq, but foreign policy issues had little traction with an electorate enjoying an unprecedented wave of prosperity. Riding high on the president's new and largely domestic mandate, in 1997 the White House unveiled a new policy of "deconflictization," a euphemism for distancing the United States from Iraq. However, Washington's hopes that the Iraqi "headache" would go away, were short lived. A series of dramatic developments in 1998 was to test the limits of Liberal Internationalism and give the neoconservative critique a new lease on life.

Failing the Reality Test: Liberal Internationalism and the "Unholy Trinity" of Terrorism, Weapons Proliferation, and Iraqi Defiance

Much as Clinton relished the image of a "domestic president," a notion supported by voters who trounced Dole, a candidate with vast foreign policy experience, by the second term, events in the Middle East increasingly encroached on the White House. Although al Qaeda's first anti-American proclamation was virtually ignored by the media, bin Laden's tireless efforts of self-promotion began to bear fruit. In 1997, he gave a number of inflammatory interviews to American and Western journalists (Weiss 2003, 177). Media accounts indicated that the al Qaeda chief was seeking to acquire nuclear weapons from Russia, where, according to reports, a hundred suitcase-size nuclear weapons went missing (Dean 2004, 122).

Such accounts fed into the already considerable anxiety about the proliferation of WMD. A large number of studies, reports, and congressional hearings seemed to confirm the observation of one expert that "it was virtually impossible to control proliferation" in spite of the international agreements and inspection protocol established by the United Nations (Bitzinger 1994; Chandler and Trees, 1996; Kincade 1995; Roberts 1997; G.D. Smith 1993; Sopko 1996–97; Steinbruner 1997–98; Trevan 1994; Zimmerman 1994, 82). Most worrisome was the fast-growing arsenal of chemical and biological weapons, whose manufacturing was simple, portable, and easy to conceal under dual use technology. Aum Shinrykio's sarin-gas attack in the Tokyo subway system on March 20, 1995, provided a chilling confirmation that even a small and bizarre cult could engage in chemical warfare. To prevent such an eventuality, on June 21, 1995, Presidential Directive (PDD) 39 made fighting nuclear, biological, and chemical (NBC) terrorism a top priority.

Unfortunately, the administration's resolve to take a stronger stand was overshadowed by the political firestorm triggered by Clinton's decision to replace Deutch with Tony Lake in 1997. The nomination of such a high-profile member of the anti-CIA crusade brought scathing criticism from the right wing and the neoconservatives, helped by the Newt Gingrich "revolution," which produced a Republican Congress and a robust foreign policy critique of Liberal Internationalism. Gingrich and other conservative Republicans took an especially dim view of what they considered to be a dysfunctional and timid intelligence community; the new House Speaker referred to it as "gelded" (Knott, 2000, 53). Threats by the Republicans to expose Lake's past association with the Chilean communist Orlando Leterier, who headed the IPS-inspired Transnational Institute, and his alleged greenlining of Iranian input into the fight in Bosnia, forced Clinton to settle on George Tenet, a career intelligence official. Tenet (2007, 9), who was recommended by Lake, got the job after a perfunctory meeting with the president on March 17, 1997.

The failed Lake candidacy served as a background for yet another round of discourse on the CIA. In spite of a growing awareness of bin Laden, advocates of openness and accountability were still very much in the foreground (Goodman 1997; Johnson 1996a, 1996b; Pekel 1998). Arthur S. Hulnick (1999, 77, 84, 112–113), a CIA official-turned academic expert, affirmed that "dealing with terrorist is another vexing problem for covert action" because "they operate in small cells and their members are prone to violence." Still, he noted that "distaste for recruiting such people is growing," and suggested the use of informants and electronic surveillance. Hulnick also urged the CIA to be more "aggressive about declassifying and releasing information about past covert actions."

Much to the dismay of advocates of New Oversight, a growing number of critics argued that there was a need to rethink covert activity in the age of Islamic terrorism. A Task Force on Intelligence of the liberal Council on Foreign Relation (1997) urged beefing up clandestine operations. L. Paul Bremer (1995), an ambassador-at-large for counterterrorism in the Reagan administration, suggested that the slow response to terrorism was caused by "Western apologists" guilt-ridden by colonialism and Vietnam and their insistence that terrorism can be fought by curing its "root cause" grievances. A 1999 conference on the future of terrorism sounded the alarm on what it called "low intensity high impact conflict." As two participants noted, a WMD terrorist attack would have a devastating impact on life and property.

More important, congressional Republican took a number of high-profile steps to restore American intelligence capability. The 1996 GOP platform stated that "terrorist states made a comeback during Bill Clinton's administration" (Beinart 2004). Soon after, Dole and Christopher Cox, a conservative House member from California, created the Congressional Policy Advisory Board. The board, which included Donald Rumsfeld, Dick Cheney, Paul Wolfowitz, and the heads of the Hoover and Heritage Institutes, was charged with providing an alternative to Clinton's tepid antiterrorist policy.

Bill McCollum, a Republican from Florida and the founder of the House Task Force on Terrorism and Unconventional Weapons, repeatedly wrote to Clinton to warn him of the dangers of bin Laden and his state sponsors (Lopez 2003). The Task Force that billed itself as an "independent voice" in alerting the U.S. government to such threats, commissioned its director, Yossef Bodansky (1999, viii), a former consultant to the State Department who spoke Arabic and Farsi, to research al Qaeda. In 1997 Congress created the bipartisan Commission to Assess United States National Security Space Management and Organization to evaluate the threat from ballistic missiles. Chaired by Donald Rumsfeld, the commission found that North Korea, Iran, and Iraq presented a "worrisome scenario" (Mann 2004, 240–242). Given such concerns, the Republicans were eager to bolster the CIA. George Tenet (2007, 21, 107) whose repeated requests for more funding annoyed the Clinton administration, managed to receive a supplemental budget through his "off the book alliance" with Gingrich.

Much as the Republicans tried to delegitimize Liberal Internationalism, they had to wait for events in the Middle East to put the White House on the defensive. To begin with, the sanction regime had turned into an increasingly embarrassing public relations problem. Virtually unnoticed by the administration, the alleged suffering of the Iraqi population became a rallying cry for a large coalition of leftist, pacifist, and antiglobalization groups. The Iraqi Ministry of Information helped to host delegations that were taken to hospitals to see starving infants and their distraught mothers. Foreign media were invited to watch mass funerals featuring little coffins and, on one occasion, a group of Iraqi women tried to hand their dead babies to Rolf Ekeus (Cockburn and Cockburn 2002, 113; Ritter 1999, 150).

The issue of Iraqi suffering was mainstreamed when, in 1995, *Lancet,* a prestigious medical journal blamed the sanction for the death of 567,000 Iraqi children annually. Although the number was disputed by other researchers, it was picked up by the *New York Times*, which declared that "sanctions kill children" (quoted in Cortright 2001). Though in 1996 the United Nations created the Oil for Food program that allowed selling oil to buy food and medicine, it did little to quell protest over the suffering of the Iraqi people. When Madeleine Albright, Clinton's new secretary of state was asked about "half a million children" dying, she compounded the problem by stating that this was a "worthy price" to pay for containment. In her memoir, Albright (2003, 275) acknowledged that her replay was a "terrible mistake," adding that she "must have been crazy."

The UN-administered Oil for Food program proved to be a huge boost for the regime. Early complaints from Chalabi and other dissidents warning that Saddam Hussein skimmed large sums of money from oil receipts were dismissed by the CIA as "sour grapes." It would take another five years to discover how the regime manipulated the program largesse to bolster its power, while doing little to help the population.

The White House apparently understood even less how Hussein manipulated the United Nations and neutralized UNSCOM. Following the embarrassing revelation of Hussein Kamal, the inspectors increased the pressure on Iraq. In 1996, Scott Ritter, the hard-charging American on the team, and the Russian Nikita Smidovitch were said to be closing on the "nerve center" of the regime (Cockburn and Cockburn 2002, 266). Ritter revealed that the inspectors were able to perfect their methods after receiving considerable intelligence help from the Israeli military intelligence Aman. The cooperation with Israel was questioned by some in the intelligence community, but was supported by Richard Butler, an Australian diplomat, who replaced Ekeus as UNSCOM's chief (Ritter 1999, 155–176). In October 1997, Butler submitted a scathing complaint against Iraq to the United Nations, but the Security Council split when France, Russia, and China abstained on a resolution to punish Iraq.

Saddam Hussein, hoping to fracture the Council even further, announced that American inspectors, whom he accused of spying for the United States and Israel, would not be welcome. A full-blown crisis was averted when Primakov and Albrecht negotiated an agreement later in October, but the tensions persisted. After the inspectors uncovered evidence of chemical experiments on prisoners in Abu Graib in January 1998, the regime blocked further inspections. A new round of hectic negotiations followed, involving the Russians and the United Nations chief Kofi Annan, who flew to Baghdad in February, where he described the Iraqi president as "a man I can do business with" (Albright 2003, 283). However, a few months later, Hussein violated the Annan agreement, and after a further round of attempted inspections and inconclusive negotiations, on December 15, Butler officially reported to the UN that Iraq had ceased to comply with the inspection regime.

The unhappiness of the administration over the humiliating treatment it received from Iraq was compounded when the outspoken Ritter (1999, 181–182) resigned in August 1998, accusing Clinton of timidity. Ritter maintained that, in its efforts to prevent him from carrying out his duties, the administration had threatened to charge him with spying for Israel. Ritter and others argued that by ending the inspection regime, Iraq was allowed to keep its still undisclosed WMD stocks. The notion that Iraq was left with considerable illicit stockpiles was widely shared. The respected military analyst Tony Cordesman wrote that "any strategy for dealing with Iraq must assume that Iraq will pursue it efforts to acquire weapons of mass destruction" (Cordesman and Hashim 1997, 336). A February 1998 report on Iraqi Chemical and Biological Weapons (CBW) of the authoritative Congressional Research Service asserted that Iraq had chemical weapons and biological agents, including the Ebola virus. The study noted that even with the inspection regime in place, Iraq had managed to acquire biological capabilities from Russia. News that after years of containment Saddam Hussein was still holding on to WMD could not have come at a worse time for the administration. According to Clinton (2004, 788–789), in 1997, he had read Richard Preston's *The Cobra Event,* a book about biological warfare and had asked Richard Clarke, his counterterrorism expert on the NSC to invite top scientists, molecular biologists, and other specialists for a series of workshops. In May 1998 the president signed PDD 62, updating the Protection against Unconventional Threat to the Homeland and Americans Overseas, but the CIA was ill- prepared to tackle the problem. Tenet was credited with lifting some of the legal restrictions imposed by his predecessor on the Directorate of Operations, but the bureaucratic and analytical culture was more difficult to change and the morale continued to be low.

The administration was also slow to react to the fatwa that Osama bin Laden issued on February 23, 1998, titled "Declaration of the World Islamic Front for Jihad against the Jews and the Crusaders." To garner more publicity, bin Laden invited ABC's journalist John Miller for an interview in Afghanistan. Miller's report, showing bin Laden touting an automatic weapon, and bin Laden's subsequent writings made some impact but, according to Michael Scheuer (2002, 188), the information that 12 Iraqi experts had arrived to assist al Qaeda in the production of chemical weapons did not receive the attention it deserved. George Tenet (2007, 109–114) and senior DO officials vetoed a plan to kidnap bin Laden from his Tarnak Farms compound because of legal constraints imposed on the CIA by Attorney General Janet Reno.

It was only the bombing of American embassies in Africa on August 7 that put bin Laden on the front page. Clarke organized a White House-based Counterterrorism Group and, on August 20, the administration responded with a missile attack on al Qaeda bases in Afghanistan and the al Shifa pharmaceutical factory in Khartoum.

Clinton's resolve, while welcomed by Republicans in Congress, was overshadowed by the growing scandal over his relations with Monica Lewinsky, a White House intern, which came to light after an investigation of the First Couple's dealings in a failed real estate deal in Arkansas. After months of denial, on August 17, a few days before the bombings, the president was forced to admit to the affair, leading to a steep drop in his public credibility. In an improbable coincidence, earlier that year Hollywood had released the movie "Wag the Dog" about a president who tries to divert attention from a sexual scandal by invading Albania.

The Sudanese government launched a major public relations offensive, with al-Turabi charging that the bombing was an effort by Clinton to distract from his Lewinsky problem. The Sudanese minister of information added that Clinton was a "proven liar" with more than a "hundred girl friends" (Berger 2002, 126; Hendrickson 2002, 109–111). Needless to say, the Sudanese vehemently denied that the factory produced chemical agents. Left-wing Web sites and even mainline media raised questions about the veracity of the al Shifa intelligence.

Under growing criticism, in a January 23, 1999 interview with the *Washington Post,* Richard Clarke defended the attack. He pointed out that the Iraqi experts were heavily involved in building and maintaining the facility and that a powdered VX substance was being produced there (Crowley 2002). A private investigation commissioned by the factory owner revealed no traces of EMPTA, a VX precursor that was allegedly found in a soil sample. A slew of subsequent reports proved to be inclusive; while some supported the American position, others backed the Sudanese version. More surprising, Tenet revealed that a decade after the attack, there was still a debate in the

CIA about "how good a target al Shifa was" (Berger 2002, 128; Hayes 2004, 195; Miniter 2003, 184–185; Tenet 2007, 117; Unger 2004, 185).

The charges of the "wag a dog" presidency and "bimbo bombings," as the journalist Barbara Ehrenreich (1999) famously described it, intensified when, on December 16, 1998, the administration launched Desert Fox, a series of bombing raids on Iraq in retaliation for Hussein's expulsion of UNSCOM. As the attack commenced a day before Congress was scheduled to start the impeachment procedures against the president, a growing array of critics on both sides of the political divide questioned the president's motives (P. Baker 2000, 232). In the Arab word, the raids became known as "Monica's war" or "Monica's missiles," adding to other conspiracy theories that had Lewinsky working as an agent of the Israeli Mossad (Bhatia and McGrory 2000, 14–16).

Both supporters and detractors of Clinton maintained that the scandal hurt the foreign policy of the administration. To begin with, Clinton's political and marital problems left him precious little time to tackle the al Qaeda and the Iraqi problems (Harris 2005, 345, 358–358; Stewart 1996, 75). More damaging was his moral deficit in international arena. Paul R. Pillar, the then deputy chief of the Counterterrorism Center, was among the many in Washington who felt that "the wag a dog" scenario "muddled the message" (quoted in Coll 2004, 412). Sidney Blumenthal (2003, 396–397, 545–546), Clinton's loyal adviser, noted that "the din of the scandal grew ever louder, even as President Clinton's deadly serious work on Iraq headed toward a possible military confutation." Albright (2003, 350) wrote that while doing her job, "the din was impossible to ignore."

Radical critics were less charitable. As Eqbal Ahmad (1998) put it, "[I]n the eyes of the world, Saddam Hussein and Monica Lewinsky "hold hands with Bill Clinton." Michael T. Klare (1998), a former ISP associate-turned professor of Peace Studies, charged that Clinton and Saddam Hussein were "brothers in arms." Some of the messages in the Internet debate were downright crude, with entries such as "no blood for blow jobs" or the "cunnilingual bomber returns" setting the tone of the discourse (P. Baker 2000, 127; Lowry 2003, 310–320; Morris 2003, 128; Unger 2004, 187; Zola 1998).

Insiders confirmed that this devastating criticism hampered the administration dealings with bin Laden and Iraq. An already risk-averse White House was apparently so paralyzed by fear of another public debacle that a number of schemes to capture or kill bin Laden were abandoned at the last minute. As the 9/11 commission indicated, some of the reasons were fear of hurting "innocents" as written into the CIA code and inability to confirm information by a second source, a CIA requirement to certify intelligence as "actionable." Sandy Berger, Clinton's NSC adviser, allegedly nixed plans that had no "significant" or "substantial" probability of success. There were speculations that Berger, who was subsequently convinced of stealing documents from the National Archives, tried to cover up the administration's decision to abort the Tarnak Farms plan because of the "legal implication" of bringing bin Laden to the United States (*The New Republic* 2004).

A similar combination of considerations worked against a decision to hit bin Laden during a hunting party for visiting Gulf sheiks in early 1999. Tenet (2007, 123) was worried about collateral damage, low probability of success, and uncorroborated information provided by one tribal group. General Anthony Zinni, who assumed the United States Central Command (CENTCOM) post on August 13, 1997, was another cautious warrior. He told the 9/11 panel about the worry that missile strikes would kill up to 2000 bystanders (Strasser 2004, 106). Zinni, who was an expert on peace-making and humanitarian interventions known as Operations Other than War (OOTW), was also critical of CIA's intelligence on bin Laden. On one occasion he was reported to have claimed that launching cruise missiles was "a long shot, very iffy" (quoted in Coll 2004, 410).

Even without the Lewinsky imbroglio, the cost of managing the containment policy became prohibitive. In spite of the Oil for Food program, the criticism of sanctions became relentless. On February 18, 1998, during a nationally televised "town hall" meeting at Ohio State University, a group of radical students from the nearby Antioch College and other activists bused from around the region harshly attacked Albright, Secretary of Defense William Cohen, and Berger (Mylroie 2000, 157).The visibly shaken Secretary of State later wrote that "it was roughest day in office to that point" (Albright 2003, 282).

The "half a million dead children" became an iconic number, supported by such figures as the Irish Quaker Denis J. Halliday who assisted the Oil for Food program. Halliday (1999) resigned, charging that the UN inflicted immeasurable suffering on the Iraqi people. Others, such as the veteran radical activist Ramsey Clark and Noam Chomsky, were less restrained; they asserted that sanctions were the real weapons of mass destruction and that genocide was being committed in Iraq (Arnove 2000). Even mainstream scholars seemed to accept this argument. A respected Middle East expert wrote that, rather than putting Hussein in a box, the "only box into which sanctions put Iraqis is coffins" (Gause III, 1999). Two other professors titled their article "Sanctions of Mass Destruction," implying that the human cost of the Iraqi sanctions compared with those of weapons of mass destruction (Mueller and Mueller 1999, 51). The author of a detailed study of the sanctions regime accused the Clinton administration of conducting a "genocidal" policy (Graham-Brown 1999, 348).

Indeed, by 1999 the notoriously fractured IR field was close to agreement that sanctions and the containment regime had not worked in Iraq. As one observer summed it up, "it is all pain without gains" (Losman 1997). Rational choice theorists pointed out that the degree of international cooperation required for containment is difficult to sustain, because self-interest drove actors to defect from the collision or engage in hidden sanction busting (Baldwin 1999–2000; Elliott 1998; Crawford 1996; E. Mansfield 1995; Pape 1998).

With new reports that Saddam Hussein might be equipping al Qaeda with WMD, the debate on how to sustain containment intensified (Auster 1998;

Venter 1999). The range of suggestions spanned the ideological gamut; some advocated the use of Iran as a renewed counterpoint to Iraq, while others put their faith in changing the international environment. The latter insisted that Iraq and all other ills could be fixed by addressing issues of international distributive justice and stopping the Untied States from acting as a hegemonic bully (Beitz 1999; Gause III 1999; Kupchan 1999; Meyer 1999). One scholar went so far as to advocate that the United States should acknowledge that "our laboratories, our corporations and other scientists" first developed Weapons of Mass Destruction and then "strive to construct security at the global level" (Tuathail 1999, 121). Bemoaning the "short fixes," Graham-Brown (1999, 348) concluded that a true solution should be based on "peace and stability and, hopefully, a more open style of government in Iraq." But she could not explain how a "more open style of government in Iraq" could be achieved on Hussein's watch. Commenting on the vagueness of these suggestions, one skeptic labeled them "a cri de coeur than a reasoned and systematic analysis" (Sterner 1997, 13).

Toward the end of Clinton's tenure, it was quite clear to Albright (2003, 272) and her team that Iraq had turned into "the most persistent headache" of the administration and, by implication, to Liberal Internationalism. The neoconservatives reached much the same conclusion and were prepared to offer their own solution.

The Neoconservative Alternative: Regime Change within the Context of Democratic Universalisms

In laying out their case, neoconservatives mustered a body of evidence to support their contention that self-interest made sanctions hard to sustain because, as Wolfowitz put it in 1993, coalition partners were "too greedy for Iraqi contracts." These allegations were confirmed by repeated congressional hearings; one, held by the Senate Foreign Relations Committee in 1999, was appropriately titled "Facing Saddam: Disarray in the International Community." Neoconservatives, drawing upon INC information, were also the first to argue that the Oil for Food program became a source of strength for the regime (Mann 2004, 227, 295).

By focusing on the manifold failures of Clinton's Iraq policy, neoconservatives hoped to promote a neo-Reaganite foreign policy that would utilize American might as a "benevolent hegemon" to push for global democracy. In line with Kantian democratic peace, neoconservatives declared that a universal democratic system was the only antidote to rogue states and weapons proliferation.

In 1998, The Project for a New American Century (PNAC), the foreign policy organ of the neoconservative movement, released a public letter to President Clinton. The letter, signed by a number of officials from the Reagan and Bush administrations, including Donald Rumsfeld, Richard Perle, Paul Wolfowitz, and Zalmay Khalilzad, asserted that sanctions and containment did not work and suggested that Saddam Hussein should be overthrown and a democratic Iraq established (Mann 2004, 239; Mylroie 2003, 135; Wurmser 1999, xi). In September, Wolfowitz (1998) praised Ritter for resigning and denounced the administration for pretending that "everything is fine "with its Iraqi policy." Wolfowitz argued that Americans did not need to send soldiers "marching to Baghdad" but should help Iraqi people liberate their country. In October, Republicans in Congress passed the Iraq Liberation Act of 1998 that called on the president to help the Iraqi opposition to change "the bitter reality of internal repression and external aggression that the current regime in Baghdad now offers" (Clinton 1999).

David Wurmser (1999, 7–8, 61), a fellow at the American Enterprise Institute (AEI), unveiled a broader case against Clinton in his book *Tyranny's Ally. America's Failure to Defeat Saddam Hussein*. He declared that overthrowing Saddam Hussein was not enough because the real force of destabilization was the "bond between internal tyranny and external aggression." Wurmser added that tyrannical regimes try to legitimize themselves by fomenting anti-American feelings, and that this "anti-American animus cannot be tamed by timid or toadying politics." Wurmser charged that the White House ignored Iraq's role in sponsoring Islamic terrorism.

Soon after, Bodansky (1999, vi), produced a detailed catalog of the Iraqi-al Qaeda connection. Among others, the director of the House Task Force drew attention to a joint Baghdad-al Qaeda effort to foment unrest in Saudi Arabia in 1998. As the prescient introduction to Bodansky's book warned, this new type of terrorism might relegate the concept of "fortress American" to history books, because "Islamist terrorists can penetrate America's geographic shield, bringing us within target range of terrorist activity." It was subsequently established that Osama bin Laden had ordered the planning of the September 11 attack in May 1998 during his stay in Khalden Camp in southeastern Afghanistan (Lopez 2003).

In spite of the fact that Bodansky's book became a bestseller the neoconservatives fought an uphill battle to popularize their message. Making little headway in Clinton's Washington, they hoped for a better hearing in the fledgling election campaign of George W. Bush.

4

September Eleven, the Bush Administration, and the Ascendance of the Neoconservative Vision of Democratic Universalism

Taken aback by the outcry over "bimbo bombings" and the charge that containing Iraq amounted to "sanctions of mass destruction," the outgoing Clinton administration had little incentive to reevaluate its policy toward terrorism or Iraq. The suicide bombing of the USS *Cole* in the Yemeni port of Aden in November 2000 did not alter the resolve of Clinton's team to muddle through until the end of its tenure. Summing up his time in the White House in a *Foreign Affairs* article, National Security Adviser Samuel Berger (2000, 31) devoted hardly a few paragraphs to Islamic terrorism and Iraq. As for future challenges, Berger urged the need to address globalization, international trade, and global warming.

Neither was George W. Bush, the Republican challenger of Al Gore in the 2000 campaign more forthcoming about the twin problems of terrorism and Iraq. Bush mentioned the terrorist threat in conjunction with weapons of mass destruction and rogue states in a speech at the Citadel in 1999 and in a May 2000 address on national security, but he was quite vague when questioned about a response to the *Cole* attack. His foreign policy adviser Condoleezza Rice (2000) was a realist in the mold of the senior Bush and his National Security Adviser Brent Scowcroft, a fact clearly reflected in her *Foreign Affairs* article on "promoting the national interest." With Bush's election team focusing on domestic problems and Gore being handicapped by the fallout from the Clinton's scandal, foreign policy was, in the words of one commentator, a "non-issue" (Dean 2004, 106–107). Louis Freeh (2005, 292) later observed that "as a measure of our unwillingness to look reality into the eyes—the 2000 presidential campaign spoke volumes."

In hindsight, a vigorous debate about terrorism was fully justified, but the virtual absence of the issue in the presidential campaign was a reflection of the larger discursive climate. In fact, neither the 1998 indictment linking bin

Laden to the 1993 Word Trade Center bombing, nor the *Cole* attack changed the view that Islamic terrorism was more of a myth than a reality.

ISLAMIC TERRORISM: ROUND TWO OF THE "MYTH OR REALITY" DEBATE

In an effort to raise the profile of international terrorism, in the late 1990s the Republicans in Congress created two commissions to study the issue. The first, named "Countering the Changing Threat of International Terrorism" chaired by L. Paul Bremer released its findings in June 2000; it urged revamping of the structure of intelligence gathering, including a closer collaboration between the CIA and the FBI and removing the legal obstacles to tracking terrorists operating in the United State. In his introduction, Bremer (2000) quoted the warning of the noted scholar Thomas C. Schelling that strategic surprise inevitably includes some measure of "genuine novelty introduced by the enemy." The second study, "New World Coming: America Security in the 21st Century," chaired by former U.S. senators Gary Hart and Warren Rudman generated a number of reports over a three-year period and the study was formally submitted to Congress in February 2001. Embracing the Lewis-Huntington thesis, Hart-Rudman argued that the modernization-driven confusion and frustration in the Muslim world would lead to an increase in terrorism. Both commissions criticized Clinton's terrorist policies as passive and reactive and urged a more proactive approach.

Much to the dismay of the Republicans, the findings of both commissions failed to attract the attention of the media and the public. The only substantial response came from the academic community, which used the occasion for a new round of the "myth or reality" debate. As noted in chapter 3, by and large, scholars and their journalistic followers had felt that "many works on Islam" were "alarmists, grounded in an obsessive fear of Islam" and the "fantasy of fear" in the West (Barber 1997–98; Sachedina 1998, 51). Loren Jenkins, the foreign editor of National Public Radio suggested in August 1998 that much of the militancy attributed to bin Laden was based "on his own braggadocio"; in reality the al Qaeda chief was more of spiritual leader and a financier (quoted in Peretz 2002).

As for Islamic radicalism, MESA scholars had continued to link it to such "root causes" as poverty, hunger, illiteracy, illness, political oppression, the Arab-Israeli conflict, or, on occasion, to a quest for a more "authentic, religiously based society" (Esposito 1997). To add a comparative dimension to Islamic terrorism, MESA experts frequently emphasize that Israel had its own terrorists such as Menachem Begin and Yitzkah Shamir (Little 1998; Mosmoudi 2001). Hart-Rudman's use of the "clash of civilizations" theory invited particular criticism. As the author of a reaction paper commissioned by the U.S. Army War College argued, the report was "based on poor social science" and was "too speculative" to support its assertions (Roxborough 2001). The U.S. Institute of Peace, a bastion of Liberal Internationalism, was particularly vocal in this respect; it decried the besmirching of the name of Islam and called on Americans to treat the "root causes" of Islamic discontent such as poverty and oppression (PeaceWatch USIP, 1998). The Institute's visiting expert on terrorism mocked the "great superterrorism scare" (Sprinzak 1998, 112).

Some in the MESA community blamed Israel and her neoconservative allies for deliberately exaggerating the Islamic threat. After Judith Miller (1996), a *New York Times* journalist, published a book on radical Islam, Edward Said (2000) accused her of "trading on the Islamist threat" and spreading the thesis that Islam is a danger to the West. Others pointed out that Miller was a student of Bernard Lewis and an "ideological soulmate" of Daniel Pipes (quoted in Moore 2004, 118). Other likeminded observers used critical theory to argue that Islamist terrorism was an "ideological construct" of the Jerusalem Conference on International Terrorism founded by the right-wing Israeli politician Benjamin Netanyahu in 1979 (Ahmed 2005, 1). After Netanyahu (1995, 75–98) published a book that discussed the possibility of Islamist attacks in the United States, critical scholars were quick to describe it as Israeli propaganda.

Continued sensitivity to negative portrayals of Islam also played a part. When, on August 19, 2001 a CBS Sixty Minutes program discussed the issue of Islamic terrorism and its purported reward of 72 virgins in heaven, a "chorus of indignation" from Middle East experts ensued (Reuter 2004, 126; Weiss 2003, 432). For these critics, the CBS broadcast was a prime example of what Said (2000) described as a Western propensity to propagate the "devil theory of Islam." Said and his MESA followers blamed Lewis, Pipes, Kramer, Emerson, and a "whole battery of Israeli academics" for creating "Western prejudice against Muslim 'terrorists'" and other "frightening" images of Muslim fundamentalism. Said and others invoked Michel Foucault's work to warn against Western tendency to "demonize" and "stigmatize" opponents (Dovi 2001).

While denying charges of denigrating the Muslim religion, opponents of MESA complained about "whitewashing of Islam under the guise of diversity." They reiterated that radical Islamism was "deeply antagonist toward the West" and bent on "creating a new order through act of wholesale destruction" through "Islamikaze," terrorism-as-martyrdom tactics (Israeli 1997; Kramer 1997, 16; Pipes 1999; 1997a, 47). Rejecting the "root cause" theory of terrorism, these and likeminded experts stressed the rival Lewis explanation, namely that the failure to modernize had created frustration and rage on which Islamism had fed. As one of them wrote, "this maddening sense of inferiority has given Islamic militancy its sharp edge" (Dawisha 2000, 90; Sivan 1998). Lewis (1998, 19) himself chastised his colleagues and the Clinton administration for not taking the 1998 bin Laden's fatwa seriously, adding that "terrorism requires only a few" to do serious damage.

Experts on terrorism furnished more specific warnings about radical Islam. Walter Laqueur (1996), who had coined the term "post-modern terrorism," maintained that this type of violence is guided by the coup de theatre factor; it seeks to created chaos through indiscriminate mass killings and devastation. Steven Emerson delivered yet another warning about the danger posed by global al Qaeda and its American cells (Emerson and Pipes 2001). Bruce Hoffman, a RAND scholar, (1998, 94; 1996, 216) wrote that "such violence is first and foremost a sacramental act or divine duty executed in direct response to some theological demand." He pointed out that the 1993 Trade Center terrorists plotted "more egregious" attacks on tunnels and other sites around New York. In what proved to be a prescient observation, Hoffman asserted that Islamist radicals who hijacked an Air France airplane in 1996 had sought to create a huge impact by planning to blow themselves up over Paris.

The literature on proliferation of weapons of mass destruction ranging from nuclear suitcases to biological agents such as the Ebola virus and smallpox supported the "catastrophic terrorism" scenario (Preston 2000). Theories of asymmetrical warfare pointed out that weak nations and terrorist groups could find such weapons to be a "cheap and effective" way to counter the overwhelming military force of the United States. According to reports published at the time, a number of Russian-made nuclear suitcase-bombs were unaccounted for and the Defense Intelligence Agency speculated that two might have fallen into the hands of al Qaeda (McCuen 1999; Schmid 2000; Stern 1999, 130; J.B. Tucker 1999; D. Tucker 2001).

To recall, biological warfare had attracted the attention of President Clinton. Experts were quite convinced that "Iraq had shown that it is prepared to use biological weapons" and that al Qaeda might get hold of them, creating the "nightmare scenario" (Cordesman 1999, 597; Garrett 2001; Leitenberg 2000; O'Toole and Henderson 2001; Tucker 2001; Venter 1999). In their view, "toxic terrorism," a collaboration of a rogue state and a terrorist organization, represented what one DIA analyst called the "sum of all our fears" (Traves 1997, 12).

Observers who followed bin Laden warned that his entrenched camps in isolated, Taliban-ruled Afghanistan afforded a haven for terrorist training (Rubin 2000). As noted, bin Laden's long-standing interest in WMD was known since his days in Sudan. In December 1998, *Time* magazine quoted him as saying that "we do not consider it a crime if we tried to have nuclear, chemical and biological weapons." The grand jury in the African embassies bombings received testimony that bin Laden had made efforts to obtain such weapons during his stay in Sudan, evidence that was incorporated in the Congressional Research Service Report of 1999 and repeated in congressional testimony in 2000 (Dolnik 2001).

Going against the popular "Lone Ranger" view of terrorism, Hoffman (1998, 186) and Laqueur (1996) argued that rogue states such as Libya and Iraq might furnish terrorists with WMD because such weapons were a "potentially a risk-free means of attacking stronger enemies." Such anonymous "donations" would protect rogues from massive retaliations, a development postulated by Second Nuclear Age theory. This scenario was part of a RAND classification of the terrorist-rogue state nexus; each category called for a different level of involvement and deniability. RAND analysts noted that a response to such clever terrorist-state networks would require a "basket" of tactics, including prevention, deterrence, and retaliation against suspect sponsor states (Lesser et al. 1999).

Viewed in light of 9/11, some of the commentaries on "spectacular terrorism" were eerily prescient, but, as noted, they faced an uphill battle against the MESA paradigm. Nor were influential IR scholars inclined to consider threats from obscure nonstate actors. In a book published a few months prior to the attack, John Mearsheimer (2001) failed to refer to Islamic terrorism or al Qaeda. Writing in the July/August 2001 issue of *Foreign Affairs*, Robert Jervis (2001, 143) was actually critical of the "current focus on WMD, rogue states, and terrorism," stating that "terrorism is not steadily increasing" and that, if anything, it was mostly a European phenomenon. While Jervis stopped short of labeling bin Laden the new bogeyman, he suggested that American preoccupation with terrorism "may be more a function of the lack of threat to U.S. security than of the magnitude of the actual menace." Andrew J. Bacevich (2001), a highly regarded security scholar, added that this line of writing is "fanning the fears that terrorists may employ WMD."

Overall, IR scholars were convinced that in the decade to come, America would be able to engage in "military deglobalization," their term for dismantling the global empire erected during the cold war and bringing troops home (Cohen 2000; Henderson and Tucker 2001; Krepon 2001; O'Hanlon 2001). Charles A. Kupchan (1999, 20), a senior fellow at the Council on Foreign Relations, stated that the "coming decade" would see a transition to a more multipolar world and a more equal distribution of resources. Joseph Nye, Jr. and his long time collaborator Robert O. Keohane conceived of a new world of "complex interdependence" where "military globalism" would decline and where "human aspirations" were becoming one. Writing months before 9/11, Nye (2001) titled his article "Military Deglobalization?" Much of this optimism was reflected in a poll of a large number of academics and lay experts conducted by the CIA's National Intelligence Council, *Global Trends, 2015: A Dialogue about the Future with Non-Government Experts.* Released in December 2000, the report did not include terrorism as one of the seven "drives" that were said to shape international relations (Ganon 2001). Reflecting some frustration, in March 2001, Hoffman (2001) wondered why experts paid only "minimum attention" to terrorism.

Making few dents in the view that Islamic terrorism was more of a myth than reality neoconservatives could only hope that the administration of George W. Bush would take a fresh look at al Qaeda and Iraq. However, the new foreign policy team did little to merit such expectations.

The Bush Administration's Foreign Policy: Finding its Way in the Murky Reality of Islamic Terrorism

Like Republican presidents before him, the younger Bush led a party whose foreign policy vision was badly fragmented. Epitomized by Patrick Buchanan

(1999), the right-wing isolationists strenuously objected to turning America into an "empire," let alone squandering American might on fighting foreign wars. In the center were somber realists such as the elder Bush and his foreign policy team of James Baker, Colin Powell, and Brent Scowcroft. As noted earlier, the realists were wary of radical changes to the status quo and accepted the limits imposed on the United States by the international community.

On the other side of the ideological divide were evangelical Christians, a large and vocal bloc, whose theology put them at odds with the view of a stable international order based on secular values and material progress. Deeply suspicious of the United Nations and skeptical of multilateralism, evangelicals considered the protection of Israel as a paramount American security interest. By the same token, they viewed Islam in a negative, if not an apocalyptic light, akin to the secular "clash of civilizations" theory (Mead 2006). Completing the spectrum were the neoconservatives who shared the evangelicals' dislike for multinational institutions, but held a highly optimistic view of an international order based on universal democratic values. While intellectually prominent, the neoconservatives had little initial impact on the new administration.

In fact, Bush's foreign policy appointments reflected a mix of political calculations and personal considerations. To fend off criticism of limited international exposure, the president picked three seasoned foreign policy players—Richard Cheney as vice president, Colin Powell as secretary of state, and Donald Rumsfeld as secretary of defense. Condoleezza Rice, the national security adviser, was a protégée of Scowcroft and a realist like Powell. So much so, that many observers referred to them as a "realist dream team" (Shore 2003, 349). Neoconservatives—Paul Wolfowitz and Douglas Feith, were given second- and third-tier positions in the Department of Defense; a lengthy confirmation process delayed their appointments until March and July 2001 respectively (Strasser 2004, 112–113). Completing the neoconservative contingent was Richard Perle whom Rumsfeld had picked to chair the influential Defense Policy Board.

In the postelection period telescoped by the Florida recount, Bush's foreign policy transition team touched only briefly upon the issue of terrorism. RAND reports, including the work of Bruce Hoffman served as a background for the deliberations. Hoffman's (2001) criticism of Clinton's law enforcement approach to terrorism was also noted (Carluci, Hunter, and Khalilzad 2000).

Shortly after taking office on January 21, 2001, the National Security Council launched a review of al Qaeda policy. According to the commission investigating 9/11, the lengthy processes, completed only on September 4, reflected the lack of urgency on the part of the administration. Democrats accused the Republicans of ignoring their warning about bin Laden, which, according to Berger, he had personally delivered to Bush and Cheney and, in a more detailed form, to Condoleezza Rice. Clinton's national security adviser allegedly told his successor that "terrorism in general and al Qaeda in particular" would be a time-consuming topic (Dean 2004, 107). George Tenet (2007, 144, 151–153, 158) maintained that he had warned Rice twice—on May 30 and July 10, 2001—that an al Qaeda attack was imminent. Tenet quoted a CTC analyst Rich B. as saying "they're coming here"; B.'s boss, Cofer Black had urged the country "to go on a war footing now."

Republicans denied this charge and noted that Berger did not consider bin Laden an urgent priority, a fact reflected in his *Foreign Affairs* article. The 9/11 commission added that Brian Sheridan, the outgoing assistant secretary for Special Operations in the Department of Defense failed to brief Rumsfeld on al Qaeda (Strasser 2004, 112–113). Condoleezza Rice rebutted Tenet's allegation and pointed out that it did not correspond to his own testimony before the 9/11 commission, where he also had praised the Bush team for making al Qaeda an "agenda item" early on (Knowlton 2007). The 9/11 report made no reference to his alleged testimony about the two meetings (Tenet 2007, 153).

Even without a final review, the new administration took a number of steps to intensify the fight against terror. In April, Attorney General John Ashcroft moved to implement the Bremer and Hart-Rudman recommendation to relax the legal restraints on counterterrorist activity in the United States (Hall and Locy 2004). On March 27, 2001 the House Subcommittee on National Security and Veteran Affairs held a hearing on the subject where RAND's Hoffman (2001) repeated his criticism of the law enforcement approach to terrorism, calling it "dangerously myopic." Sensing a change of climate in Washington, Freeh (2005, 28, 31, 243) successfully petitioned Bush and Rice to give the FBI a free hand to pursue the investigation of the Khobar Towers that had languished under Clinton. The FBI chief who accused Clinton of sidelining the Khobar inquiry in order to pursue "rapprochement with Iran," described Rice as a "breath of fresh air."

While Freeh and others in the law enforcement community welcomed these steps, congressional Democrats, the American Civil Liberties Union, and academics expressed alarm that tightening surveillance might target the Arabs in the United States. To recall, intelligence experts spent the better part of the 1990s arguing that protection of civil liberties should not be sacrificed on the altar of intelligence. Richard K. Betts (1998, 40) maintained that in spite of WMD terrorism, loosening legal restraint might not be wise as "a panicked legal system would roll over Arab Americans." An analyst for the Congressional Research Service came to the same conclusion, writing that a proactive antiterrorist strategy might lead to "a curbing of individual rights and freedoms" (Perl 2001).

Administration efforts to implement the Bremer and Hart-Rudman recommendation for restructuring the CIA proved even more of an uphill struggle. In spite of the growing awareness of al Qaeda, opposition to clandestine activity did not disappear. The prominent commentator Garry Wills (1999, 50) complained that too much "old secrecy" had turned the United States into a "bully of the free world" and accused the right-wing activist Richard Mellon Scaife of fomenting the "danger scenario." Robert David

Steele (2000, 422), the president of Open Sources Solutions, an anti-CIA group, argued that "national intelligence must be redefined away from secrets" and another observer worried that a push for counterterrorism would return the CIA to "zealotry," not seen since the days of James Angelton, its counterterrorism chief and anticommunist crusader (Thomas 1999–2000, 406). Some Liberal Internationalists urged the Agency to focus on demographics, environment, competition for resources, and other "real issues" of the twenty-first century (Klare 2000a).

Going against tradition, Bush retained George Tenet as intelligence director and Richard Clarke as his "terrorism tsar," a decision that disappointed some CIA insiders. Melissa Boyle Mahle (2004, 196–197) described Tenet as "risk averse" and argued that until September 11 the CIA was "in denial" about terrorism. Michael Scheuer (2006, 215) added that with the exception of Reagan-Casey, the Agency had done little to fight terror. He was equally uncomplimentary about Clarke whom he called a "blusterer in chief" appointed by Clinton to "deflect the media from the president." Drawing on this and other sources, the journalist James Risen (2006, 33) described the CIA director before September 11, as "paralyzed by political correctness and risk aversion." John L. Halgerson, the CIA inspector general, would later blame Tenet, along with other key officials, for failing to take aggressive steps against al Qaeda (Mazetti 2007).

Perceived failure of Tenet's leadership aside, other critics questioned whether it was possible to turn around a long-standing institutional culture on short notice. Reuel Marc Gerecht (2000, 2001) a former DO agent who joined The Project for the New American Century, asserted that the CIA is a "risk averse" organization reflecting the take-no-risk culture of the American society. He contended that the Agency had failed to penetrate the Taliban and al Qaeda, adding sarcastically that bin Laden and his men stayed awake "around the campfire...scared stiff about us." Frederick P. Hitz (2000), a onetime CIA council general, complained that excessive legalism all but undermined counterterrorism. He explained that terrorist groups were "notorious[ly] difficult to penetrate," often requiring a criminal act as part of initiation that would have created a legal "bedlam" for American handlers.

Another difficulty stemmed from the highly bureaucratic structure of the Agency. John F. Lehman (2004), a member of the 9/11 commission, denounced "the CIA incompetence, careerism and bureaucratic narrowness," which, in his view, detracted from the Agency's ability to hire qualified candidates. Early in the 1990s, Congress described the number of Arab speakers in the CIA as "abysmal," but more than a decade later, and in spite of Woolsey's efforts to hire Arab-speaking personnel, critics still decried the "linguistically bereft" case officers (Leebaert 2002, 619; Perry 1992, 346). Gerecht (2000, 2001) doubted whether the Directorate of Operation had a "single truly qualified Arabic speaking officer of Middle East origin" who could pass for a "believable Muslim fundamentalist." Writing under the name of Edward G. Shirley (1998), Gerecht described the DO as a "sorry blend of Monty Python and Big Brother"; he noted that senior officers rose through the hierarchy "without ever learning much about the language, culture, or politics" of the countries in which they served.

To complicate matters, until September 11, the Agency was beholden to the diversity drive mandated by President Clinton. Although some considered diversity an antidote to the white, male-dominated intelligence culture, others viewed it as an exercise in "political correctness." Detractors would later note that instead of looking for qualified Arabic-speaking agents, Tenet had exhorted the Agency to promote "minorities, women, and people with disabilities." In their view, hiring based on affirmative action goals, coupled with a long-term decline in the number of Ivy League applicants, made American agents less "sophisticated and cultured" than their European counterparts (Callum 2001; Clarridge with Diehl 1997, 303; Schoenfeld 2005, 49).

The continued culture of risk aversion in the DO, which one scholar termed the "Seymour Hersh" effect, was even more resistant to change. After years of being scrutinized and criticized by the media, counterterrorism and covert operations were not a popular destination for career-minded intelligence officers (Hersh 2001; Jones 2006; Nolan 1999, 18). John R. Bolton (2001, 121, 125–126), then vice president of the American Enterprise Institute blamed "thirty years of ... congressional and media exposures" of covert operations for a culture of "timidity" and "paralysis."

Bolton and his fellow neoconservatives tried to inject a sense of urgency into fighting terrorism. But some influential CIA insiders shared the general skepticism about a megaterrorist attack. In a book published months before 9/11, Paul R. Pillar (2001, vii, 4–8; 50, 53, 56, 114, 122, 206, 224), intelligence officer for Near East and South East Asia and a former deputy head of the Counterterrorism Center blamed Lewis and Huntington for adopting a confrontational posture toward Islam, a critique that he also extended to the National Commission on Terrorism. He accused "minorities,"—a reference to AIPAC, a pro Israel lobby—of fomenting a terrorist panic. Quoting approvingly the works of John Esposito, Pillar argued that the "United States should not become preoccupied with any one terrorist as it has been with Osama bin Laden," because there is "an absence of terrorism international." He implied that bin Laden became the "bete noire of the moment" and urged Americans not to get fixated "on a single foe." Pillar revealed that Clinton had asked the Counterterrorism Center to assess the probability of an attack on New York, but he dismissed the scenario of large-scale American casualties as not greatly plausible.

Pillar rejected the idea of "developing and applying a terrorist profile" for identifying terrorists on the grounds that there "is nothing close to a single profile of terrorists." He expressed doubts about the efficacy of retaliatory raids against the al Qaeda network and, by and large, objected to the resumption of assassination attacks because it would resurrect "old suspicions" about the CIA. Emphasizing that terrorism has deep "root causes," Pillar urged accommodation and negotiations. In a spirit of comparison, he reminded readers that "not only were Yasir Arafat and Gerry Adams leaders of terrorist groups; so were Menachem Begin and Yitzhak Shamir." Michael H. Armacost, president of the liberal Brookings Institution that published the book, hailed Pillar's conclusion that "terrorism is a challenge to be managed, not solved."

The views of the intelligence officer for Near East and South East Asia contrasted sharply with Tenet's subsequent recollection about an imminent al Qaeda attack. The opinions of some of Pillar's retired colleagues-turned-media-experts were equally sanguine. Larry C. Johnson (2001) a former terrorist expert in the CIA and the State Department and a media expert on terrorism, wrote in July 2001 in *New York Times* about the "declining threat of terrorism." Johnson charged that the National Commission on Terrorism described the "terrorist threat in vastly exaggerated terms." He accused the "bureaucracies in the military agencies and intelligence agencies" of trying to find new enemies to justify their budgets and blamed "news reports" and "popular entertainment" for the fact "that Americans are bedeviled by fantasies of terrorism." Another former intelligence official contended that "somewhere out in the great global unknown, some wacko group could raise to hammer U.S. facilities; this danger American intelligence can't predict or do much to forestall." Instead, he urged a study to investigate why so many people despise America (Chapman 2001, 130).

If the threat of Islamic terrorism was controversial, the link between al Qaeda and Iraq was even more debatable. While theoretically appealing, tracking a terrorist-rogue state collusion is difficult because, as noted in chapter 3, there is a certain "phantom" quality to such relations.

Tracking the "Phantom Link": Saddam Hussein, Bin Laden, and Weapons of Mass Destruction

With the expulsion of the inspectors in 1998, the United States lost its only reliable source of information on Saddam Hussein's lethal weapons program. However, there was a general consensus that, unencumbered by the UN oversight, Hussein was busy restarting his production lines. Richard Butler (2000a, 146; 2000b), the last UNSCOM chief was an ardent proponent of this theory. Blaming Kofi Annan for the UNSCOM "sale out," Butler warned that Iraq was the primary threat to world peace. Tim Trevan (1999, 384–390), Butler's spokesman and a specialist in biological warfare, suggested that Hussein's complex deception scheme left the world in the dark about biological and other lethal weapons. David Albright, the head of the Institute for Science and International Security who collaborated with Khidir Hamza, a dissident Iraqi nuclear scientist, called attention to Hussein's plans to reconstitute his production of nuclear weapons (Albright and Hamza 1998). Albright helped Hamza (2000) to publish a book on the subject, fueling more speculations on the extent of the program. By and large, the CIA confirmed these views in its August 2000 report, "Iraq, and Weapons of Mass Destruction." Tenet (2007, 336) noted that "the consistency of our views on the issue of [Iraqi] weapons programs was carried forward to two presidents of different political parties."

The issue of Iraqi ties to al Qaeda was also discussed in this context. Press reports mentioned that, in a quest for deniability, Saddam Hussein, might "outsource" catastrophic terrorism to bin Laden. In 1999 *Newsweek* wrote about the growing al Qaeda-Iraqi ties, noting that portable nuclear weapons would make such an alliance "highly alarming" (Dickey et al. 1999). Vincent Cannistraro, a former CIA counterterrorist official, speculated that the sophisticated bomb used against the *Cole* might have come from Iraqi intelligence (Borger 2002).

Information on Iraqi assistance to al Qaeda's highly secretive unconventional weapons production was harder to come by. After the bombing of al Shifa in 1998, Ayman al Zawahiri asked an Egyptian expert Midhat Mursi al Sayyid Umar, known as Abu Khabab, to create a chemical-biological program codenamed *al Zabadi* in Afghanistan. A number of other scientists joined, including Yazid Sufaat and Rauf Ahmad who worked on anthrax, Sayf al Adl, and Mohammed Abdel al Aziz al Masri, the so-called nuclear CEO. In fact, efforts to obtain a nuclear device predated *al Zabidi*; during the African embassy bombings trial in February 2001, Jamal Ahmad al Fadl testified that al Qaeda had tried to buy uranium in Sudan but had been apparently scammed. Bin Laden had also approached Abdul Qadir Khan, the father of the Pakistani nuclear bomb, but had been rebuffed (Tenet 2007, 272–287).

Still, in the summer of 2001, two members of *Umma Tameer-e-Nau* (UTN), an Islamist group founded by retired Pakistani nuclear scientists, engineers, and military officers to help the Taliban, met with bin Laden and al Zawahiri in Kabul to discuss building a nuclear device. One of them, Sultan Bashirrudan Mahmood, a former head of his country's Atomic Energy Commission, was the author of the 1989 *Doomsday and Life after Death: The Ultimate Faith of the Universe as Seen by the Holy Quran*. The treatise, considered the "Islamic bomb" manifesto, discussed the role of science in jihad and predicted a nuclear Armageddon in fulfillment of Koranic prophecies. Mahmood, a highly devout Muslim was an admirer of the Taliban leader Mullah Omar, a sentiment shared by others in Pakistan's atomic and security establishments, especially in the powerful intelligence service, the Inter-Service Intelligence Agency (ISI) (Mishra 2003; Tenet 2007, 272–287).

Overall, Pakistani leadership felt that Americans had "ulterior motives" in eliminating the Taliban. A return to chaos would have prevented the construction of a natural gas pipeline from Turkmenistan to Afghanistan and Pakistan, which the Pakistani government had negotiated in 1995 with the Central Asia Gas Pipeline Corporation, a consortium of Unocal, the Russian Gazprom, and Saudi interests. Indeed, after the strike against bin Laden's camp in 1998, Unocal, citing security concerns, withdrew from the project. Already alienated by U.S. sanctions, the Pakistanis redoubled their effort to help the Taliban and their protégé, al Qaeda. According to Tenet (2007, 140), the ISI cold-shouldered all American requests for cooperation on bin Laden.

While the extent of al Qaeda's WMD program was unknown to the CIA, there were rumors that a few Iraqi experts were sent to assist with *al Zabadi*. In 2000, the CIA's Iraqi Operation Group (IOG) in northern Iraq received information that *Ansar al Islam*, a fundamentalist Kurdish group, sponsored by the Iraqi intelligence services to counter the American-allied Kurdish Democratic Party and the Patriotic Union of Kurdistan, had set up a chemical production facility in Khurmal. Abu Musab al Zarqawi, a senior al Qaeda operative attached to the group, along with approximately a hundred al Qaeda fighters, was reported to have received training in chemical weapons in Baghdad (Tenet 2007, 154).

The Iraqi regime was also said to have offered sanctuary to bin Laden, whose relations with the Taliban had deteriorated in the late 1990s. Although the al Qaeda chief declined, limited tactical cooperation apparently continued. For instance, there were speculations that Iraqi doctors had treated bin Laden for an acute renal failure, allegedly caused by an effort to poison him in 1998 (Dolnik 2001). In October 2000 an Iraqi intelligence operative Saleh Suleiman was arrested near the Afghan border after he visited bin Laden (Lopez 2003). A few months later a CIA liaison officer in Prague learned about an April 21 meeting between Ahmad Khalil Ibrahim Samir al-Ani, an official in the Iraqi embassy, and Mohammad Atta, the ringleader of the September 11 terrorists.

Adam Dolnik (2001, 8–9), a Czech researcher in the Monterey Institute of International Studies included these and other alleged contacts in his study "America's Worst Nightmare? Osama bin Laden and Weapons of Mass Destruction" posted on the Internet on September 12 by PIR, a Russian research center dedicated to nonproliferation. Dolnik explained that Iraq was seeking al Qaeda's assistance in bombing Radio Free Europe in Prague and other targets in Europe. Dolnik also noted that the "Iraqis have extensive WMD research experience" and stockpiles of such weapons in Sudan, adding that al Qaeda "collaboration with Saddam Hussein's secular regime in Iraq" was in line with bin Laden's "pragmatic alliance building" strategy.

In time the so-called Prague connection would become part of a highly controversial debate about the nature of Saddam Hussein's links with bin Laden. Naturally, the question of whether Saddam Hussein had played a part in the 9/11 plot attracted most of the attention. But this particular "murky relation," as the CIA termed it, had raised more basic issues in analyzing the nexus of terrorist networks, lethal weapons, and rogue states (Gordon and Trainor 2006, 126).

Two interlocking factors hindered such an investigation. The first pertained to the origin of information on terrorist groups and their linkage to state sponsors such as Iraq. With virtually no independent intelligence on the ground, the Agency had to rely on a bewildering array of sources. Tips about al Qaeda-Iraq collusion came from Arab, British and other foreign intelligence services, Sudanese opposition figures, the anti-Taliban Northern

Alliance, Arab media, opportunistic profiteers and Iraqi defectors working independently or through Ahmed Chalabi's Iraqi National Congress, and Iyad Alawi's Iraq National Front. While there is a standing intelligence assumption that bias, self- serving and deception are inevitable, it was virtually impossible to sort out the veracity of each source in such a miscellaneous ensemble.

The second factor touched on the epistemology of intelligence analysis, that is, the set of rules guiding perceptions of international reality. As already noted, during the cold war, the CIA faced a relatively stable environment defined either explicitly or intuitively by rational choice theory concepts. In the turbulent era of international terrorism and weapons proliferation, dissimulation, deception, ambiguity, and randomness raised the level of epistemic complexity. A former chief of the Israeli Mossad observed that "the purveyors of terror and WMD proliferation were diabolically sophisticated; their culture and modus operandi did not lend itself to the traditional methods of data gathering" and, more important, analysis (Halevy 2006, 181).

CIA's epistemology was shaped by Sherman Kent, "the father" of the analytical branch, whose vision was permeated by a strong positivist belief in a rational political universe where objective experts could parse reality in order to reach a "truthful" conclusion based on incontrovertible evidence. To preserve this objectivity, the CIA instituted a total physical separation between the analytical and operational environments (Kessler 2003, 123). Kent's leading rival Willmore Kendall rejected the notion that such predictive "truth" can be separated from personal beliefs of analysts or isolated from the strategic culture of a deceptive adversary, but was forced out in 1949. In the 1970s a number of critics, including the influential strategic expert Albert Wohlstetter and the historian Richard Pipes, challenged the CIA analytical tradition with regard to the Soviet Union, resulting in the Team B exercise (Seliktar 2004, 67–72).

In yet another blow to the Kentian tradition, experts on terrorism such as Claire Sterling (1981) questioned the CIA conclusion that the Soviet Union and its satellites had no role in supporting international terrorism. The then CIA director William Casey, a strong critic of Kentianism and legalism commented that the Agency was permeated by "the air of a lawyer's pleas, arguing there should not be an indictment because there is no strong evidence." When the Soviet archives were opened, Moscow's deep involvement with terrorist groups surprised even the harshest critics of the CIA (Gates 1996, 204; Mylroie 2001, 247–248).

The failure to predict the collapse of the Soviet Union gave CIA's longstanding critics such as Abram N. Shulsky (1993, 183) an opportunity to mount a new attack on the Kent-inspired standards of "objectivity" and "exactitude." In Shulsky's view, such a methodology befitted a "world-class think tank…a kind of living encyclopedia or reference service." Donald P. Steury (1994, vii, xviii), a CIA official involved in researching the Soviet debacle, commented that the Kent-like aura of "Olympian detachment" was born out of a naïve belief that a truly objective assessment could be produced.

The rise of Islamist terrorism prompted these and other observers to urge the Agency to adopt a new methodology for discerning complex deception systems; "to determine whether the adversary is deceiving us or denying information" (Shulsky and Schmitt 1996). Indeed, the former CIA operative Melissa Boyle Mahle (2004, 265) claimed that the Agency was a victim of deception when it failed to foresee the Indian nuclear test in 1998. Admiral David Jeremiah, the head of the commission that investigated the failure concluded that such deceptions are especially difficult to the American "mind-set" that defines what is implausible in ways that "have nothing to do with how a foreign culture might act" (Tenet 2007, 45). Laurie Mylroie (2001, 114–115, 248), a harsh critic of American intelligence, added that high evidentiary standards are "frequently not available" when dealing with terrorist organizations. Consequently, intelligence officials who "say that they do not have proof" often mean that they "have no evidence." In a particularly prescient article, the leading intelligence expert James J. Wirtz (1991, 8), noted that the ethnocentricity and mirror imaging of the cold war, was "pale in comparison" to the cultural gaps between analysts and the third world.

Cheney, Rumsfeld, and Wolfowitz had their own misgivings about the CIA. Cheney was among the very few in the first Bush administration to argue that the Soviet Union was on the verge of collapse (Seliktar 2004, 188–207). He also faulted the Agency for ignoring Saddam Hussein's plans to invade Kuwait and for missing Hussein's nuclear program. Rumsfeld chaired the 1998 commission to assess the ballistic missile threat to the United States; the panel concluded that rogue states such as North Korea could develop intercontinental missiles in as little as five years, contradicting the CIA's much longer estimate of ten to fifteen years. Wolfowitz, who correctly predicted that Saddam Hussein was serious about Kuwait in 1990, was even more dismissive of the CIA, referring to it as "priesthood" (Ackerman and Judis 2003; Boyer 2004; Clarke 2004, 232–233; 2006; Decter 2003, 110–11; Gordon and Trainor 2006, 126). Tenet's (2007, 44) candid admissions to having "no clue" about the Indians served to reinforce the image of incompetence.

While the president developed camaraderie with Tenet, Cheney and Rumsfeld sought ways to supplant what they considered a chronically failing and dysfunctional organization. It was well known that both officials believed that the CIA was either unable, or unwilling to effectively challenge terrorism or provide the Pentagon with timely operational information. Creating more tension, the Defense Department had long-standing reservations about the working of the broader intelligence community. In this view, the frequent disagreements in the Agency, amplified by the discord among other intelligence organs, made reaching a solid and timely conclusion on any issue virtually impossible.

To address some of these problems, Bush asked Cheney to evaluate the performance of the intelligence community, especially with regard to WMD. The vice president's office was also tasked with generating "worst-case scenarios" and enhancing homeland security. Cheney discussed this mandate in an interview with *New Yorker* in May 2001. He disclosed his concern about the poor state of homeland security and pointed out the real threat of a terrorist attack against the United States, possibly with weapons of mass destruction supplied by rogues such as Iraq, Iran, or North Korea (Dubose and Bernstein 2006, 166–167). Soon after, in a virtually unnoticed development, Cheney hired retired admiral Steve Abbott to oversee the program (Woodward 2004, 29). In a separate review, Brent Scowcroft, whom Bush appointed to head the President's Foreign Intelligence Advisory Board (PFIAB), conceded that the CIA was still geared to cold war realities.

For his part, the secretary of defense argued that intelligence gathering should be closely related to Special Operation missions in the mold of the Intelligence Support Activity of the early 1980s, which blended intelligence gathering, analysis, and covert activity in real time. While the new approach was derived from the overall philosophy of Cheney's Strategic Guidance document of 1992, concentrating much of the intelligence effort in the Pentagon had the added advantage of what Rumsfeld called the "one dog to kick" approach, namely improving the accountability for intelligence failures (Arkin 2002; Risen 2006, 67).

Critics would later charge that the shift of intelligence to the Department of Defense was motivated by the quest to link Saddam Hussein to al Qaeda and thus justify an invasion. In fact, steps to ensure a larger role for the Pentagon were taken in the spring and summer of 2001. Robert J. Newberry, the head of the Special Operations and Low Intensity Conflict in the Department of Defense was ordered to enlarge the intelligence-gathering functions of the military. Andrew Marshall, the veteran defense analyst in the Office of Net Assessments was asked to produce the plan for a "Revolution in Military Affairs," first mentioned in the missile commission report. Rumsfeld also appointed Stephen Cambone, his aide on the commission and a critic of the CIA, as his special assistant. Later on, Rumsfeld created the Policy Counterterrorism Evaluation Group (PCTEG) within the Office of Under Secretary of Defense for Policy (OUSDP) headed by Douglas Feith. The PCTEG, whose personnel were detailed from the Defense Intelligence Agency, was charged with studying the "policy implications of terror and their sources of support" (SSCI, 2004, 307).

In a memorandum announcing these changes, Rumsfeld noted that with the decline in "orderliness and predictability" of the bipolar world, a more dynamic approach to intelligence was needed (Suskind, 2004, 81). By all accounts, Rumsfeld's thinking was influenced by the work of Thomas Schelling and Roberta and Albert Wohlstetter on strategic surprises. Schelling, in particular was convinced that surprises emanated from "poverty of expectations," that is, the "tendency to confuse the unfamiliar with improbable." In Rumsfeld's terminology, such "unknown unknowns" should be given serious consideration if surprise was to be avoided (Goldberg 2003; Gormley 2004).

In fact, Pentagon's work on terrorist worst-case scenarios preceded Rumsfeld. In 1993 the Pentagon commissioned a private study to chart terrorist trends until the end of the decade. Among others, *Terror 2000* looked into a scenario involving an airplane flying into important targets in the United States and concluded that Islamic "superterrorists" with WMD posed a grave danger to American security. At the time, Norman J. Rabkin, a national security expert in the General Accounting Office, reported that these findings "appear to be at odds with judgment of the intelligence community." Apparently expressing a CIA position, Rabkin chastised the private study for a failure to "distinguish what is possible and what is likely." The rise of al Qaeda did little to modify this view. The White House terrorism tsar Richard Clarke testified before the 9/11 commission that his notion of airplanes flying into building was derived from novels, but that "he did not pursue the systemic issues of defending aircraft from suicide hijackers or bolstering wider air defenses" (Reeve 2002, 259; Strasser 2004, 327; Warrick and Stephens 2001).

Much as the Pentagon was prepared to entertain such scenarios, as noted, key Middle East specialists were skeptical. Moreover, the State Department, an important bureaucratic player in the administration, showed little anxiety. The department's Intelligence and Research Office, which was involved in the preparation of the annual *Patterns of Global Terrorism* expressed optimism in its 2000 write-up. During its official release, on April 27, 2001, Colin Powell stated that "the results are clear; state sponsors of terrorism are increasingly isolated, terrorist groups under growing pressure, terrorists are being brought to justice." The Congressional Research Service echoed State's conclusions in a report published on September 10, one day before the attack. Its lead author Kenneth Katzman (2001, 10), argued, seemingly oblivious to the 1998 court ruling, that the "1993 bombing of the World Trade Center" was not linked to al Qaeda.

With little progress in proving the "phantom link" between Iraq and al Qaeda, the administration realists, Collin Powell and Condoleezza Rice, saw little need to fashion a more aggressive policy toward Saddam Hussein.

From Sanctions to "Smart Sanctions": The "No Pain, No Gain" Approach

By all accounts, Iraq was not a major priority for the administration until September 11. Still, the White House was compelled to look for ways to respond to the alarming erosion in the sanctions regime. As noted, in 1999 Congress held hearings on the subject. In a testimony before the U.S. Senate Committee on Banking, Housing, and Urban Affairs on February 7, 2001, Richard T. Cupitt (2001), associate director of the Center for International Export Controls at the University of Georgia, repeated the warning that nonproliferation controls were easy to evade. Gary Milhollin, the director of the Wisconsin Project on Nuclear Arms Control, detailed how Iraq, using Jordanian and other Arab middlemen, had evaded monitoring efforts (Milhollin and Motz 2001).

In addition to violations, the public relations costs of containing Iraq were mounting. By 2001, sanction opponents in the United States seemed to have gained the upper hand; attacks on Madeleine Albright, as the "hideous harridan" and a "poster child" for callous American foreign policy filled the Internet and the left-wing press (Szamuely 2000). The antisanction community, augmented by a number of church-based groups, mobilized to publicize the sufferings of the Iraqi people. The radical Institute for Policy Studies mounted a major campaign to lift sanctions altogether (Bennis 2000, 2002). American activists received considerable support from the international community. In January 2001, Hans von Sponeck, who replaced Halliday as UN Humanitarian coordinator, launched a scathing attack on sanctions and declared that the "no-fly zone" should be abolished (Simons 2003, 212). Dozens of flights carrying human rights activists and sympathizers landed in Baghdad, followed by politicians, businessmen, and even a head of state, the Venezuelan president, Huge Chaves (Hiro 2002, 149–150; Simons 2003, 205).

In a belated effort to counter criticism, the State Department rolled out an initiative to blame Saddam Hussein for much of the suffering. An official Web site and other publications showed that the Iraqi dictator had built numerous palaces while starving his people. There were also reports that Hussein curtailed water use for farmers during a severe draught, causing food shortages (Washington Files, 2000). A number of journalists who visited Iraq in the late 1990s confirmed stories of deliberate efforts to block food supplies (Kelly 2002). A joint study of the UN Food and Agricultural Organization and the World Health Organization indicated that half of the Iraqi population was overweight and, as a result, hypertension and diabetes were among the leading causes of death. A detailed article by Baram (2000) blamed the cases of malnutrition on the regime's discrimination against the Shiites in the South.

However, much of this information was either ignored or rejected. Baghdad, which assisted the antisanction movement and provided much of its statistics, registered its satisfaction. During the Arab summit in March 2001, Saddam Hussein implied that after finding ways to outwit the sanction regime, Iraq had used the international sympathy to bolster the legitimacy of his government (Ghabra 2001, 49).

Indeed, the opposition to sanctions, once limited to the radical left, had come to dominate much of the foreign policy discourse in Iraq. David Cortright, the president of the Fourth Freedom Foundation, a pacifist-disarmament organization, and George A. Lopez, the policy director of the left-leaning Joan B. Kroc Institute for International Peace Studies at Notre Dame University, urged a new "bargaining model" of sanction combining sanctions with positive incentives and dialogue. To minimize the suffering of the civilian population, they called for "smart sanctions" that would enable civilian trade but block arms and dual use technology. The study urged, among other measures, a closer cooperation of the international community, a system of border monitoring and verification, and a stronger role for the

United Nations (Cortright and Lopez, 2000; Lopez and Cortright 2000, Cortright 2001). The Cortright-Lopez plan received a substantial boost from the Brookings Institution's Study Group on the Utility of Economic Sanctions as an Instrument of American Foreign Policy headed by Richard Haass, the Institute's director of Foreign Policy Studies. The Haass group came up with its own version of smart sanctions and argued that a more liberal approach would provide Saddam Hussein with incentives to modify his behavior (Haass 1998; Haass and O'Sullivan 2000).

Smart sanctions, were enthusiastically received in liberal circles. The Carnegie Endowment for International Peace featured smart sanctions as part of its global issues program for 2001. Michael Ignatieff (2001), the director of The Carr Center for Human Rights Practices at Harvard University, urged for a replacement of "dumb sanctions" with smart sanctions, a call that was repeated by *Foreign Policy* and other elite foreign policy publications. By mid-2001 there was a growing demand that smart sanctions should replace the failed containment policy toward Iraq (Mellinger 2001). On June 20, 2001, the Library of Congress convened a conference titled "The End of Dual Containment: Iraq, Iran and Smart Sanctions." The panelists called for a more "nuanced" Middle East policy, a "dialogue" with "countries" and a "broader regional effort to discourage weapon proliferation" (Katzman 2001).

But neoconservative observers were much less sanguine. Reflecting on the sanction debate, Michael Rubin (2001), an expert on Iraq with inside knowledge of the country, argued that smart sanctions were essentially a theoretical construct that would not stand up to reality. Richard Butler (2000a, 105–117) created something of a diplomatic stir when he accused Yevgeny Primakov, the former Russian prime minister and Hussein's friend, of facilitating an extensive network of business relations between Moscow and Baghdad. The Project for the New American Century (PNAC) emphasized that Saddam Hussein was contravening sanctions and pursuing his WMD program. Neoconservatives and their Iraqi protégés hoped that such charges would persuade the Bush administration to embrace the Iraqi Liberation Act to change the regime in Baghdad (Eisenstadt 2001).

To promote regime change PNAC created the Committee for Peace and Security in the Gulf. The committee was joined by the Iraq Foundation, a human rights group organized by Kanan Makiya whose revelations about Saddam Hussein' abuses made him a household name among neoconservatives and Iraqi expatriates (Aburish 2000, 363). Chalabi's INC intensified its own lobbying campaign in Washington and the *Weekly Standard* exhorted Bush to "get serious about toppling Saddam Hussein" (Gerecht 2001). Taking a page out of the democratic peace book, neoconservatives argued that once Hussein was "rolled back" by opposition forces, Iraq could become a pivot for democracy and stability in the Gulf.

If neoconservatives hoped that the Committee for Peace and Security would impact the discursive community, they were bound to be disappointed.

Objection to regime change came from many quarters. Former Middle East diplomats, Clinton administration officials, and academics decried it as the "rollback fantasy" and warned that the use of Iraqi opposition would result in a new "Bay of Pigs" (Byman 1999; Byman, Pollack, and Rose 1999; Peck 1998).

Most scholars were equally pessimistic about the chances of bringing democracy to Iraq. The author of a well-timed book on the history of Iraq observed that "sectarian identity" trumps any sense of national cohesion, especially among the Kurds (Tripp 2000, 274–276). Thomas Carothers (1999, 99–128), director of the democratic transition project at the Carnegie Foundation, stated that Arab exceptionalism might present a problem in Iraq. He was also less than persuaded that civil society was a panacea for all the ills of autocracy. The isolationist Cato Institute warned that overthrowing Saddam Hussein would plunge Iraq into a violent civil war and an eventual split (Isenberg 1999). The academic left was openly hostile to the Democracy Project because it promoted market economy. A well-publicized study argued that democracy is an American vehicle to create a global empire based on "irresistible and irrevocable globalization of economic and culture exchange" (Hard and Negri 2000, xi).

For their part, realist IR scholars rejected the notion that the character of the regime matters. Mearsheimer (2001, 367, 371) admitted that "democratic peace" was among the "strongest challenges to realism," but went on to argue that his own formula of "offensive realism," a blend of international and unilateral measures, would restrain the most recalcitrant of actors. Emulating Tony Lake, some IR experts objected to the practice of turning select states into international outlaws. Robert S. Litwak (2000a, 2000b), a former director of nonproliferation on Clinton's NSC and the head of International Studies Division at the Woodrow Wilson International Center for Scholars argued that the "rogue" label was too simplistic and inflammatory and driven by the American view of international relations. In other words, a "rogue state is whatever the United States says it is" (Strauss 2000). Blaming the "fear of American military primacy" for triggering "defensive reaction" by some actors, Walt (2002, 148–149) counseled the United States to eschew "large offensively capabilities." Klare (2000b, 46) proclaimed that the rogue state doctrine was strategically obsolete.

Not all IR experts accepted the notion that, by design or default, rogue states are an American creation. Addressing Walt, Hoyt (2000) noted that rogue states pose a challenge both to the United States and realist theory because they act in an irrational way, defined as opposition to the international order in spite of high cost to the regime (Rotberg 2000). Commenting on this exchange, one scholar would later note that the "debate at the level of theory mirrored what was happening at the level of policy" (Haslam 2002, 242–243).

Indeed, the public debate on the Iraqi sanctions was reproduced in the Bush administration. Hardliners were skeptical that smart sanctions would work, given Saddam Hussein's record of manipulating a stringent containment regime. From his perch at the head of the Defense Policy Board, Richard Perle argued that that the United States had to make clear its resolve to get rid of the dictator (Mackey 2002, 338).

But Colin Powell viewed regime change as an anathema to the cautiously realistic course he hoped to pursue with regard to Iraq. Well aware that sanctions posed a public relation problem the secretary of state felt that smart sanctions would create a more humane image for American foreign policy at home and abroad. Powell picked Richard Haass to head policy planning and draft the State Department's version of smart sanction. In a hearing before the House International Relations Committee on March 7, 2001, Haass assured the lawmakers that the new policy would reenergize the international coalition and alleviate the humanitarian crisis in Iraq. According to the Haass plan, sanction policy would be liberalized, allowing Iraq to purchase a wider variety of goods. Liberals applauded the State Department and praised Powell for his vision. In the words of Lopez (2001), "U.S. Secretary of State created a new momentum in the tragic and puzzling quagmire of U.N. sanctions on Iraq."

But Rumsfeld and his neoconservative appointees, Wolfowitz and Feith, were upset by the State Department embrace of smart sanctions. *The Weekly Standard* was openly dismissive of what was dubbed "the no pain, no gain" approach. Still, Powell's arguments carried with President Bush who was wary of international intervention and nation building associated with regime change (Mackey 2002, 378; Mann 2004, 301). Analysts who followed the internal debates in the administration were quick to conclude that the pragmatic realists were firmly in control. With no significant political constituency of their own, and out of tune with mainstream Republican party, let alone its isolationist right wing, the neoconservatives were left holding the short end of the power stick. As one leading journalist put it, in the summer of 2001, the "war party" was "losing to Powell" (Ricks, 2006, 28).

All this was to change on September 11. The unprecedented attack on American soil separated, in the words of one observer, "a naively complacent past from a frightfully vulnerable future" (Miller 2002, 15). This new sensibility provided the neoconservatives with a unique chance to reshape the American foreign policy in their own image.

SEPTEMBER 11 AND ISLAMIC TERRORISM: THE VINDICATION OF THE NEOCONSERVATIVE VISION OF FOREIGN POLICY

Like Pearl Harbor and other unexpected traumas in American history, 9/11 was akin to a Kuhnian-like alteration in the paradigm used to understand and predict the future. To recall Kuhn's proposition, revolutionary change in knowledge occurs when a dominant paradigm is overthrown and a new set of assumptions about the essence of reality comes to fore. Scholars and practitioners associated with the old epistemic community are discredited and their intellectual rivals move in. In terms of American discourse on the

Middle East, the al Qaeda attack had undermined the MESA paradigm and vindicated the Lewis-Huntington "clash of civilizations" theory. An even more important change occurred in the core assumptions used to analyze reality, as outlined in chapter 1.

First, there was serious questioning whether the positivist, secular humanistic view of perfectible human nature could explain political reality. The alternative model of people choosing between good and evil, once the exclusive domain of Christian evangelicals, was gaining ground in the newly reconfigured discursive space. As one critic put it, the "liberal mind" has a basic difficulty in comprehending evil because of its belief in the perfectibility of human nature moving along a "linear path" toward enlightenment (Hannity 2004, 2–3). Another observer claimed that al Qaeda presented the most profound challenge to liberalism since its inception; it restored a view of human nature based on an essentially "illiberal revealed theology" of Judeo-Christianty and Islam (Owen 2004, 325). Equally surprisingly, some of the most trenchant critique of liberalism came from the intellectual left. Todd Gitlin (2002, 3; 2006, 32) was among those who admitted that "9/11 jammed my intellectual circuits" as he struggled to come "to grips with apocalyptical suicidal-homicidal fanatics." He also decried the "glaring lacuna" in the philosophy of liberalism, that is, its "longstanding failure to address the problem of evil."

Second, there was the closely related issue of morality in international relations. As already discussed, realists had little use for moral factors. The postmodern critical scholarship with its emphasis on "narratives" and multiculturalism has favored outright moral relativism. Applied to the international realm, moral relativism has mutated into the creed of moral equivalence. Neoconservative critics contended that the "corrosive effect of moral equivalence" led the intellectual left to defend the Soviet Union during the cold war and radical Islam later on (Elshtain 2003, 145). The political philosopher Michael Waltzer (2002) went further; he accused the left of a "willful denial" of any difference between premeditated murder of civilians by terrorists and the unintended killings caused by response to terrorist attacks.

Third, the magnitude of the predictive failure raised doubts whether the largely secular academic community, famously defined by Sir Isaiah Berlin as "stone dry atheists," was qualified to understand the force or religious beliefs in human life (Ignatieff 1998, 291). With a host of scholars proclaiming the "twilight of atheism" and the "fall of disbelief," the God-is-dead gospel of the 1960s that guided social sciences for four decades seemed to be on the defensive (McGrath 2004, 175). Kevin Phillips (2004, 228), the onetime Republican analyst-turned critic of the Bush administration, was forced to acknowledge that "several layers of disbelief vanished in the aftermath of 9/11," shaking the "underlying skepticism of modern secular elites."

Much of the new focus on the religious underpinning of human action was applied to the Middle East. The MESA view of terrorism as emanating from socioeconomic "root causes" came under harsh attack. David Horowitz (2004, 37, 437–438), a leading conservative critic, asserted that addressing "real causes of timeless phenomena like terrorism...was a code for the utopian agenda of the left." Another conservative scholar added that the "futile search for root causes" was part of a broader apologetics for Marxism and Islamism (Radu 2002). Some observers pointed out that since the collapse of the Soviet Union, the left had strengthened its intellectual links with radical Islam to fight the perils of globalization. First conceived by Ali Shariati in France, this so-called red and green alliance was given a strong impetus by the writings of Roger Barodi, a French Marxist who had converted to Islam, and disseminated in the United States by Eqbal Ahmad, the editor of *Race and Class* (Horowitz 2004; Kurlantzick 2004).

While suicide bombings were certainly not new phenomena, the magnitude of the attack made it easier for observers to define Islamic terrorism as a moral evil. As one expert put it, it was "deliberate suffering" imposed on "sentient beings" through the use of immoral means (Stern 2003, xxiii, 281–283). Others described al Qaeda as detached from society and intent on an abstract and apocalyptical vision of a global war "between good and evil" (Reuter 2004, 17; Sageman 2004, 151). The "root cause" theory of terrorism was further discredited when it was learned that the September 11 hijackers came from privileged middle-class backgrounds. A Harvard study that found that any connection between poverty, lack of education and terrorism is "indirect, complicated, and probably weak" was widely quoted in the press (Charen 2003, 248; Krueger and Maleckova 2004, 27–33).

A growing scrutiny of Hasan al Bana, Sayyid Qutab, and other formative figures of Islamic fundamentalism frequently quoted by bin Laden further questioned the "root cause" theory. Al Bana and Qutab called for jihad against the West where, in their view, the "jahilyya society" of secularism, modernism, and materialism took root (Emerson 2001; Euben 2002; Lewis 2003, 77; Rapoport 2001; Shepard 2003). While careful to distinguish between Islamic masses and hard-core jihadists, observers noted that "Osama bin Laden inexorably linked [Islamic] religion with a war against Jews and Christians, a war devoid of any remorse or shame." As one scholar argued, this new terrorism was not about poverty versus wealth but rather a "confrontation between a theistic, land based and traditional culture...and the secular material values of the enlightenment" (Howard 2002; Nisan 2004).

In his widely read book *What Went Wrong? Western Impact and Middle East Response* and other writings, Bernard Lewis (2002, 7; 2003, 374–375) rounded out the "clash of civilizations" theme. Lewis noted that the cultural antecedents of economic well-being present in Europe "found no way to the Middle East" and that historical-religious hatreds were compounded by Arab envy of the success of West. Accordingly, it was difficult if not impossible "to be strong and successful and to be loved by those who are neither the one nor the other." What is more, with the "clash of civilizations" theory seeming to be vindicated, the opposing argument that blamed the Arab-Israeli conflict for all the problems in the Middle East lost much of its luster. As the attention to the writings of Islamic fundamentalists replaced the traditional preoccupation with Israel and the Palestinians, even those who disagreed with Lewis had to admit that he was "a rare intellectual" whose influence was "considerable" (Benjamin and Simon 2005, 264).

Blaming MESA scholars for misleading Americans about Islamic radicalism was also on the rise. As already detailed, in his well-timed book and subsequent writings, Martin Kramer (2001, 2003a) chastised academics who "adamantly denied the potential for terrorism" and showed contempt "for those who argued that large scale terrorism was possible." Kramer argued that John Esposito, whom he called "America's foremost apologist for Islam," blocked efforts to discuss fundamentalism and radicalism in the Islamic context. Lewis (2004, 389–393) was even more scathing in his denunciation of "political correctness" in Middle East Studies. He wondered how political reality could be understood in a field where rewriting of history and creating of mythology were buttressed by "amnesia sustained by concealment," and "invention sustained by fabrication." Some commentators felt that the willful whitewashing of militant Islam and its "capacity for monstrous bloodletting" was synonymous with the "Stockholm Syndrome," where Western intellectuals played the role of captives sympathizing with and exculpating their "terrorist captors" (Hotaling 2001, 144, 167). In their own effort at deconstruction, neoconservatives attacked Said and his followers for using the guise of objective research to pursue a radical anti-American agenda. In this view, the refusal of prominent MESA scholars to acknowledge the danger of Islamist terrorism caused real damage to American national security. The charge received national attention when Congress decided to probe Middle East programs offered in colleges nationwide (Kramer 2003b).

Sensing public damage, Joel Beinin (2003, 15), the then MESA president, rejected the claim that Middle East scholars failed to warn about Islamist terrorism. He described such allegations as "scurrilous attacks" and denounced them as "an amalgam of outright mendacity and tendentious readings of a highly selective body of the scholarship and popular writing of some MESA members." Above all, he denied that MESA was "unpatriotic" and "uninterested in warning the United States about the danger of terrorism." Beinin, who had coined the term "terrorology," argued that "terrorolgists did not accomplish much" because they focused on "tactics and symptoms," without an "investigation into historical and social causes," including the Arab-Israeli conflict.

Beinin was not the only one to defend the notion that the Arab-Israeli conflict and American support for the Jewish state were to blame for September 11. Days after the attack, Stephen Walt (2001) stated that to avoid terrorism in the future, the United States needed to change its approach to the conflict, even if such as "shift of policy would leave many American Jews uneasy." In an effort to deflect from the "clash of civilization" theory, Mearsheimer (2002) argued that there were real grounds for the hatred of America and suggested that the United States should pressure Israel to create a viable Palestinian state.

Further to the left, the so-called blowback theory, first given academic credibility by Chalmers Johnson (2000), charged that U.S. actions around the globe—whether supporting Israeli or spreading hegemonic capitalism—triggered intense anti-American hatred (Cooley 2002; Kolko 2002, 102–140; Wallerstein 1997). Turning the Unocal episode on its head, antiglobalists explained that American oil companies supported the Taliban in order to build a pipeline through Afghanistan. A variation on this theme held that the United States was also the leading international terrorist and thus fully deserving of the attack. Crossing the threshold of blowback were fringe conspiracy theories that alleged that September 11 was a joint CIA-Mossad venture designed to frame Islamic fundamentalists. A more generalized version held that the United States, which in the past had helped Hitler and Mussolini, had created the Taliban and supported bin Laden (Said 2002b, 2000a).

Neoconservatives denounced the blowback interpretation of September 11, calling it a "myth" and "bad history." They pointed out that "blame America first" was possible because of the "permissive" anti-Americanism attitude of academic and intellectual elite, amplified by a large number of pundits and a long list of publications such as *Nation, Progressive, Counterpunch, ZMagazine* and others (Henriksen 2002; Horowitz 2003, 426). Neoconservatives alleged that this anti-Americanism was even built into mainstream IR theory where accusing the United States for third world behavior was de rigueur.

As if to illustrate this point, when Robert Snyder (1999) published a paper claiming that American involvement in third world conflicts in the 1960s and 1970s was a response to provocations by local revolutionaries backed by the Soviet Union, he created a storm that preoccupied the IR discipline virtually until 9/11. A special International Studies Policy forum condemned Snyder's thesis; the then president of the International Studies Association complained that the younger generation of IR experts were "more conservative" than their predecessors. Others expressed fear that the field was becoming a "tool of propaganda" of the American government and urged that students should be taught more progressive values (Ghibbs 2001; Murphy 2001). In an unprecedented move, *The Chronicles of Higher Education* covered the debate.

That the neoconservative critique of academia benefited from the September attack was obvious. Although it is difficult to measure paradigmatic shifts, anecdotal evidence based on Internet searches seems to indicate that after 9/11, there was a dramatic increase in the conjoint occurrences of terms terrorism and Islamic fundamentalism (Goldberg 2003; Kramer 2003a).

More important than scoring points in an intellectual debate, September 11 gave the neoconservatives an opportunity to translate their vision into a new foreign policy model.

The War in Afghanistan and the Triumph of Democratic Universalism

In light of the September attack, much of the neoconservative critique of intelligence looked prescient, if not prophetic. The sea change in attitudes toward covert action and domestic surveillance was especially noticeable, with former opponents now eager to acknowledge that "with hindsight," the reluctance to "mount an aggressive surveillance and search" operations was a failure (Betts 2002, 51; Hulnick 2004, 170; Johnson 2003–04; Steele 2002). Without admitting his role in muzzling the CIA, Seymour Hersh (2001) described Reul Marc Gerecht articles as "prescient." Even the far left *Mother Jones* declared that the Agency was "clueless" and blamed the Carter-Turner reforms for "privileging" the "clean" signal intelligence (SIGINT) (Gup 2002).

A number of prominent intelligence and security officials expanded on this criticism. Bobby R. Inman (2001), maintained that the CIA had never regained its covert capacity after "Turner's devastation" during the Carter administration and the legalism of some of his successors. William J. Perry (2001) suggested that the "dark arts" in the Agency suffered from years of excessive legal restriction and stringent separation of intelligence and law enforcement. In a sign of the times, Oleg Kalugin (2004) a general in the former KGB, received a respectable hearing when he urged the United States to adopt Soviet-style covert operations, sabotage, and other interventionist tactics.

CIA's methodology was also assailed. Considerable criticism was leveled at the Kentian dictate for "objective" truth and high evidentiary standards. Echoing Shulsky, a number of observers charged that such standards were unfortunate in managing information uncertainty created by complex terrorist networks and their hidden state sponsors (Feder 2002; Homer-Dixon 2002; Rothmell 2002). These and other critics pointed out that President Clinton's decision to call off a number of attacks on bin Laden because, in his words, "there was no sufficient evidence," was a case in point (Clinton 2004, 925). The 9/11 Commission would subsequently criticize the Clinton team for its reluctance to link the Iranians to the Khobar Towers bombing because there was a lack of "definitive evidence" (Kean and Hamilton 2004, 64–65). In defending his decision to abort strikes against bin Laden, Tenet (2007, 109) blamed the "high hurdles" of gathering sufficiently clear evidence required by Clinton's Justice Department.

That bin Laden could have been eliminated, had evidentiary standard been lower, was quickly turned into a stock neoconservative argument. As Wolfowitz contended, the lessons of 9/11 demonstrated that "we can't always wait for clear cut evidence" and made acting upon "murky evidence" a necessity (quoted in Ferreira 2003). A number of studies on "losing bin Laden" made the point that "smoking gun" proof was too exacting for cracking the al Qaeda network and eliminating its chief (Coll 2004; Miniter 2003, 121).

Terrorism practiced on the scale of al Qaeda added poignancy to the long-standing neoconservative unease over traditional thinking on deterrence. To recall, only a handful of analysts such as Payne (1996), had warned that classic state-based theories of deterrence were not adequate in the post–cold war era. As terrorist organization had no "return address," and deterrence had to be replaced by preemption. With WMD added to the mix, the chance that a small terrorist group could inflict "catastrophic damage" on a country created a novel challenge to the international system. Abraham D. Sofaer (2003) a former State Department's chief council advocated a change in international law to legalize preemption. Although liberals strenuously objected to this, Rumsfeld made it clear that preemption would become an integral part of the Bush doctrine. True to form, the secretary of defense used the Schelling-like proposition that "the greater the threat the greater the risk of inaction," a notion that was echoed in the administration's 2002 "Fighting Global Terror" document (Arend 2003, 96; Decter 2003, 142; Fukuyama 2006, 67; Hersh 2004, 203).

Perhaps most significantly, the al Qaeda operation in Afghanistan highlighted the perils of Islamic and Arab autocracy. There was a virtual consensus that the Taliban theocracy was an extreme example of an illegitimate Islamo-fascist regime ruling over its citizens with singular brutality verging on the grotesque. That such a regime represented a "swamp" in which Islamist terrorism could flourish gave rise to calls to transform Afghanistan into a democracy. To persuade critics of the virtues of Kantian democratic peace, neoconservatives argued that by harboring al Qaeda, the Taliban endangered the security of the United States. Upon launching Operation Enduring Freedom in October 2001, the president emphasized his determination to crush the Taliban and turn Afghanistan into a "demonstration model" for extending the process of democratization to the Islamic world (Suskind 2004, 186–187).

By adding democratic transformation to muscular militarism, the neoconservatives drew on Woodrow Wilson's idealism to create a hybrid model often referred to as "Wilsonianism in boots" (Ash 2004, 120). But unlike developmentalists or Liberal Internationalists, neoconservatives were not eager to embrace nation building and social engineering. The swift and low cost victory over the Taliban followed by a provisional democracy under Khamid Karzai bolstered the standing of the neoconservative creed. To its architects, the success in Afghanistan was a highly propitious sign that the United States could extend the vision of Democratic Universalisms to Iraq.

5

The Buildup to Operation Iraqi Freedom: Implementing Democratic Universalism

If the quick victory against Taliban and the preliminary process of democratization in Afghanistan seemed to vindicate the democratic peace, it did not allay concerns about al Qaeda's potential for perpetuating further attacks. On the contrary, as more information on the secretive group began to emerge, there was growing alarm that bin Laden was determined to use lethal weapons against the United States.

The series of anthrax letters greatly unnerved the administration. Coming so close after the 9/11 attacks, it seemed a logical extension of the "toxic terrorism" script. Although the "scenario from hell," as Condoleezza Rice termed it, was contained, the uncertainly about its origin was unnerving. For one thing, a summer 2000 State Department simulation pointed a finger at the Iraqi plant *al Hakam* as a possible producer of anthrax to be used in such an attack. Richard Sperzel, a former UNSCOM expert on biological weapons, concluded that the anthrax was professionally produced, either in Iraq or the former Soviet Union (Miller, Eghleberg, and Broad 2002, 298, 321). President Bush was reported to "be obsessed by the danger," pointing out that if a culprit could not be found the entire notion of "deterrence was out the window" (Schweitzer and Schweitzer 2004, 523–524).

More fundamentally, the president was moved to reflect on how the United States could reform the type of "countries that produced ideologies and people" with the goal of "killing Americans." In the view of Michael Gerson, Bush's speechwriter, the president decided that the only way to prevent such an ideology from spreading was to bring democracy to the Arab world (Woodward 2004, 89).

When Bush included Iraq, along with Iran and North Korea, in his "Axis of Evil" State of the Union address in January 2002, he provided a preview of what would eventually become the Bush doctrine. The speech offered a strong belief that the domestic policy of a country matters in international relations and that the United States would seek to democratize countries to maximize its own national security. Journalist Bob Woodward (2004, 87, 91) suggested that Bush was convinced that he and his generation were called to fight a new and more sinister evil than his father's cohort. This twenty-first-century threat was "malicious, ruthless but elusive and unpredictable." In this context, bin Laden, and Saddam Hussein embodied a connection between weapons of mass destruction and international terrorism that could put humanity on "the road to Armageddon" (Kengor 2004, 124).

Terrorism practiced on the scale of al Qaeda added poignancy to the debate about deterrence in the Second Nuclear Age. As terrorist organizations had no "return address," deterrence had to be replaced by preemption. With WMD added to the mix, the chance that a small terrorist group could inflict "catastrophic damage" on a country created a novel challenge to the international system. Abraham D. Sofaer (2003) a former State Department chief council, advocated a change in international law to legalize preemption. Although liberals strenuously objected, Rumsfeld made it clear that preemption would become an integral part of the Bush doctrine (Arend 2003, 96; Decter 2003, 142; Fukuyama 2006, 67; Hersh 2004, 203).

During a speech in West Point on June 1, 2002, Bush elaborated upon the fatal crossroad between radicalism and technology and called for proactive steps against proliferation and for regime change. The 2002 National Security Strategy of the United States released in September formalized the Bush doctrine. In a language reminiscent of Second Nuclear Age reasoning, the document reminded Americans that "traditional concepts of deterrence would not work" against the new constellation of threats and, as a result, the United States "must be prepared to stop rogue states and their clients before they are able to threaten" other actors (www.whitehouse.gov/nsc/nss.pdf).

Behind the scenes, the administration was receiving alarming news that the "Armageddon" scenario could be closer than expected. The British Intelligence service M16 passed on information that a Pakistani nuclear scientist, subsequently identified as Abdul Qadeer Khan, the "father of Pakistan's nuclear program," had developed a lucrative black market in nuclear designs (Woodward 2004, 47). CIA had no proof that bin Laden obtained nuclear technology such as dirty bombs from Khan, but American forces in Afghanistan came across evidence of the *al Zabadi* project, including chemical experiments, blueprints for chemical attacks and, in Khandahar, high-grade anthrax. More important, a number of captured al Qaeda operatives, including Mohammed Mabruk, Ibrahim Sayyied al-Najjar, and Ibn al Sheik al Libi claimed that Iraqis were helping in developing unconventional weapons. Even though al Libi recanted his confession in 2004, Cheney and Rumsfeld were unhappy with the CIA's scant knowledge of al Qaeda's unconventional production line. The Senate Intelligence Committee subsequently faulted the CIA for underestimating the size and sophistication of bin Laden's WMD program (SSIC 2004; Suskind 2006, 122, 251). To his credit (Tenet 2007, 260), admitted that assuming that al Qaeda was not developing WMD "was simply wrong."

Bin Laden's long-standing efforts to obtain a fatwa legitimizing his use of lethal weapons from a number of religious scholars received a more serious scrutiny. In a June 2002 post, al Qaeda's spokesman Suleiman Abu Ghaith claimed that al Qaeda had a Koranic right to kill four million Americans; in May 2003 a respected Saudi cleric Sheik Nasir bins Hamid al Fahd, issued "A treatise on the Legal Status of Using Weapons of Mass Destruction against Infidels." Al Fahd justified WMD attacks on the ground that they could produce a large number of casualties, especially in densely populated cities such as New York or London (Bennet and Walt 2004; Dolnik 2001; Ledeen 1996; Lieber 2003; Scheuer 2004, 74–75; Williams 2006, 187). As already noted, the Iraqi Operation Group passed on information about Abu Musab al Zarqawi and the Khurmal facility. General Tommy Franks (2004, 331–332) wrote that the evidence was "not air tight" but he believed that al Zarqawi and other al Qaeda leaders were given safe passage by Iraqi security forces.

Given the long-standing suspicion that Iraq helped al Qaeda to develop lethal weapons in Sudan and then Afghanistan, the White House ordered the CIA to review all ties between Saddam Hussein and al Qaeda.

Bin Laden, Saddam Hussein, and Weapons of Mass Destruction: Trying to Flesh out the "Phantom Link"

Surprised by what Tenet (2007, 342–343) called the "intensive focus" of "some" in the administration on the Iraq-al Qaeda linkage, the CIA had initially few details to offer on the issue. This was especially true compared to the intensive work performed by the PCTEG and its successor, the Pentagon Office of Special Plans (OSP) directed by Abram Shulsky and overseen by Under Secretary of Defense William J. Luti. Using advanced network analysis the PCTEG/OSP analysts found a much more evolved operational relations between bin Laden and the Iraqi Intelligence Services than the CIA had found, especially with regard to Abu Musab al-Zarqawi. The Pentagon group was also convinced that one of the 9/11 hijackers, Mohammed Atta, had met with an Iraqi official in Prague in April 2001, a notion that surfaced, among others, in the Dolnik paper posted by PIR (Gordon and Trainor 2006, 127; Kean and Hamilton 2004, 97).

To respond to the Pentagon, the Counterterrorism Center and the DI's Near East and South Asia Office (NESA) produced two preliminary papers; a longer report "Iraq and Al Qaida: Interpreting a Murky Relationship" was issued on June 21, 2002. The report cautiously concluded that there might be "limited offers of cooperation between bin Laden and Saddam Hussein," but found no "smoking gun" evidence (SSCI 2004).

Even this mild conclusion was deeply contested by some NESA analysts who, among others, were skeptical about *Ansar al Islam* and the role of the then virtually unknown al Zarqawi. Although Pillar conceded that "some tactical cooperation" between the Islamists and Saddam Hussein was possible, NESA stood by its conclusion that there was no alliance between Baghdad and al Qaeda. To press their point, some regional analysts complained informally to the Agency's ombudsmen about politicization of the estimate (Tenet 2007, 345). The Robb-Silberman Commission and the

Senate Intelligence Commission that investigated the matter noted that such differences were due to the requirement of "juridical evidence" (Goldberg 2003; Robb and Silberman 2005, 309; SSCI 2004, 309, 329–330).

What the CIA viewed as "murky," Cheney, Rumsfeld and his top aides considered yet another example of the Agency's long-standing incompetence culminating in September 11. Although Tenet was spared public criticism, neoconservatives and other commentators excoriated the Agency for its misjudgment of al Qaeda and supporting the theory of freestanding terrorism. Some of these critics singled out Paul Pillar for downplaying the idea of megaterrorism in his 2001 book (Coll 2004, 277; de Wijk 2002; Mylroie 2003, 126; Tucker 2001; Woolsey 2001). Bruce Berkowitz (2002, 290, 292), who served on the Congress-appointed committee to study the Soviet intelligence failure, contended that the timid "mindset of the CIA was not suitable for analyzing elusive terrorism" and urged the Agency to become "fiercely proactive."

Pentagon's own misgivings about the CIA were summarized in a theoretically oriented brief "Fundamental Problems with How the Intelligence Community Is Assessing Information." The paper listed a number of perceived faults: insistence on "juridical evidence for findings, ignoring the deception that al Qaeda and Iraq used to hide their relations, and adhering to a rigid hypothesis that secularist and Islamists cannot cooperate." On August 15, 2002 the Pentagon team met with Tenet and his deputies for intelligence and operations to present their findings. Tenet (2007, 342–349) rejected the Czech report on the meeting as not credible, but had a more nuanced view on other connections between Iraq and al Qaeda. A September meeting between Vice President Cheney, his chief of staff, Lewis "Scooter" Libby, and Tenet failed to resolve the dispute, but, under considerable pressure from the White House, the CIA pushed to clarify its position on the Iraq-al Qaeda ties. However, as Tenet subsequently admitted, the continued disagreements in the Agency, primarily between regional analysts and counterintelligence officials, made writing the report difficult. While the former believed that bin Laden's fundamentalist Islam was a grave danger to a secular Iraq, the latter noted that there was a "deeper relationship" in terms of safe haven, training, and contacts.

In the fall, the CIA received intelligence about "greater contacts regarding Iraqi training of al Qaeda, leading to yet another round of debates within the Agency. In December a draft report, "Iraqi Support for Terrorism" was circulated and a final version in January 2003 identified three "areas of concern: "safe heavens, contacts and training." Tenet mentioned this finding in his congressional testimony in March 2003, but insisted that it did not show any Iraqi "authority, direction, or control over any of the many specific terrorist acts carried out by al Qaeda."

The "murky" nature of the relations would continue to fuel controversy. The Prague connection was definitively discredited when the CIA received incontrovertible evidence in 2006 that the person who met the Iraqi official was not Mohammed Atta (Tenet 2007, 355). For that matter, no evidence has been found to support the contention that Iraq was involved in any of the al Qaeda attacks. In 2007 the acting inspector general of the Pentagon Thomas F. Gimble called the actions of Feith team "inappropriate," because it developed "dubious intelligence" inconsistent with the "consensus of the wider community" (Stout 2007). Yet, as Tenet (2007, 351) admitted, the Iraqi-al Qaeda contacts in the "areas of concern" could not be refuted, leading to further debate. Using his position as the national intelligence officer for Near East and South Asia, Paul Pillar (2006) continued to fight the idea that there was a significant cooperation between al Qaeda and Iraq, a centerpiece of the Department of Defense's argument for war. Emile Nakhleh, Director of the Political Islam Strategic Analysis Program in the CIA was another high-level analyst who claimed that "we had no evidence that there was a Saddam-bin Laden axis" (Silverstein 2006).

If the hardliners had hoped to portray bin Laden as Saddam Hussein's sorcerer's apprentice ready to unleash a WMD attack on the United States, they were gravely disappointed. Nor was the White House more successful in eliciting a consensus on Saddam Hussein's WMD program. CIA's longstanding position was that Saddam Hussein had retained parts of his program, including approximately five hundred tons of yellow cake, the raw material for producing uranium. Tenet (2007, 315), disclosed that, over the year, the Agency had written in key publications, including the President's Daily Brief, "very assertive" pieces about Iraq's WMD.

However, the extent to which Iraq was reconstituting its nuclear program became the subject of a considerable debate after 9/11 that focused on Iraq's alleged procurement policies. Early in 2001 the Jordanians notified the CIA that they had seized a shipment of aluminum tubes destined for Iraq. Joe T., an analyst in the CIA's Weapons, Intelligence, Non-Proliferation, and Arms Control division (WINPAC), who worked on this issue, concluded that the tubes were purchased to serve as centrifuges, a finding that was supported by the DIA. However, a team of experts from the Department of Energy and Greg Thielmann, the head of Strategic, Proliferation, and Military Affairs Office in the State Department's Bureau of Intelligence and Research (INR), rejected this assumption. The highly arcane debate, joined by experts from a number of foreign intelligence services, split the intelligence community. Thielmann, whose personal relations with John Bolton, the undersecretary for weapons control, were strained, would later resign in protest (Gordon and Trainor 2006, 123; Richelson 2006, 478–479; Risen 2006, 112).

Evaluating alleged Iraqi efforts to purchase uranium from Niger proved to be even more divisive. The information originated with a number of Western intelligence services, including Britain's MI6, Italy's Military Intelligence and Security Service (SISMI), and France's GDES. In 1999, the MI6 learned from a number of different sources that the Iraqi ambassador to Vatican visited Niger to discuss the purchase of uranium, which was mined by a consortium controlled by the French company COGEMA. In 2000, an Italian businessman Rocco Marino provided documents from Niger's embassy in Rome indicating that Iraq was interested in buying yellow cake.

While the Marino document was subsequently ruled to be a forgery by the International Atomic Energy Agency, the British believed that some of their sources were credible.

While the CIA was seeking to determine whether the claim had any merit, the debate about the extent of Saddam Hussein's unconventional weapons was getting more heated. Ironically, the growing realization that the White House was ready to use its preemptive doctrine to change the regime in Iraq mobilized some inside the intelligence community to intensify their scrutiny of the evidence. Outside critics turned to the Internet, which served not only as an ongoing referendum on the Bush war plans, but also an arbiter of the evidence mustered to support it.

The Antiwar Coalition as an Intelligence Watchdog: Second-Guessing the Administration

Leading the charge against the war in Iraq was a loose alliance of groups and individuals that spanned the entire political spectrum. While both the radical right and the radical left had a known ideological agenda, the middle-of-the-roaders—former foreign policy, military, and intelligence officials—were well positioned to question the rationale for the war and cast doubts on the relevant intelligence.

Among the first to organize was Marc Ginbsurg, co-chair of Al Gore's foreign policy election committee, who founded the Alliance for American Leadership, a loose network of antiwar speakers, some with ties to the Clinton administration. Among them was Ambassador Joseph Wilson, a career diplomat with stints in Iraq and Gabon and an official on Clinton's NSC, who was loosely affiliated with Gore's election campaign. The former vice president himself launched a vigorous attack on the Bush administration through the MoveOn Website established by two Silicon Valley entrepreneurs and supported by George Soros and Tides Foundation who were listed among its benefactors, and Teresa Heinz Kerry, the wife of Senator John Kerry, a prospective Democratic presidential contender. Soros, a billionaire financier, was a bitter critic of Bush whom he described as acting upon a "misguided messianic impulse" (Johnson 2004; quoted in Schweitzer 2005, 154).

On the Republican side, James Baker, Brent Scowcroft, C. Boyden Gray, and other realists who served in the first Bush administration were joined by Senator Chuck Hegel, and self-described "old guard Republicans," a mix of Taft-style isolationists and libertarians such as Ron Paul, a congressman from Texas. The libertarian Cato Institute provided much of the intellectual argument against the war, which mirrored the reservations of the "Bush realists." In due course, Christopher Preble, Cato's director for foreign policy, would join forces with Gray to form the Committee for the Republican Old Guard, a center of realist opposition to the war (Gross 2005).

The Middle East Institute under Edward "Ned" Walker, a former assistant secretary of state for Near East affairs, emerged as an early war opponent.

Ambassador Wilson, an adjunct scholar at the Institute, was also close to the circle of war critics associated with the Middle East Council led by Chas Freeman, a former ambassador to Saudi Arabia. A sizeable contingent of high-ranking retired military officers and intelligence officials bolstered the legitimacy of the civilians. General Anthony Zinni, whom the neoconservatives blasted for being overly cautious in targeting bin Laden, was perhaps the most prominent military critic. In a major address to the Middle East Institute in October 2002, Zinni disputed the view that the war was "either inevitable or desirable" (Strother 2006). He was backed by General Wesley Clark, another high-profile war skeptic. The Veteran Intelligence Professionals for Sanity, founded by a retired CIA agent Raymond McGovern, in collaboration with Larry Johnson, the former counterterrorism expert in the State Department and Greg Thielmann, was most effective in raising questions about the intelligence on Iraq.

Richard Clarke, whom the Bush administration had retained as its terrorism tsar, was also becoming a vocal critic. By 2002, Clarke, who in 1999 had asserted that al Shifa was targeted because of the Iraqi-al Qaeda connection, became more guarded. Daniel Benjamin, Clinton's NSC official in charge of terrorism had a similar change of memory. Benjamin recalled that, following the criticism of al Shifa, Clarke had ordered a review of the information on al Qaeda, Iran and Iraq, but in spite of a stack of papers "three feet high" there was no "smoking gun" (Benjamin and Simon 2003, 263). In a book published after September 11, Clarke (2004, 142) wondered whether Sudan, using bin Ladin's money could "have hired some Iraqis to make chemical weapons." Such discrepancies prompted critics to accuse Clarke of politicizing intelligence (Ijaz 2004).

Scott Ritter, the former weapons inspector who denounced Clinton for "mollycoddling" Hussein in his 1999 book was perhaps the most surprising convert to the view that Iraq had no WMD. In June 2000, Ritter (2000, 2001) published an article in *Arms Control Today* stating that a less aggressive monitoring regime in Iraq should suffice because Saddam Hussein had little to conceal. In July, the former inspector was in Baghdad filming a documentary on the impact of sanctions on the Iraqi population; on September 8, 2002, Ritter addressed the Iraqi parliament, a rare honor for a foreigner (Crossette 2000; Hiro 2002, 206–207; Lynch 2000). Ritter subsequently joined forces with William River Pitt, the head of the leftist Progressive Democrats of America, to offer a scathing denunciation of the administration's handling of the Iraqi intelligence (Pitt and Ritter 2003). In his new book *Iraq Confidential,* Ritter (2005, 289–292) claimed that, far from trying to disarm Iraq's arsenal, the United States had used the UNSCOM apparatus to undermine the United Nations and overthrow Saddam Hussein.

Numerous observers speculated on the dynamics driving this loose alliance that questioned so effectively the administration's efforts to flesh out the "phantom link," or indeed, prove that Iraq harbored lethal weapons. Though separating personal, political, and bureaucratic factors is virtually impossible, there were speculations in the press on the motivation of some participants. For instance, Ritter's dramatic change of heart was attributed to apparent money problems, possibly compounded by his legal entanglement for soliciting sex with a minor on the Internet. The Oil for Food disclosures indicated that Shakir al-Kafaji, who financed Ritter's documentary, was one of the businessmen who profited from Saddam Hussein's oil vouchers program (Crowley 2002; Gilmore and Laurence 2003; Miller and Lipton 2004). Wilson was a consultant for the Rock Creek Cooperation, which was associated with Mohammed Alamoudi; the latter was affiliated with Delta Services, a Swiss subsidiary of Delta Oil, a recipient of Oil for Food business (Fedora 2004). Tenet (2007, 148) wondered whether Clarke might have been upset because the Bush team did not accept his Blue Sky proposal, an aggressive plan to counter al Qaeda with help from the Northern Alliance. The counterterrorism chief was also accused by critics of trying to secure a position in the Kerry campaign and of drumming up publicity for his book, which defended Clinton's record while blaming the Bush administration for September 11 (Clarke 2004, 227–229, 242). Indeed, Thomas Kean and Lee Hamilton (2004, 154–155), who co-chaired the 9/11 commission, expressed their irritation with Clarke, until then a relatively unknown official, for moving up the publication date of his book to coincide with his scheduled appearance before the commission. Louis Freeh (2005, 297–298) described Clarke as a publicity-seeking, second-tier player not averse to spinning a "nice tale." For his part, the former terrorist expert expressed disappointment that, unlike other presidents, Bush did not care about "root causes" of terrorism (Clarke 2004, 244).

Whatever their individual interests, members of the alliance shared four concerns. First, many of them were members of the epistemic community that blamed Israel for the authoritarian governments in the Middle East. Skeptical of democratic universalism, they viewed regime change as a highly destabilizing development with far-reaching consequences for the United States and its allies. In April 1999, while heading CENTCOM, Zinni had conducted a war game, Desert Crossing; the exercise concluded that regime change in Iraq "may cause regional instability" and "fragmentation along religious and ethnic lines." Not surprisingly, Zinni was inclined to think that bad as Saddam Hussein was, "stable Iraq is better than instability" (quoted in Hersh 2004, 175; Strother 2006).

Second, the antiwar coalition was concerned that the Bush doctrine injected too much idealism into American foreign policy. That the proposed regime change in Baghdad was enthusiastically supported by evangelical Christians was especially unsettling to realists wary of the "messianic" zeal in the White House. As Ambassador Wilson (2002) cautioned in a Middle East Policy Council Symposium in October, the combination of pro-Israel evangelicals and Jews was bad news for America.

Third, members of this group strongly resented the influence of the neoconservatives on the Bush administration. To the military and intelligence men in particular, Perle, Wolfowitz, and other Pentagon civilians were "chicken hawks," officials with no military background, pushing for a war that was likely to produce a large number of American casualties. Zinni was known to detest Wolfowitz whom he considered to be the architect of Operation Iraqi Freedom (Ricks 2006, 65). Wilson (2004, 432–434) called the neoconservatives a "small pack of zealots whose dedication has spanned decades," adding that "never in the history of our democracy has there been such an influential and pervasive center of power" capable of skewing "decision making practices."

Fourth, war opponents charged that the largely Jewish neoconservatives advocated a regime change in Iraq on behalf of Israel and against American national security interests. Ambassador Walker complained that the Jewish lobby was working hard against Saddam Hussein, a notion that was strongly supported by Raymond McGovern (Lipsky 2001; Tobin 2005). The libertarian-leaning congressman Ron Paul (2003) was a particularly vigorous promoter of the theme that the White House was "neo-conned" into a stand inimical to its interest and subservient to Jerusalem. Michael Scheuer (2004, 227) echoed this allegation, stating that "the Israelis have succeeded in lacing tight the ropes binding the American Gulliver to the tiny Jewish state." Scowcroft was reported to have said that the then Israeli Prime Minister Ariel "Sharon just had him [Bush] wrapped around the finger" (Kessler 2004).

Blaming Israel for having undue influence on American foreign policy was not a new phenomenon. While many of the war opponents had well-documented reservations about the quality of intelligence that was driving Operation Iraqi Freedom, criticism of Israel's alleged prominence in Washington was a staple of both the radical right and the radical left. Indeed, the notion of a Jewish "cabal" running Washington was often discussed in Lyndon LaRouche's *Executive Intelligence Review* and *The Washington Report on Middle East Affairs,* a fringe magazine that specialized in conspiracy theories (Steinberg 2001). At one point, the *Review* claimed that, in an attempt to draw America into the war, Michael Ledeen, a Jewish neoconservative, traveled to Rome to help fabricate the Niger document (Steinberg 2005). Matt Hale, the leader of the white supremacist World Church of the Creator, disseminated a book about Jewish and Zionist complicity in September 11 (Stern 2003, 274–275). Similar conspiracy theories were circulated on thousands of Web sites, with some going so far as to assert that Colin Powell was part of the Jewish "cabal" because of his Jewish ancestry and his command of the Yiddish language (Muravchik 2003; No War for Israel.com 2003; Rubin 2004).

Lost in this emotional debate were the finer points of the threat potential embedded in the Bush doctrine. As noted earlier, well before September 11, Shulsky, who parleyed his expertise for an appointment to the Office of Special Plans, and other disciples of Albert Wohlstetter and Thomas Schelling had concluded that absence of clear information about a terrorist-rogue state nexus should actually increase the urgency of the preemptive imperative. Wohlstetter was also a strong advocate of the notion that states should tackle emerging threats before they are fully formed. The September attack and the anthrax scare, followed by the discovery that al Qaeda had a fairly advanced chemical capability, prompted the administration to formalize a response to a high-level impact, low-probability event. Dubbed the "one percent doctrine," it stipulated that traditional notions of deterrence would not work in a world where dictators could use small apocalyptical groups to wage an unconventional war against the West. Alternatively, "rogue scientists" such as A.Q. Khan, could either sell lethal technology for profit or give it away for ideological reasons. According to Cheney, the combination of less than sufficient intelligence, the norm in such cases, and the low threshold for error mandated a preemptive strategy (Suskind 2006, 47, 65).

President Bush used this argument in April 2002, stating that "the worse thing that could happen would be to allow Saddam Hussein to develop weapons of mass destruction and then team up with terrorist organizations" (quoted in Woodward 2004, 12). On another occasion Bush asserted that "until we get rid of Saddam Hussein we won't get rid of uncertainty" (quoted in Suskind 2004, 306). His national security advisor Condoleezza Rice was even more succinct; she argued that though it was not possible to eliminate all uncertainty about how quickly Saddam Hussein can acquire nuclear weapons, "we do not want the smoking gun to be a mushroom cloud" (quoted in Risen 2006, 92).

Although chastened by their denial of the danger of Islamic terrorism, IR experts seemed to have mixed feelings about preemption. Jervis (2002a; 2002b, 40–41) agreed with the administration that "warding off 99 terrorist attacks does little good if the 100th succeeds, especially if weapons of mass destruction are used." Yet he felt that such "strategy makes more sense in theory, rather than practice" because preemption, or prevention, as he called it, is justified only if the "government is quite certain that failing to do so will lead to a disastrous attack." The celebrated historian John Lewis Gaddis (2002, 52) found parts of the Bush doctrine "plausible," but was far from eager to endorse it. G. John Ikenberry (2002, 45) argued that "preemption was a cover for America's nascent neo-imperial grand strategy." Only a minority of scholars were ready to concede that the Second Nuclear Age, with "complex and often pathological strategic dynamics of players" is dangerous enough to warrant preemption. As one of them put it, "Iraq, with a GDP 15 percent of the annual revenue of Wal Mart" could find WMD an attractive cheap alternative to traditional military power (Bracken 2003, 412).

Unlike the relatively straightforward assessment of stockpiles, analyzing threat potential, which was at the core of the Bush doctrine, was more difficult because it required an understanding of the mind of totalitarian leaders in general and Saddam Hussein in particular As already noted, there was little consensus about Hussein's intentions, rationality, and deterrability. Still, with the growing prospect of a war, speculating on Hussein's psychology turned into a virtual cottage industry.

THE "REAL" SADDAM HUSSEIN: RATIONALITY IN THE EYE OF THE BEHOLDER

In theoretical terms, the new round of writings drew on a large number of approaches, generating a wide variety of assessments. The unitary (state) actor model and individual rational choice theory competed with cognitive psychology, clinical evaluations, and more than a passing nod to psychoanalysis. Further muddying the waters was the "seat of the pants" approach based on the observer's report about the state of the mind of the Iraqi dictator. Much of the difference stemmed from the gap between the rigorous epistemics of rational choice and deterrence theories and the softer definitions of clinical pathology and cognitive psychology. In the former, knowledge about the future action of an adversary is based on the assumption of a rational actor capable of making a cost benefit calculus. The latter try to predict behavior from personal characteristics, but behavioral sciences have been hard pressed to determine how personality traits affect such a calculus.

Not surprisingly, Post and Baram (2002) reiterated that Hussein was a malignant narcissist prone to taking risks, but added in a somewhat ambiguous manner, that he was in "touch with psychological reality, but out of touch with political reality." Ofra Bengio (1998, 210), an Israeli expert on Iraq, found that Hussein exhibited "cool political reasoning with an obscure mysticism closer to the language of dervishes." Bengio emphasized that Saddam was not haphazard and tended to plan in advance, but was "prone to miscalculation." The publication of Hussein's historical novel *Zabiba and the King* in the spring of 2001 increased the psychological scrutiny of the Iraqi leader. However, beyond a general sense that Hussein was preoccupied with his security and place in history, CIA's profilers and outside experts could not agree on the exact interpretation of *Zabiba*'s plot (Bengio 2002; Sciolino 2001). Cognitive studies of Hussein were equally unclear as to the degree of his rationality (Hermann 2003; Suedfeld 2003).

In an effort to bridge the gap, Betty Glad, a noted expert on the psychology of leaders, linked personality traits to the processes of decision making. Using the example of Nazi Germany, Glad showed that, isolated from external reality, surrounded by sycophants, and unencumbered by procedural checks on his decision making, Hitler had become erratic, delusional, and irrational over time. Glad speculated that an equally distorted decision-making process in Iraq could isolate Hussein and contribute to his delusional divorce from reality.

A number of studies seemed to bear out Glad's hypothesis. In a detailed analysis of Iraqi decision making during the Iran-Iraq war, Karsh (2002) found that Hussein made decisions with virtually no planning or debate. Worse, he would brook no opposition, disposing of naysayers in his entourage by either having them arrested and tortured, or killed. Other observers noted that the family pathologies and the out-of-control tribal dynamics strained the already brittle personality of the dictator (James 2000; Mackey 2002, 332–333; O'Neill 2001). A former regime insider suggested that Saddam Hussein had become delusional to the point of morphing into a "Stalin-Saladin" while trying to turn Iraq into a "Middle Eastern Soviet Union" (Aburish 2000, 67). Scholarships and politics became inextricable in the fall of 2002 when preemptive war against Iraq became a distinct possibility. Kenneth M. Pollack (2002a, 2002b), a Gulf expert on Clinton's National Security Council made a cogent argument for preemption and regime change. In a widely discussed book, *The Threatening Storm*, Pollack suggested that the mischief-making Iraqi dictator had to be taken down before he "crosses the thresholds to nuclear weapons." In a companion *New York Times* op-ed, Pollack suggested that Hussein was "unintentionally suicidal," because he "miscalculates his odds of success and frequently ignores the likelihood of catastrophic failure..." While in UNSCOM, Scott Ritter (1999, 155) made the observation that WMD-equipped Hussein was both extremely dangerous and unpredictable.

Whatever the merits of these arguments, other observers adamantly rejected the view that Hussein was irrational and undeterrable. Leading the way were a number of prominent IR experts, including Kenneth N. Waltz, Robert Jervis, Walt, Mearsheimer, and Betts, who signed an antiwar ad in the New *York Times* on September 26, 2002. In articles written around the time, they took issue with the "war party's" portrayal of Saddam Hussein as a "serial aggressor." The professors rejected Pollack's finding that Hussein was "unintentionally suicidal"; on the contrary, they found that during the Kuwait crisis, the dictator "was neither mindlessly aggressive nor particularly reckless." In their view, the historical record "shows that the United States can contain Iraq effectively," even if Saddam has nuclear weapons. Indeed, they noted that, on the whole, "Saddam's record...is no worse than that of neighboring states such as Egypt and Israel" (Betts 2002; Mearsheimer and Walt 2002, 3; 2003, 56).

Former opponents of sanctions and critics of the rogue-state doctrine cast their own vote of confidence in Hussein's rationality. In a change of opinion, these observers now claimed that sanctions actually did work because Saddam Hussein was rational enough to be subject to what Jentleson (2000, 9) called "coercive prevention" by diplomacy (Halperin 2002, 2003). In July 2002 George Lopez and David Cortright (2000) testified to the same effect before Congress. Belief in Hussein's rationality was especially high among MESA academics, many of who considered his action to be a reasonable response to American provocations (Esposito 2002; Said 2002b). Speaking for the far left, Noam Chomsky stated that "Saddam Hussein had proven himself to be a brutal tyrant but a rational one. If he had chemical and biological weaponry, they were kept under tight control."

While different methodologies accounted for some diversity of opinion, there is little doubt that the debate about Saddam Hussein's rationality was a template for the larger issue of a preemptive war. Jervis (2003c, 370; 2003a) and Litwak (2002–03) were among the many scholars who critiqued Bush's "calculus of preemption." Jervis noted that "it is no accident" that Albert Wohlstetter, trained "many of the driving figures" in the administration. In Jervis's view, while theoretically plausible, preemption was problematic because relevant information about threats was difficult to obtain ahead of time. Even in the case of Hitler, "it was far from clear that he would turn to be such a menace."

Neoconservatives and other war supporters were quick to retort that professions of Saddam Hussein rationality were a ploy to avert the war. In what became a rather vitriolic exchange, war proponents suggested that after dismissing the probability of a terrorist attack, scholars should not be trusted with forecasting Hussein behavior. They also accused war opponents of lacking intellectual integrity. Max Boot (2002), a *Wall Street Journal* editor, went so far as to decry the hypocrisy of the "left's new love affair with containment."

With much of Saddam Hussein's rationality confined to the eye of the beholder, it was left to the president to make a judgment call about Iraq's deterrability. The administration argued that Baghdad possessed weapons of mass destruction and that Saddam Hussein could be neither contained nor deterred. Government spokespersons emphasized Hussein's long history of confounding the sanction and inspection regimes; they found him reckless enough to either use unconventional weapons or transfer them to third parties.

As noted, the White House labored under the constraints of the "one percent doctrine" that left little margin for error in assessing the degree of threat posed by Iraq. Unlike academics, administration officials had little room for nuanced theoretical debates. Frank Anderson, the former chief of the Near East division in the Directorate of Operations noted that Saddam "could probably be deterred from using weapons of mass destruction should he acquire [them]" but added that "the bad news is that if I'm wrong, I'm wrong big time" (quoted in Marshall 2002, 408). For others, Hussein's history of erratic and unpredictable behavior was weighted heavily on the side of preemption. Richard J. Kerr, a former deputy director of the CIA, argued that given what was known about Saddam Hussein, coming to the alternative conclusion that Iraq "was not a threat was not an acceptable option" (quoted in Kessler 2004, 205). Tenet (2007, 328) expressed similar sentiments, stating that "it [the war] was about unwillingness to risk surprise."

Perhaps more significantly, those acquainted with the reasoning of the president after September 11, detected a certain "Churchilian" determination not to negotiate with "evil." For Bush, an evangelical Christian, the conviction that evil leaders cannot be contained or deterred might have carried a certain a moral certitude. Bush was not alone among American presidents to draw on the lessons of the 1930s. John F. Kennedy, a great admirer of Churchill, reached the same conclusion in his book *Why Britain Slept*, a harsh denunciation of Chamberlain's appeasement. As one historian suggested, the Munich experience left a lasting impression on Kennedy who was fond of repeating that "aggressive behavior, if allowed to grow unchecked, ultimately leads to war" (Smith 2004, 315).

Biographers of the Bush family pointed out that, like Churchill, Bush was "willing to defy pundits" who advocated "appeasement" of dictators. Stretching this analogy further, the president felt that the "fact that so many academics and other highly educated people did not see the [Nazi] threat was a commentary on higher education" (Kessler 2004, 276). Bush's own experience at Yale left him with a lasting sense of liberal bias and double standards in academy, apparently compounded by a run-in with the leftist

Yale chaplain, Reverend William Sloan Coffin. Both father and son shared a keen frustration with Ivy League liberalism, as expressed in a letter that became part of family lore. Writing to the then Yale president, Bartlett Giamatti, the older Bush wondered "why it was all right for [Rev. William Sloan Coffin] to urge defiance on Vietnam, tolerance on Khomeini, or advocate gay marriages" at a time when the Religious Right was denied the opportunity to work against abortion or prayer in school (Kengor 2004, 14; Mandel 2005; Schweitzer and Schweitzer 2004, 290).

Churchill's belief that evil cannot be controlled or appeased was the antithesis of the realist school, which, as noted, lacked the language of moral discourse. Jervis (2003b, 319) spoke for many of his colleagues when he stated that it would be "clearly a mistake to jump from the fact that Saddam is evil to the conclusion that his possession of WMD threatens the US and world peace." In a last ditch effort to avert the war, IR scholars and sanction specialists produced a new round of proposals for containing Iraq, including "vigilant containment" (Mearsheimer and Walt 2003, 58). But to hardliners in the administration, Hussein's ability to maneuver the sanctions regime was proof positive that containment was a sham.

Regime Change as an Alternative to Containment: The Decision to Launch Operation Iraqi Freedom

A special meeting of the Defense Policy Board on September 19 and 20, 2001 was tasked with reviewing Iraqi policy; it noted that in an apparent effort to test the new administration, the regime initiated attacks on coalition planes patrolling the no-fly zone. The 18-member board composed of high-ranking officials in past Democratic and Republican administrations, including Harold Brown, Carter's secretary of defense, James R. Schlesinger, Ford's secretary of defense, Henry Kissinger, and Admiral David E. Jeremiah concluded that Saddam Hussein was defiant and unpredictable and needed to be overthrown. James Woolsey, another board member, was reported to have been building a legal case for the proposed regime change (Sciolino and Taylor 2001).

Early in November, the retired General Wayne Downing began preparing a plan based on his counterinsurgency experience in Iraq (Kessler 2003). In December, Ahmed Chalabi was asked to present a new plan for deposing Saddam Hussein. The newly reinvigorated Iraq Operation Group (IOG) in the CIA was also providing inputs, leading to the so-called modified Chalabi plan for overthrowing Hussein.

"Modified Chalabi" was incorporated in a top secret order of February 11, 2002, authorizing the CIA to depose the dictator. The new plan vastly expanded the Clinton-era steps; in addition to working with opposition groups and third countries to destabilize Iraq, it called for disinformation and deception operations, the disruption of the regime's finance and banking system, and sabotage. A key element in the plan aimed at interdiction and sabotage of shipments of Baghdad's illicit weapons and goods to sow distrust in Hussein's inner circles (Hersh 2004, 171; Risen 2006, 81).

However, during an April meeting with IOG operatives, CIA station chiefs in the Middle East were reported to be taken aback by the "IOG zealots," arguing that sabotage of vessels carrying contraband would cause civilian casualties. In any event, the new head of the IOG was convinced that Hussein's security apparatus would defeat any covert action. According to this assessment, the extraordinary level of the regime's brutality made covert activity or even an uprising, an unrealistic option. The IOG operatives found that recruiting Iraqis was very hard because of the extreme retribution against spies and dissenters; they could be expect to be tortured, their wives and daughters raped, and the whole family eventually killed (Mann 2004, 332; Woodward 2004, 108).

Alongside plans to destabilize Iraq through counterinsurgency, on November 27, 2001, Rumsfeld ordered General Tommy Franks (2004, 315–355), the head of CENTCOM, to upgrade operational plan for a war with Iraq known as OPLAN 1003. On December 27, Franks briefed the president on his ideas to depose Saddam Hussein. Franks did not rule out the use of counterinsurgents, but the new plan envisioned a full-scale American invasion.

While Franks and his staff were updating the contingency plans, new concerns about the cost and efficacy of containing Iraq through sanctions surfaced. During a trip to the Middle East in March 2002, Cheney learned from his hosts that Islamist radicals in their countries emulated bin Laden in using the plight and humiliation of the Iraqi people to bolster recruitment. Complaints that sanctions were channeling the younger generation into "bitter radicalism" were not new, as Albright (2003, 272) had recalled in her memoir, but Cheney found Saudi ambivalence toward American troops on its soil perplexing, if not alarming (Randal 2004, 108).

Upon further investigation, the White House discovered that the troops issue played into the ongoing succession struggles among the 7000 royal princes of the House of Saud that Robert Baer (2003, xxix) famously described as "five extended, dysfunctional families." So much so, that the pro-American Crown Prince Abdullah apparently proposed to Bush in April to spend up to a billion dollars for a covert operation to get rid of Saddam Hussein. As the hitherto ignored writings of Osama bin Laden were read anew, there was a growing realization that the containment policy was an important tool in the rise of al Qaeda and revival of Muslim brotherhood in Egypt (Baer 2003, 184; Bodansky 1999, 219; Callinicos 2003, 80–81; de Borchgrave 2005; Hersh 2004, 194; Unger 2004, 274, Woodward 2004, 229).

On July 10, 2002, Richard Perle, an outspoken critic of Saudi Arabia, asked the Rand analyst Laurent Murawiec to brief the Defense Policy Board on the issue. The meeting was sensationalized because of Murawiec's former association with LaRouches's *Executive Intelligence Review,* but its essence was sobering. The analyst confirmed that some powerful royal critics of the crown prince had intensified their support for Islamist causes, including terrorism. When details of the meeting leaked, the administration was embarrassed and issued a quick denial (Callinicos 2003, 80–81; de Borchgrave 2005; Hersh 2004, 194; Unger 2004, 274).

Along with the rising appreciation of the cost of containment, there was a growing doubt about its effectiveness. Although the CIA found Chalabi's repeated complaints about corruption in the Oil for Food program not credible, by the beginning of 2002, Kurdish contacts told IOG's operatives that Baghdad had managed to reach high into the UN bureaucracy that administered the program. The Kurds also shed light on the regime practice of inflating its profits by buying poor quality products and reselling them to the population for high prices (Babbin 2004, 28). The scale of Hussein's manipulation was public knowledge in Iraq where it was also known that many UN officials received bribes. As one high-ranking Iraqi general recalled, third world UN officials were especially likely to take "bribers to look the other way" (Sada with Black 2006, 203).

Much of this information was confirmed in a "Revenue for Saddam & Sons: A Primer of the Financial Underpinning of the Regime in Baghdad" compiled by the Coalition for International Justice (CIJ) and made initially available to journalists in the summer of 2002. The human rights watchdog revealed that the Iraqi regime manipulated supplies to create shortages and mass suffering, an important part of Baghdad's public relations campaign. The CIJ confirmed earlier intelligence about the regime's profiteering through sale of inferior quality goods and price gauging. The *London Times* defense correspondent reported that Hussein used Oil for Food revenues to buy and ship arms through Syria (Blaustein 2002; Evan 2002). Ironically, the flow of cash enabled Saddam Hussein to purchase large quantities of weapons and munitions that were smuggled through Syria. Taking stock of the situation, the *Financial Times* proclaimed that, with the exception of the United States, adherence to containment was all but dead (Khalef 2002).

The CIJ report took an especially critical view of the United Nations' "undue deference" to Saddam Hussein. As Baghdad was allowed to dispense the vouchers through which oil was sold, it used them to manipulate the Security Council. For instance, Yuri Shafranik, the head of the Russian-Iraqi cooperation board and a voucher recipient, and Yevgeny Primakov were reported to have been Hussein's direct conduit to the Russian president Vladimir Putin. Oil for Food revenues apparently continued to support the political ambitions of Jacques Chirac of France. In addition, Hussein deposited millions of dollars in French banks in the hope that France would block U.S. proposals in the Security Council. In return, France and Russia were said to have obstructed American initiatives at the Council. A book published in 2002 listed many of these cases, noting that clandestine business with Baghdad was the "prime motive that had informed the stances . . . of three permanent members [France, Russia, and China] of the Security Council" (Hiro 2002, 155).

Paul A. Volcker, chair of the commission investigating the Oil for Food scandal, would later back these allegations. The commission found that

Sadden Hussein disbursed vouchers to journalists, politicians, and other well-connected individuals in return for speaking out against sanctions. The Volcker panel also found that high-ranking UN officials such as Benon V. Sevan were on Baghdad's payroll (Babbin 2004, 28–29; Baker and Baker 2005, 223; Frum and Perle 2003; Miller 2004; Miller and Hogue 2004; Morris 2003, 117; Sachs and Miller 2004).

With much of this evidence in place by the summer of 2002, "sanction skeptics" in the administration, including Cheney and Rumsfeld, were ready to take on the "smart sanction" advocates in the State Department. Richard Haass, the sanction's architect was the first casualty of the power struggle. Although Secretary Powell was publicly holding his own, behind the scenes, his opponents were able to discredit many of the assumptions on which his sanction plan was based. For their part, top state officials such as Richard Armitage intensely disliked their counterparts in the Department of Defense; Armitage allegedly referred to Wolfowitz, and William Luti, the deputy assistant secretary of defense for Near East and South Asian affairs, as "right wing crazies" obsessed with the removal of Hussein (Hersh 2004, 177). Still, the sheer scale of sanction busting made it hard for the State bureaucracy to argue that Iraq could be contained by a system that depended on good faith efforts by self-interested individuals and countries. To dispel any further illusions, the conservative Heritage Foundation began compiling its own list of sanction violations, including detailed charges against France, Germany, Russia, and China, first published in 2002 and then periodically updated (Satterlee 2003).

Hussein's ability to circumvent a decade of containment looked especially ominous in light of continued worries about weapons of mass destruction (Woodward 2004, 195). However, as mentioned above, the extent of to which Iraq was trying to conceal its program was intensely debated throughout the intelligence community. To settle the yellow cake issue, Cheney ordered the CIA to check out the information on the ground in Niger. Acting upon the recommendation of Valerie Plame, an official in the DO Counterproliferation Division (CPD), the Agency asked her husband, Joseph Wilson, to travel to Niger in February 2002. Wilson, whose activities in the nascent antiwar coalition were not known to the White House, reported that he had found no credible evidence to support the yellow cake claims, a conclusion seconded by INR's Thielmann. However, the British intelligence insisted that its own sources in Niger were solid, a view that Tenet was reluctant to dismiss. With or without the Nigerian uranium, other European and Middle East intelligence services were convinced that Saddam Hussein was planning to reconstitute his lethal weapon program (Franks 2004, 418–419).

The intelligence community was also split over the veracity of information provided by an Iraqi defector codenamed Curveball, an asset of the German Federal Intelligence Service (BND). The Germans notified the DIA that Curveball, an engineer later identified as Rafid Ahmed Alwan, provided information about some 20 mobile trailers capable of producing biological weapons. The BND refused to disclose Curveball's identity but Tyler Drumheller (2006, 60, 105), the chief of CIA's covert operations in Europe, was told that the defector was not reliable, a message that was included in a letter from a CIA agent in Berlin. According to Drumheller, he called his boss to warn him about Curveball, but Tenet (2007, 375–383) disputed this charge: he stressed that Drumheller had failed to forward the Berlin letter and issue a "burn notice" on Curveball, standard procedure to flag a discredited source. Moreover, analysts from the CIA's Center for Weapons Intelligence, Nonproliferation, and Arms Control were "passionately" convinced that Curveball's sketches of the mobile trailers were specific enough to pass the reliability test (Risen 2006, 112–116; Warrick 2006).

More important, in late summer of 2002, the CIA managed to recruit the Iraqi Foreign Minister Naji Sabri who disclosed that the regime was producing and stockpiling chemical weapons. Sabri claimed that Iraqi scientists were pursuing an "amateurish" biological program and that Iraq had mobile launchers armed with chemical warheads to be used as weapons of last resort. The foreign minister was not aware of a working nuclear program but emphasized that Saddam Hussein was keen on restoring one. Sabri's evaluation matched the CIA's information that Hussein had retained his nuclear scientists and had met with them in 2001(SSCI 2006, 144).

By August 2002 tensions between the State Department and the Department of Defense were running high. According to a later account, Powell called the Rumsfeld team "the JINSA crowd," a reference to the staunchly pro-Israeli Jewish Institute for National Strategic Affairs (DeYoung 2006, 356). Alarmed that the hardliners were gaining ground, Colin Powell met Bush on August 5 to warn him that an invasion would destabilize the Middle East and hurt the war on terror. Powell also urged the president to build a new containment coalition through the United Nations. Although Powell was reported to have felt that he had scored some points, the National Security Presidential Directive (NSPD) of August 14 "Goals, Objective, and Strategy" stated that the United States would pursue its objective of regime change "with a coalition of committed countries," but did not rule out going it alone, "if necessary" (Woodward 2004, 149, 153, 173).

As was customary in Washington, internal divisions were soon paraded in public. A particularly damaging disclosure came from Pentagon dissenters who leaked information from a top secret CENTCOM meeting in March 2002; it accused the Central Command of "gross incompetence and strategic ineptitude" (Franks 2004, 382). According to Wilson (2004, 293), by June 2002 it was clear that the war debate was "going places," prompting the antiwar coalition to speak out more vigorously. Brent Scowcroft warned against an invasion in a *Wall Street Journal* op-ed of August 15, 2002. Wilson (2004, 312, 318) began a series of antiwar speeches, attracting the attention of *The Nation* editors who were looking for highly placed officials to legitimate their own increasingly vocal critique of the war.

To counter the perception that the administration was split on Iraq, the White House Iraq Group (WHIG) composed of Rice and a number of senior staffers, began working on a new policy draft at the beginning of September.

Bowing to the pressure from the State Department, the White House decided to ask for a new United Nations resolution to disarm Iraq, a message delivered by President Bush on September 12. For Cheney and Rumsfeld, highly suspicious of the United Nations, this was a politically necessary but ultimately a futile step, The "UN skeptics" in the administration scored an important victory when, on September 18, the *Washington Post* published a summary of the CIJ report on the Oil for Food scandal (Farah and Lynch 2002). However, the State Department did not react to the revelations and there was virtually no follow-up in the media. Nor did the Education for Peace in Iraq Center (EPIC), which boasted Mearsheimer, Walt and Anthony Cordesman among its speakers, refer to the problems raised by the CIJ report.

On the contrary, as anxiety about a possible war increased, the call to engage the United Nations and the international community became louder. The professors who signed the New *York Times* ad, a forerunner to the Coalition for a Realistic Foreign Policy, wanted the United Nations to play a major role in the "vigilant containment" of Iraq. Undoubtedly, questions about the ability of the international community to sustain containment would have undermined antiwar protest, ahead of the congressional vote on the Iraqi war scheduled for October.

Instead, war opponents intensified their criticism of manipulation of intelligence by the neoconservatives. Ian Lustick (2002), a prominent Middle East expert, charged that the preexistent "neoconservative cabal" used the "window of fear" created by September 11 to suppress "bureaucratic intelligence and military opposition" to press for regime change in Baghdad. Worries about the quality of intelligence were shared by Democrats in Congress; on September 11, 2002, Bob Graham, on behalf of the Senate Intelligence Committee, set in motion the process for producing a formal National Intelligence Estimate on Iraq's WMD.

The request presented a huge challenge because, as Tenet (2007, 321–322) admitted, he did not think it necessary to start drafting of a NIE on Iraq's WMD earlier in the year. Substantively, the intelligence community was divided over Iraqi procurement policy while being pressed by critics to provide a product that would "connect all the dots" and avoid the type of equivocation that earned the CIA analysts the name "academics on testosterone." Stuart Cohen, the acting chair of the National Intelligence Council, was keenly aware of the difficulty of balancing a less than ironclad set of data with the need to provide a strong conclusion. Seared by September 11, John McLaughlin, Tenet's deputy and other analysts apparently felt that "they had to dare to be wrong to be clear in their judgment" (Woodward 2004, 196–197).

Written by Robert Walpole, National Intelligence Officer for Strategic and Nuclear Programs and presented to the Senate Intelligence committee on October 2, the 92-page NIE reflected this predictive predicament. The analysis stated that "Iraq has chemical and biological agents," but was less sure about nuclear weapons, noting that Saddam might "gain access to fissile material." Saddam's state of mind was a major factor in the assessment; echoing Post, the analysis surmised that if desperate enough, the dictator would either unleash his arsenal or use al Qaeda to hurt America and the West. In a 9-page appendix the State Department listed its disagreements, especially about nuclear capability. The NIE asserted that "Iraq has no integrated and comprehensive approach to acquire nuclear weapons." Four days later, the CIA released an unclassified White Paper version that glossed over the finer points of the internal dispute (Richelson 2006, 483–489; Woodward 2004, 193–201).

With the intelligence community divided and the evidence less than stellar, the White House chose to emphasize the high threat potential posed by Hussein. In an October 7 speech in Cincinnati, Bush reiterated that "facing clear evidence of peril . . . we cannot wait for the final proof, the smoking gun that could come in the form of a mushroom cloud." On October 11, Congress passed a resolution authorizing the president to use military force against Iraq. Although both chambers gave the president a comfortable majority, the dispute over the intelligence and the motives of the administration did not subside.

In a testimony before the Senate Armed Services Committee, Clinton's former national security adviser Sandy Berger (2002), urged to make a distinction between Saddam Hussein's capability and his intentions and the urgency of the threat. Members of the antiwar coalition scoffed at the idea that Hussein would use lethal weapons, although most admitted that Iraq had a WMD arsenal. In an October op-ed, Wilson (2002; 2004, 367) wrote that Saddam Hussein could be disarmed by a credible show of international resolve and a muscular inspection regime.

The three major television networks, ABC, NBC, and CBS did not carry the Cincinnati speech, but in the Senate, Senator Ted Kennedy denounced the Bush doctrine as a "call for 21st century American imperialism" (Woodward 2004, 203). By December, some prominent antiwar activists such as Zinni felt that the war was a forgone conclusion, but others, including Wilson (2004, 312) intensified their antiwar efforts. Wilson and other activists joined the "Win without War: Advocating Alternatives to Preempt War against Iraq," an umbrella group launched on December 11 by the National Council of Churches, MoveOn.org, the IPS-linked Center for International Policy (CIP), and other administration foes.

A new move by the UN Security Council to tackle the Iraqi unconventional program offered the State Department and other war opponents a glimmer of hope. But the Bush team, mindful of the UNSCOM debacle, directed NSC to demand a tough inspection regime. The White House was especially wary of the United Nations Monitoring and Verification Commission (UNMOVIC), which the Security Council had established on December 17, 1999 to replace the defunct UNSCOM. In spite of American backing for the hard-charging Rolf Ekeus, under pressure from France and Russia, Hans Blix was picked to head the new monitoring group. Critics argued that Blix was at best ineffectual, as attested by his failure to uncover

Iraq's WMD before 1991 or, worse, "soft" on Saddam Hussein. His admission that "the IAEA was fooled by the Iraqis" did little to help his credibility (Borger 2002).

To stiffen the proposed inspection regime, the NSC and the Department of Defense wanted a no-drive zone along the routes that the UN inspectors would travel. To increase deterrence, they wanted the UN resolution to automatically trigger a war, should Baghdad violate any of its provisions. But Powell felt that such constraints would torpedo his efforts to enlist France and other Security Council members. In the end, the United States proposed a softer version that did away with the no-drive zones and the automatic war trigger clause. Even so, the secretary of state, apparently unaware of the collusion between Hussein, Jacques Chirac, and Vladimir Putin, was "surprised" by the opposition that the French and the Russians were putting up (Woodward 2004, 224). When, on November 8, the Security Council unanimously passed Resolution 1441 authorizing UNMOVIC to pursue an aggressive inspection policy, Powell and his deputy Robert Armitage nursed a modest hope that a diplomatic solution could avert an invasion. The antiwar movement welcomed the resolution, describing it as a healthy return to healthy multilateralism.

However, for Cheney, Rumsfeld, and other neoconservatives already highly critical of Kofi Annan's "coddling" of Saddam Hussein, the UNMOVIC represented a continuation of the old UN policy of "see no evil." Sperzel (2003) warned that Blix would turn the inspection process into a "circus." Surveillance of the UNMOVIC team ordered by Bush revealed that Blix "was not reporting everything and [not] doing all the things he maintained he was doing." The vice president considered the slow pace of inspection to be part of a larger international diplomatic agenda of wrapping things in "red tape," of passing resolutions, calling it "good," and going "home" (Cockburn and Cockburn 2002, xxviii; Woodward 2004, 235, 240).

Viewed from the White House perspective, Blix provided the Iraqi leader with an international seal of approval without tackling his WMD program. To challenge UNMOVIC, Bush sought further clarifications from the CIA. During a December 21 meeting in the White House, George Tenet assured the president that the case for the existence of such weapons was a "slam dunk." Aware that his credibility in making the case before the jury of public opinion was at stake, the president cautioned Tenet to make sure that no one should "stretch to make our case" (Risen 2006, 121; Woodward 2004, 250). Tenet (2007, 3602) subsequently explained that "slum dunk" was an intentional "misrepresentation" of his position at the meeting.

With the final decision on Iraq approaching, the CIA, the DIA, and the Office of Special Plans in the Department of Defense intensified their efforts to come up with more conclusive intelligence. Robert Richer who took over DO's Near East and South Asia Division on November 4, 2002, was instrumental in this drive. The Northern Iraq Liaison Element, which began moving paramilitary teams into northern Iraq, was successful in recruiting some

Iraqi insiders. Through its contacts, NILE debriefed a large number of Iraqi officers who all claimed that Hussein had WMD, but hard evidence was still scarce (Tenet 2007, 388–390). The National Security Agency intercepted a number of communications that could be interpreted as Iraqi efforts to hide WMD ahead of UNMOVIC visits, but they too fell short of the "smoking gun" evidentiary standards. DIA's highly secret Weapons of Mass Destruction Master List (WMDMSL) listed 946 possible production or storage sites, but there were little fresh data in the database (Boyer 2004; Woodward 2004, 89, 93).

Foreign intelligence services were also consulted. The most supportive information came from the British intelligence dossier published on September 2, 2002. The MI6 suggested that Iraq had dispersed its "special weapons" to strategic storages around the country to be used during an invasion (Coughlin 2006, 243–244). The Egyptian president Hosni Mubarak claimed that Iraq had biological laboratories and King Abdullah of Jordan personally told Franks that his intelligence service had reliable information about Hussein's WMD, a view that was also shared by French intelligence (Blix 2004, 128; Franks 2004, 418–419; Woodward 2004, 312). Other information suggested that the Iraqis had an Unmanned Aerial Vehicle (UAV) program potentially capable of delivering chemical or biological weapon in the United States. The Israeli Military Intelligence (Aman) identified unmanned aerial vehicles that have been modified for long-range attacks However, the Iraqi engineer who worked on the UAV project, then living in Australia, refused to cooperate unless 21 of his relatives were relocated out of Iraq (Kam 2004; Woodward 2004, 246).

The case of the UAV engineer was illustrative of the larger problem of recruiting insiders, defectors, and expatriates. Given the brutality of the regime, fear for self and family was a formidable barrier. For instance, when Charles Allan, the CIA's assistant director for collection, conceived of a plan to send U.S.-based relatives of Iraqi nuclear scientists to question them on the status of the program, the scientists assumed that it was a ploy of the Iraqi security services to test their loyalty. After reviewing the interviews, the IOG concluded that the "fear factor" contaminated the result (Risen 2006, 89). Pervasive fear of the regime derailed a CIA plan to enlist senior Iraqi commanders for a prewar deception plan; they too assumed that that it was a loyalty test set up by Saddam Hussein (Gordon and Trainor 2006, 109).

While evaluating defectors and expatriates, political agendas, personal gains, and the desire to extricate family members left behind had to be taken into account. Critics would later claim that the administration was manipulated by contacts provided by INC, but there were very few good options for obtaining conclusive information from highly secretive areas such as Iraq. James Bamford (2001, 545), a harsh critic of the administration, was forced to admit that Iraq was "the most denial-and-deception orientated target that the U.S. has ever faced." Even David Albright, the head of the respectable

Institute for Science and International Security, was taken in by one of his "star" sources, the nuclear scientist Khadir Hamza. Albright, who had employed Hamza as a consultant, would later claim that Hamza "deliberately distorted his past credentials and his statements about Iraq nuclear capability" (www. global security.org/wmd/Iraq/tuwaita-imagery.htm-24k).

The UNMOVIC mandate made provisions for interviewing Iraqi insiders and safeguarding their families, but the administration was skeptical, especially after Blix did nothing to secure the cooperation of the UAV engineer. Further American surveillance indicated that Blix was reluctant to provide the Americans with a pretext to invade Iraq. In late December, Rice informed the president that the inspectors were less than aggressive in pursuing unconventional weapons and took time off for holidays (Woodward 2004, 250). UNMOVIC interim report of January 27, 2003 noted that "Iraq appears not to have come to a genuine acceptance" of the transparency "which was demanded of it," but fell short of the strong indictment that the administration was hoping for.

On February 5, 2003, Secretary Powell delivered the American response. In what some described as his "J' accuse" speech, Powell presented a methodically constructed argument that Saddam Hussein was determined to keep and develop weapons of mass destruction. Powell and his aides prepared the speech in the CIA headquarters, where they could ascertain the veracity of intelligence (Tenet 2007, 373). But, as expected by the White House, Blix's final report on February 14, found no "smoking gun" that would warrant holding Iraq in "material breach" of Resolution 1441. The UNMOVIC chief asked for more time to search for the forbidden weapons, a request that was supported by France, Russia, and other Security Council members (Woodward 2004, 293).

If the White House considered UNMOVIC to be a predictable part of the "wrap it in red tape and go home" strategy, the behavior of France and Russia also upset the State Department. Powell, who still hoped that the Security Council would move against Iraq, was reported to have been appalled by his French counterpart who took to arguing that "nothing justifies war." Conversely, the staunch opposition of President Chirac and de Villepin to a new UN resolution authorizing the invasion cheered war opponents and energized war critics. The Win without War Web site was one of the many organizations that carried de Villepin's speech praising Blix and castigating the administration (Punditwatch 2003).

The French position was all the more puzzling because, according to Blix himself (2002, 127), the GDES sided with the CIA on the WMD issue. But to hardliners in the administration, the French maneuvers were yet another indication that the United Nations was too corrupt and beholden to Saddam Hussein to compel Iraq to disarm. As the president would later note, "when de Villepin speaks, it made me realize that Saddam would try to skate even more because he had people that were unknowing[ly] helping him" (Woodward 2004, 284–285).

With or without a new UN authorization, the momentum for regime change became irreversible. Shortly before Powell's speech, on January 24, General Franks presented to Rumsfeld the final war plan; on February 22 the president was expected to make a final decision on the war. Meanwhile, the American military buildup in the Gulf had intensified, with approximately 140,000 troops scheduled to be deployed by mid-February.

Alongside military planning, the administration took some steps to bolster plans for democratic transition. On January 10, Bush and Cheney met with three prominent Iraqi dissidents—Hatem Mukhlis, Kanan Makiya, and Rend al Rahim Francke, the director of the Iraq Foundation. Makiya, an ardent critic of Arab exceptionalism, assured the president that a democratic Iraq was the only guarantee against the WMD threat. The dissidents argued that a democracy based on the Afghan model under Hamid Karzai was highly possible in their country (Woodward 2004, 258).

While the focus was on Iraq, the White House hoped that the Democratic Project would change "the way things were done" in Iran as well (Suskind 2006, 122; Woodward 2004, 231). As already noted, the assumption that a swelling democracy movement in the Middle Eat would eventually sweep away the Iranian theocracy was bolstered by a long line of academic experts on Iran. In their view, the overwhelming popular support for the moderate president Mohammed Khatami testified to the long-awaited arrival of an Iranian "perestroika," if not "Islamic Reformation" (Abdo 2001; Hiro 2003; Hunter 1998; Masoud 1998). Regime change in Iran would have been most welcome. Although not publicized at the time, the White House was deeply concerned about Teheran's nuclear ambition. In August 2002, an Iranian dissident group publicized the fact that Teheran, aided by North Korea and A.Q. Khan, was developing a uranium enrichment program in Natanz. Satellite pictures taken by National Security Agency fleshed out the information. After American complaints, in June 2003 the IAEA official accused Iran of hiding its nuclear program (Hersh 2005; Triplett II 2004, 170–172).

Much as the White House regarded democratic universalism a panacea for American security problems, it was well understood that public opinion would not stand for a foreign policy project driven by such ambitions. Indeed, the Win without War coalition and other antiwar groups intensified their efforts to paint the forthcoming war as an exercise in empire building. On March 3, Ambassador Wilson (2003) wrote in *The Nation*, a leading antiwar player, that Americans should make a clear choice between a republic and empire. He charged that the neoconservatives have a "stronghold on the foreign policy of the Republican party," lamented the "administration's imperial tradition" and predicted that the experiment of forcing "revolutionary change in the region" may turn into a bitter lesson.

War critics were also unlikely to buy into the administration's assertion that high-stakes threat potentials should relax evidentiary standards. An exchange between Condoleezza Rice and Carl Levin, a Democrat on the Senate Armed Services Committee, on the day of Powell's UN speech illustrated this point. Pressed by Levin about "smoking gun" evidence, Rice noted that Blix could not say they "don't have them," prompting the senator to comment that "Blix also says he can't tell you they have them" (Woodward 2004, 308).

With Operation Iraqi Freedom looming on the horizon, both sides in the discourse hoped to vindicate their assumptions.

6

Operation Iraqi Freedom: The Rise and Fall of Democratic Universalism

Much as the administration tried to create a consensus around its Iraqi policy, the considerable skepticism in the discursive community did not subside in the weeks leading up to the invasion. On the contrary, the deep divisions among both practitioners and academic experts were reflected in the prognostication offered on issues ranging from the cost and duration of the operation to the prospects for successful democratization of Iraq.

The Invasion of Iraq: "Cakewalk" or Bloodbath

Burned by the predictive experience in the first Gulf War, when some leading experts had warned of thousands of American casualties, pundits were more cautious in assessing the human cost of the invasions this time around. Still, the difference between the two sides was unmistakable, Taking an early lead, scholars in the liberal Brookings Institute estimated that both American and Iraqi casualty count would be "high"; Brent Scowcroft warned that the invasion could be "bloody" (Dubose and Bernstein 2006, 213; Gordon and O'Hanlon 2002).

War proponents dismissed these prognostications as "fearmongering" and "quagmire chatter." Fox Channel commentators Lt. General Thomas McInerney and Maj. General Paul Vallely (McInerney and Vallely 2004, 1) predicted that the actual invasion could be accomplished with less than a thousand casualties and in record time. Kenneth L. Adelman (2002; 2003, 147), a leading neoconservative, stated that the battle would be a "cakewalk," because it was a "cakewalk last time." Supporters of the administration contended that the Rumsfeld transformation of the military and new precision technology would save both American and Iraqi lives.

As belief in Iraqi WMD was almost universal, the only caveat offered to this rosy scenario was that a "cornered Saddam" might unleash a chemical or biological catastrophe. As Jerrold Post (2003a; 2003b, 22) put it, with his "back to the wall," Hussein "will not go gently into the good night." In a

February 8 memo to President Bush, the Veteran Intelligence Professionals for Sanity expressed alarm that the use of chemical weapons could result in "thousands of casualties" (Steering Group 2003).

Pentagon planners counted on the regular Iraqi army, especially the low-ranking Shiite recruits, to turn themselves in before the ground offensive began. This assumption was supported by Kanan Makiya, Ahmed Chalabi, and other dissidents who assured the administration that large sectors of the military repudiated the Ba'ath regime and would not sacrifice their lives for the brutal dictator. What is more, they and other commentators argued that, with the exception of hard-core Sunni supporters of Hussein, the population would welcome the Americans as liberators.

Among the pessimists were MESA scholars who acknowledged that Hussein was a bad dictator but were adamant in their belief that the Iraqis would fight the invading force. Writing in the *London Review of Books* in the spring of 2003, Edward Said blamed Bernard Lewis and Fouad Ajami for persuading the administration to embark on such a "stupid war." Said dismissed Lewis as "generalist, an ideologue, and an old fashioned Orientalist" with no knowledge of contemporary Middle East and charged that Ajami was "adopted" by the Zionist lobby (Said 2005, 263–265). Juan Cole made his reservations known on his popular antiwar blogsite. Joel Beinin (2003) held the Jewish neoconservatives, acting on behalf of Israel, responsible for persuading the administration to look for an easy victory in Iraq. In the multilayered discourse on Iraq, forecasting the outcome of the invasion was never far from the larger debate about the prospects for democracy in the Middle East. As in the first Gulf War, prognostication about the behavior of the "Arab street" served as a crude indicator of the belief in the legitimacy of the American endeavor. Indeed, dire warning about upheaval in the "Arab street" started pouring in well before Operation Iraqi Freedom was off the drawing board. Leading Democratic politicians took to quoting President Mubarak that "a war will be seen in the streets of Cairo and Damascus as an attack on Islam" (Graham with Nussbaum 2004, 219). A number of scholarly publications affirmed the view that the regional fallout would be considerable, if not dire (Lynch 2000; Yamani 2003).

But proponents of the Middle East Democracy Project were scornful of what they considered to be the "Arab street" scare. In the words of two observers, the "Arab street" which hunts the "dreams and waking thoughts of many journalists, academics and government officials" did not materialize during the Afghan war and was just "footage for the nightly news" (McInerney and Vallely 2004, 115). Ajami (2003a, 2003b), a long-standing critic of the "Arab street" congratulated President Bush for breaking with long-standing orthodoxies and daring to bring democracy to the region.

As already discussed in the theoretical chapter, the "Arab street," shorthand for Arab political culture, was part of the intramural discourse on the issue of Arab exceptionalism. The pending invasion not only transformed this arcane academic debate into a hot political issue, but also reconfigured the line of argument in ways that would have been difficult to imagine only a short time earlier.

Arab Democracy or Arab Exceptionalism: Iraq and Beyond

To recall, many ranking MESA members had long argued that democracy in the region was possible and blamed the Arab-Israeli conflict and American realpolitik collusion with local dictators for its absence. By 2000, a large number of Middle East scholars had come to support John Esposito's tenet that Islam and democracy were compatible (Sadiki 2000). The Carnegie Foundation Project for Democracy was more cautious about the universality of the democratic impulse, but Thomas Carothers (1999, 63), the project director, acknowledged that, in the face of considerable skepticism, democracy had taken root in Guatemala and other unexpected places.

However, many of the same observers opposed the administration plan to impose democracy on Iraq and the region. Carothers (1999) and his Carnegie Foundation colleagues cautioned that "the increasingly popular idea in Washington...to democratize Iraq...and create a democratic tsunami in the Middle East is a dangerous fantasy" (Ottaway et al. 2002). Another scholar on the team argued that the best chance for enhancing democracy in the region was through a long-term policy of "high-level engagement with Arab governments in the region" (Hawthorn 2003). Others repeated the argument that in order to democratize the Middle East, the United States needed to solve the Arab-Israeli conflict first. Mearsheimer and Walt (2003), along with many of their colleagues in the Coalition for a Realistic Foreign Policy, reiterated that democracy led through Jerusalem and not Baghdad. Jervis (2003c) was also skeptical about the democratic contagion theory, asserting that it was unreasonable to expect a democratic "domino effect."

The CIA's views on the feasibility of democracy in Iraq were not published at the time, but key Middle East analysts were quite pessimistic. Paul Pillar and Emile Nakhleh were among those who claimed that, given its violent past and sectarian proclivities, Iraq was a most unlikely venue for democratization. According to the latter, "these were not minority views in the intelligence community" (Silverstein 2006). The Agency had also prepared the so-called Perfect Storm forecast, a worst-case-scenario paper that listed anarchy and breakup of Iraq, destabilization of the region, and a surge in anti-American terror. But, as Tenet (2007, 318) noted, this was more an exercise in worst-case thinking than an empirically grounded conclusion.

Whatever was the methodology, neoconservatives and democracy activists based in the Middle East strongly rejected these views. They warned against the traditional trap of viewing the developments in the region through the prism of the Arab-Israeli conflict. The high-profile 2002 Arab Human Development Report, which blamed "democratic deficit" rather than the Arab-Israeli conflict for many of the problems in the region, provided a strong endorsement of this view. Saad Eddin Ibrahim, an Egyptian academic and human rights activist, received a high-profile welcome in the United States along with Azar Nafisi (2003, 20), an Iranian dissident, who denounced the Western elite for refusing to believe in the "possibility of genuine democracy in the Muslim world." The author of the best-selling *Reading Lolita in Teheran,* Nafisi asserted that the "Islamists," as Communists before them, "have become popular among America's intellectual leaders, most emphatically in the field of Middle Eastern studies."

Contrary to Said's claim, Bernard Lewis (2002, 96, 100; 2003, 111–113; 2005) cautioned that bringing democracy to Arab countries would not be easy. In his opinion, the lack of civil society, the failure to develop the concept of a "legal person," and the absence of "native secularism" were only some of the most obvious impediments. Empirically minded scholars were also guarded. In a large survey of attitudes toward democratic norms in Arab countries, Tessler (2002) found that "support for Islamic guidance is inversely related to democratic attitudes," but that there was no "consistent pattern between personal piety and nondemocratic norms." Other studies sponsored by the Center for the Study of Islam and Democracy produced equally mixed results.

Divested of much of its academic nuance, the question of whether Iraq and the region could be democratized was vigorously debated in prime time television. In a widely covered speech on February 26, 2003, President Bush told an audience at the American Enterprise Institute that democracy was not only possible but also crucial to the Middle East. In a March 5 segment of *Nightline,* Senator John McCain and James Woolsey backed the president's confidence, but their counterparts, Senator Levin and Ambassador Wilson were not persuaded. With the debate turning emotional, Woolsey accused Wilson of promoting the racist view that Arabs are not "up to task" (Wilson 2004, 322).

To assure a successful transition to democracy, the administration worked on a number of postwar programs, including a large State Department report "Future of Iraq," compiled from recommendations of experts and Iraqi dissidents. Thomas Warrick, a former State Department liaison to north Iraq and Meghan O'Sullivan, the sanction specialist, supervised the study. Condoleezza Rise, a former political science professor, asked one of her colleagues at Stanford University, Larry Diamond, the renowned expert on democratic transition, for additional inputs. On January 20, 2003 a National Security Presidential Directive created the Office of Reconstruction and Humanitarian Assistance (OHRA) to help with postwar management of Iraq. However, according to reports, there was considerable behind-the-scene feuding over the project. The Pentagon objected to the input by Edward Walker, because the Middle East Institute was considered hostile to Chalabi. What is more, in the view of some observers, by early 2003, the relations between the State Department and the DoD were "intensely acrimonious" (Phillips 2005, 7). There is little doubt that such tensions detracted from the "Future of Iraq" project and contributed to what a biographer of Colin Powell called "an absence of buy-in" from the secretary of state (DeYoung 2006, 398).

External criticism of postwar planning and, by implication, American political and social intelligence on Iraq was also cropping up. The Council on Foreign Relations and the James A. Baker III Institute for Public Policy of Rice University published their "Guiding Principles for U.S. Post-Conflict Policy in Iraq" in January 2003. The report warned that a failure to reconstruct Iraq properly might cause the United States to "lose the peace, even if it wins the war."

Under the best of circumstances, creating a blueprint for a democratic transition was a huge endeavor. However, a number of factors made Iraq a special challenge. First, even the "democratic optimists" were concerned that the ethnoreligious divisions could, under some circumstances, turn into a civil war and fragment the country. The administration engaged in a number of debates on how to best calibrate the delicate balance of power between the Shiite majority and the Sunni and Kurdish minorities. Second, the future of the largely Sunni Ba'ath party was also intensely argued, with the Pentagon, advised by Makiya and Chalabi, advocating a total de-Ba'athification and State Department officials holding out for some measure of "national reconciliation" modeled on South Africa.

Third, the lingering doubts about Chalabi and, to a lesser degree, other opposition figures such as Iyad Alawi, worked their way into the debate about the prospects for Iraqi democracy. Dislike of the head of the Iraqi National Congress was not confined to State Department and segments of the CIA; General Franks (2004, 421) described Chalabi as a "Gucci leader" with no popular base at home. There were persistent rumors that some in the intelligence community preferred General Nizar al Khazraji, a former chief of staff of the Iraqi army-turned leader of the National Liberal Movement, as a replacement for Saddam Hussein (Hashim 2003; Lake 2001; Rubin 2002). Such sentiments were not lost on the Department of Defense and Vice President Cheney who questioned the State Department's commitment to democratization of Iraq. According to Woodward (2004, 284), Cheney refused to settle for anything short of a fundamental change, arguing that "we've got to give the Iraqi people a chance at those fundamental values we believe in."

With American troops poised to invade in March, the administration hoped that democratic reforms in Iraq, as other assumptions about the war would come true. In this context, the length of American presence in the country was a major concern. According to a top secret Power Point briefing, the war plan assumed that only 5000 troops would continue to be needed by 2006 (Battle and Blanton 2007). War opponents were equally eager to prove the fallacy of the Bush doctrine. Although not privy to this rosy forecast, critics warned of a long military presence or even "another Vietnam."

For both sides the stakes were enormous. In the view of one observer, Operation Iraqi Freedom was a historical "tipping point"; a successful outcome would have justified Washington's "ownership" of international security through a program of democratic and market reforms in the remaining authoritarian states (Barnett 2003). A failure would not only damage the

Bush administration but also discredit the tenets of democratic universalism that the paradigmatic switch September 11 made possible.

Reality Check: The View from Baghdad as Refracted in Washington

Of all the prewar forecasts, the easiest to evaluate was the conduct of the invasion. The 21-day war and the number of casualties—122 American and 33 British—astounded even the most optimistic prognosticators. According to accounts, the Pentagon had initially planned for approximately 125–225 days of major combat operations and a much higher number of American troops possibly being killed or injured (Hanson 2004). Although civilian casualties were more difficult to ascertain, the number was well below the thousands projected by war opponents.

Subsequent assessments, notably of the United States Joint Force Command (USJFC) "Iraqi Perspective Project," based on debriefings of Saddam Hussein, senior regime officials, and top military commanders, found that, as expected, the regular army failed to engage in battle and spontaneously disbanded. More surprising, the elite Republican Guard divisions did little fighting and essentially blended into the population. The only element to offer resistance was the Saddam Fedayeen, irregular counterinsurgency units created in 1994 in reaction to the Shiite uprising at the end of the Gulf War. In addition, there was the Quds Army, a regional militia with a nominal membership of half a million, some of whose members offered a spirited defense (Gordon and Trainor 2006, 61; Woods, Lacey, and Murray 2006).

The USJFC study also revealed that after years of Hussein's highly personalized rule, the army was reduced to a virtual phantom force. Hussein, who trusted no one outside his small inner circle, appointed Qusay to head the Republican Guards in 2001. Lacking in military experience, Qusay took to imposing his father's strategic vision on the army that amounted to little more than a spiritual exhortation to fight the "American infidel." In a short propaganda film discovered after the war, Hussein, surrounded by some of his senior military commanders, is seen to urge Iraqis to use slings and bows and arrows to resist the invader (Klein 2006; Shane 2006). The psychological cost of the ever-increasing security measures of the feared military intelligence Istikhbarat and the gruesome punishment meted out to those suspected of disloyalty paralyzed the already mediocre officer corps, which Hussein promoted from among the least talented and least threatening individuals.

The army decision to forgo almost all resistance and defend Baghdad within four concentric circles was also attributed to Hussein. Even after the invasion, the then largely delusional leader continued to believe his own information minister Muhammad Said al-Shahaf, the infamous "Baghdad Bob," who maintained that the Iraqi military was winning the battle. At the very end, surrounded by sycophants or those too intimidated to speak the truth, Hussein, like Hitler, was reduced to commanding nonexistent divisions (Gordon and Trainor 2006, 135; Woods, Lacey, and Murray 2006).

If the invasion of Iraq vindicated the "cakewalk" scenario, the failure to find weapons of mass destruction proved to be a major setback. To quote one commentator, "the Bush administration officials never anticipated this predicament," expecting the WMD to be uncovered quickly (Gibbs and Ware 2003). Indeed, an analyst for CENTCOM planning confirmed that the military based its strategy on the assumption that Iraq might use WMD, either in the course of the invasion or as a last resort in Baghdad (Hooker 2005, 65–66). Other sources revealed that a crew attached to the Army's 75th Exploitation Task Force was sent to film the expected sites. In May, the DoD formed the Iraq Survey Group (ISG) that numbered about 1,400 personnel under the CIA-appointed David Key, a former UNSCOM inspector. In spite of intense efforts, the ISG found no concealed weapons, a fact duly acknowledged in an interim report in December. Following Key's resignation in January 2004, the CIA named Charles A. Duelfer, another former UNSCOM inspector, to head the group, which produced its final report in September 2004. Both Key and Duelfer concluded that, although Iraq had retained some capabilities, the inspection regime had forced Saddam Hussein to abandon its WMD program in the early 1990s (www.cia.gov/cia/reports/Iraq_wmd_2004/_8k).

Some staunch war supporters remained undaunted by the absence of weapons. To them it was proof that Saddam Hussein had outwitted the outside world again. According to this view, the regime managed to either bury or transport its WMD stock to Syria just ahead of the invading forces (Mylroie 2004a, 2004b). But for war opponents, the failure to find the WMD was a prime example of the misuse of intelligence by an administration determined to carry out its war design.

For their part, Democrats were quick to realize that the issue of intelligence could play an important role in the 2004 presidential race. In March 2003, Rand Beers, Richard Clarke's short-lived successor as Bush's counterintelligence chief, resigned to join the Kerry campaign; Clarke was rumored to consider a similar step (Prothero 2003). It was around this time that Kerry asked Wilson to join his election campaign. To raise the profile of the intelligence issue, in May, the Senate Democratic Policy conference asked the ambassador to speak about his Niger trip. Wilson gave the *New York Times* correspondent Nicholas Kristoff permission to mention the allegations anonymously in his May 5 column. On June 12 Walter Pincus from the *Washington Post* followed up on the theme. On July 6 Wilson went public with an op-ed in the *New York Times* "What I Didn't Find in Africa."

Wilson's disclosure that, in his opinion, there was no credible evidence to support the yellow cake intelligence was an important success for the antiwar lobby. The administration reacted with a mixture of puzzlement and alarm. Richard Armitage was the first to publicly, albeit inadvertently, disclose that Valerie Plame was the wife of the ambassador, but for Vice President Cheney and his staff, the larger issue was whether Wilson was chosen "by someone in the CIA who wanted to discount the yellow cake evidence" (Dubose 2006, 214).

Apparently still unaware of Wilson's record in the antiwar coalition, Scooter Libby allegedly chose to discredit the ambassador by leaking the identity of his wife to a number of reporters. As Plame worked undercover, the move misfired badly, making the ambassador and the plight of his "outed" wife front-page news. In August, Wilson was invited to address a rally of ROAR (Retain Our American Rights), an antiwar organization, and in September the Nation Institute, created by *The Nation* magazine, awarded Wilson the Ron Ridenhour Award for Truth-Telling (Hersh 2004, 242; Wilson 2004, 360–362).

While Wilson became the public voice challenging the administration's prewar intelligence, the Democrats could count on Michael Scheuer, Paul Pillar, and other CIA insiders. Scheuer's (2004) unhappiness with the CIA, as expressed in his first anonymous book, soon turned into a scathing attack on the administration Iraq's policy in *Imperial Hubris*, his second anonymous book. Whether the censors approved the publication of the second book because higher-ups agreed with his message or were afraid to turn Scheuer into another prominent dissenter, as some alleged, the decision to approve the publication testified to the unprecedented internal turmoil in the Agency (Schoenfeld 2005).

Critics were equally emboldened by the failure to find more supporting evidence for the Iraqi-al Qaeda connection. Pillar, who at one point reluctantly acknowledged that low-level cooperation between the bin Laden group and the ISS (Iraqi security services) could not be ruled out, used a lecture at Johns Hopkins University in October 2003 to downplay such a scenario. Adding the Iraq-al Qaeda connection to the list of alleged intelligence manipulations by the White House was high on the Democrats agenda. War critics were particularly eager to target the Office of Special Plans in the Department of Defense from where much of this intelligence had originated. Responding to a request by Senator Levin, on October 27, 2003, Douglas Feith submitted a memorandum on the relation between Iraq and al Qaeda.

The memo was leaked to the press and used by neoconservatives to mount a vigorous defense of their case. In his article "Case Closed" and a subsequent book, Stephen F. Hayes (2003a, 2004), a *Weekly Standard* editor, provided a detailed account of all known contacts between al Qaeda and the Iraqi security services. To prove that the list was legitimate, Hayes reminded his readers that information about al Qaeda and Iraq had made it into the mainstream press in the 1990s. In her new book, Laurie Mylroie (2003) went as far as to accuse the "beltway" of fighting Bush and ignoring all indications of Iraqi sponsorship of bin Laden. Woolsey made essentially a similar claim in an introduction to the book.

Much as the neoconservatives hoped to "close" the case on the al Qaeda-Iraq relations, the 9/11 commission could not confirm that it amounted "to an operational level collaboration" (Gold 2004, 216; Kean and Hamilton 2004, 97). What is more, by 2004, fueled by the election campaigning, the entire Iraq intelligence came under vigorous partisan scrutiny. Elements in the intelligence community that gravitated toward the Kerry camp provided much of the momentum. A pessimistic 2004 NIE on Iraq was leaked to the press; a journalistic account implicated Paul Pillar, the NIE's author. Sensing danger, Republicans upped the ante. Senator John McCain accused the CIA of being something of a "rogue agency"; of being "dysfunctional," unwilling to change, and leaking information detrimental to the reelection of Bush (Jehl 2004). A *Wall Street Journal* article called the upheaval "the CIA insurgency" and accused Pillar of "protecting his own lousy track record in misjudging the terrorist threat," a reference to his 2001 book (*The CIA insurgency*, 2004). Another commentator wrote about "a full scale mutiny" of the CIA against the president and charged it with "betting" on Kerry (Novak 2004; Roberts II 2004).

To fend off charges that his team had exaggerated the danger of Iraqi WMD, the president was forced to appoint a committee of inquiry in February 2004. Chaired by Charles S. Robb and Laurence H. Silberman, the Commission on the Intelligence Capabilities of the United States Regarding Weapons of Mass Destruction, absolved the administration of pressuring CIA analysts and manipulating the intelligence on Iraq. The Senate Intelligence Committee launched its own investigation whose initial reports echoed the Robb-Silberman conclusions (www.wmd.gov/report/-11k).

Lost in the partisan skirmish were some more dispassionate explanations of how Saddam Hussein's behavior and his dysfunctional regime could have distorted the Iraqi estimate. Perhaps the most nuanced material came from the USJCF study, which indicated that Saddam Hussein's reasoning proved to be a big problem for intelligence officials and scholars alike. Those who had claimed that Hussein was a rational albeit ruthless leader missed his dissent into delusion, as attested by the debriefings of Tariq Aziz and other insiders. According to the inner circle, the Iraqi leader had claimed to be "unimpressed" with the new Bush administration and had decided to challenge the American and British air patrols in the no-fly zones. While grossly underestimating the United States, Hussein's paranoia about homegrown dangers to the regime was overwhelming. Right up to the invasion, the Iraqi dictator was convinced that the Shiites and Kurds would rise up against him. Consequently, the principal mission of the Iraqi military was "to ensure the internal security of the Ba'athist dictatorship," and prevent a recurrence of the 1991 uprisings. Even the paramilitary forces (the Saddam Fedayeen, the al Quds Army, and the Ba'ath party militia), which analysts considered to be part of Iraq's external defense, were actually created to protect the regime (Woods, Lacey, and Murray, 2006).

Anxiety about an internal uprising was only surpassed by fears of a military coup. Hussein beefed up his secret security service and increased the internal suppression, making the last years of his rule the most brutal in what was already a hugely oppressive dictatorship. Hussein's son Qusay, who took over most of the security operations, was particularly active against senior officers, creating a number of new "elite" units. This never-ending action to "coup-proof" the regime eroded whatever little professional standing the military had retained (Gordon and Trainor 2006, 66).

Even less understood was the fact that Hussein lost control of his corrupt and fear-ridden country, a process that, as described in chapter 2, started with his decision to create an alternative "sultanist" system of governance. To recall, Glad speculated that Hussein's delusion and wanton brutality were exacerbated by an extreme form of centralized power. The USJCM analysts found that even the simplest messages to the dictator had to be embellished with effusive praise; it was "understood that his need to hear only good news was constantly growing and that it was in their best interest to feed that hunger." Those inclined to speak their mind were deterred by "rumors . . . that summary execution awaited anyone who dared to contradict the dictator."

The weapons program was a prime victim of Saddam's acute misperception, if not outright delusion. In the words of the report, "when [Hussein] ordered [underlings] to initiate weapons programs [e.g., WMD] that they knew Iraq could not develop [in the late 1990s], they told him they could accomplish the projects with ease," and "when [he] asked for updates . . . they . . . faked plans and designs to show progress." Iraq's Military Industrial Commission (MIC) was a case in point. In 2002–03, MIC had 170 projects, with a budget that amounted to approximately 1.5 percent of the GDP. But many of the projects, including some with WMD potential, were not realistic, but a product of Hussein's imagination. Fearful of retribution, scientists produced reports based on fabricated results. Positive incentives offered by the regime worked in the same way; Tariq Aziz recounted that "people lied to get money and cars out of Saddam Hussein." Kay and other inspectors would subsequently argue that the CIA missed the "disarray in Iraqi arms program." Another analyst noted that the U.S. intelligence services could not see through the "Potemkinazation of Iraq" (Elliott 2003; Risen 2006; Woods, Lacey, and Murray 2006).

The mixture of fear, corruption, and incompetence could have accounted for some of the more disputed parts of the WMD intelligence. For instance, Kay, who interrogated many of the scientists, concluded that the MIC had purchased the nonstandard aluminum tubes because the propellants for the rockets, produced by a friend of Qusay, were too weak to carry conventional artillery shells. Afraid to anger Saddam's son, the engineers decided to modify the shell specifications, opting for the smaller and lighter casings in the hope of compensating for the weak propellers. In hindsight, this unorthodox solution probably convinced Joe T. and others that the tubes were destined as centrifuges (Woodward 2006, 242).

However, a cache of documents seized in Iraq and posted on a number of Web sites demonstrated that even in its dysfunctional state, the regime was intent on rearming. In spite of the sanctions, the scale of Iraqi illegal weapon program was considerable, if unfocused. Among others, it boasted the Jenin missile project with a range of 600 miles, well beyond the 90-mile limit imposed on Iraq and a clandestine network of small biological laboratories located in Mukhabarat safe houses, which contained dual use equipment (www. freerepublic.com/focus.f-news/1620565/post-46k).

Hussein's way of reasoning could also explain the failure of Iraq to fully "come clean" as the UNMOVIC mandated. Isolated from the outside world and confident that France and Russia would protect him in the United Nations, the Iraqi dictator hoped to outwit and outwait the Bush administration in the same way that he had maneuvered Clinton. To retain his status as a regional player, Hussein apparently decided on a strategy of "deterrence by ambiguity"; he notified the Revolutionary Command Council that Iraq had no deployable WMD in December 2002, but refused to publicly remove any lingering doubts.

Hussein's tactics left even some insiders in the dark. Ali Hassan al Majid, his top aide known as "Chemical Ali," recalled being taken aback by the December disclosure. Other senior officials actually believed that Saddam Hussein had lethal weapons, a topic of many rumors in military and civilian circles. Kay observed that "none of Iraqis had actually seen any WMD, but they all believed that such unconventional weapons existed somewhere else in Saddam's arsenal" (Woodward, 2006, 242). Tenet (2007, 331–332) explained that Hussein's deterrence by ambiguity created an "implausible truth." "We knew plenty of countries [with WMD]...trying desperately to conceal [it]. Be we had no previous experience with a country that did not posses such weapons but pretended that it did."

The regime's efforts to comply with UNMOVIC created more confusion. NSA intercepts of Iraqi communications were interpreted by intelligence analysts as commands to hide weapons. USJFC analysts commented that "what was meant to prevent suspicion thus ended up weighting it" (Woods, Lacey, and Murray, 2006).

If the postwar understanding proved that Saddam Hussein fell short of the image of a rational, but narcissistic Machiavellian, the record was ambiguous enough to keep the question of the dictator's deterrability alive. Not surprisingly, war critics have continued to claim that, like Stalin, the Iraqi leader was ruthless but cautious and calculating enough to be deterred (Record 2004, 55). Neoconservatives and administration officials have marshaled the same evidence to argue that, like Hitler, Saddam Hussein was delusional and reckless and, ultimately, not deterrable. Some went to so far as to accuse war opponents of "putting the best face on Saddam Hussein's record to justify the assumption that containment and deterrence work" (Lieber 2003). War supporters also asserted that, if left in power, the regime could have followed the A.Q. Khan model of clandestinely spreading lethal weapons to terrorist groups, either by design or, more likely, by default (Kessler 2004, 187–188; Pipes 2003b).

The Democracy Project: Evaluation from a Short-Term Perspective

The hazards of speculating on such a major endeavor as democratizing of a country are well known. As one observer put it, "when history is written" a few decades later, "historians may find benefits from the war that were not apparent at the time," or they may see that the American exercise in Kantian peace "had set world on a downward trajectory" of even greater violence (Judis 2004, 185).

Until such time, the reviews have fluctuated with the news from Iraq. In 2003, in spite of an initial wave of chaos and looting, forecasting about the future of Iraqi democracy tended to be positive, especially among neoconservatives (Elshtain 2003; Haass 2003; Hanson 2003a, 2003b; Muravchik 2003). Even the cautious Carothers (2003) seemed to allow that "gradualism" may not be the only approach to spreading democracy in the Middle East. Anthony Lake, another unlikely new believer was said to be cautiously optimistic. Commenting on these apparent "conversions," one analyst wrote that the Bush administration put the Democrats "in the box"; they, the Democrats, professed commitment to spreading democracy but were unhappy to acknowledge that a military action may work better than the gradualist "soft power" (Dionne 2003).

By 2004 sporadic violence turned into a lethal insurgency aimed at both the American forces and Iraqis who collaborated with the new authority. The scope and the ferocity of the attacks raised doubts about the Democratic Project. Detractors were quick to proclaim that Bush's goals were "unrealistic" not only in Iraq but also in the wider region (Salmoni 2004). Zbigniew Brzezinski (2004), a long-standing critic, blamed "the extremist foreign policy" of the administration for "the increasingly messy Iraqi adventure." A veteran intelligence analyst declared that the prewar "rosy picture" of democracy was put to rest by the unrelenting violence (Yaphe 2004). *Current History and The New Republic were* among a dozen or so forums that held symposia on "what went wrong." Larry Diamond (2004), back from his stint as a senior adviser to the Coalition Provisional Authority, added his personal observations on "what went wrong."

Amidst all this gloom, only a few ventured to defend the invasion. Ajami (2004) stated that "even it fell short...it was an honorable and noble expedition;" adding that the "sour realists" who had doubted Bush's democratic doctrine would be proven wrong. Natan Sharansky (2004, 278), the former Soviet dissident-turned Israeli politician, made his case for democracy in a book quoted by the president. Drawing upon his own experience in fighting communism, Sharansky asserted that Islamofascim, as all tyranny, would be "wiped of[f] the face of the earth."

But critics were quick to call Sharansky's book a piece of Israeli propaganda. In fact, with the difficulties in Iraq mounting, the argument that Jewish neoconservatives tricked the United States into an unnecessary war was getting a more vigorous hearing. In his high-profile book, Wilson (2004, 432), put the blame for the war squarely at the feet the Jews in the Bush administration. Using a more coded language, John B. Judis (2004, 168) blasted the "various generations of neoconservatives in the American Enterprise Institute." Even those who did not blame directly the "neoconservative cabal" were back to warning that without solving the Arab-Israeli conflict, democracy in Iraq and the Middle East was unattainable (Ottaway and Carothers 2004). Amatol Lieven, a scholar with the Carnegie Endowment, emphasized that the Israeli-Palestinian conflict is "a tremendous obstacle to democratization" because it influences the "most regressive aspects of Arab nationalism and Arab culture" (quoted in Joffe 2005).

A number of impressive democratic achievements in Iraq, including the ratification of a constitution and a free and democratic election in 2005 revived hope in the Democratic Project. In a provocative piece on the politics of "risky peace," one observer raised the question of whether doves or hawks "deliver peace" (Schultz 2005). A leading liberal critic of the war, "reluctantly admitted" that President Bush "might be right after all" (Fein 2005). A senior associate at the Carnegie Endowment was ready to concede that after all, the wave of Arab political modernization may be real (Hamzawy 2005). With former critics warming up to the democratic transformation, Hanson (2005) was optimistic enough to proclaim that the president's model of democratic contagion was working.

Yet not everyone was swept by this wave of optimism. In their new book, Daniel Benjamin and Steven Simon (2005, 205) decried the "democratization industry" spawned by the administration. The former president Jimmy Carter (2005, 99) averred that "dependence on military force" to expand democracy "dramatically reduced the attractiveness of our political, cultural offering."

In spite of a new Iraqi government and a working parliament, by 2006 the grim pattern of violence in Iraq was unmistakable. The number of American casualties passed three thousand and the civilian toll was staggering, What is more, the fighting morphed from an insurgency against American forces and the Iraqi government to sectarian clashes between Shiites and Sunnis, prompting commentators to speak about a full-fledged civil war.

The scope and the intractability of such violence undermined the faith of some former war supporters. Francis Fukuyama (2006, 116), a leading public intellectual, wrote that "there was a tendency to believe that democracy was a default condition to which societies would revert once liberated from dictators." Patrick Clawson, a scholar at the neoconservative Washington Institute for Near East Studies, suggested that the " 'best scenario' would be a weak but united Iraq." As a matter of fact, some observers proclaimed Iraq to be a failed state. The Fund for Peace (FfP), a nonprofit group tracking failed states in collaboration with *Foreign Policy*, listed Iraq as a premier failed state (The Failed States Index 2006). FfP's president, Pauline Baker argued that dividing Iraq into a Kurdish, Sunni, and Shiite states would be a preferable solution, a view shared by Peter Galbraith (2006), a onetime congressional liaison to the Kurds and Clinton's ambassador to Croatia. In its 2007 listing of failed states, Iraq was ranked second, after Sudan.

Commentary on Iraqi democracy was part of a larger literature on "why things went wrong." In a nutshell, one school of thought blamed technical problems of postwar management and reconstruction. One popular theory held that the "catastrophic success" of coalition forces left many Iraqi military personnel to fight another day in the insurgency. Other theories listed the paucity of American troops to safeguard the transition, the administration's decision to de-Ba'athify the country, and the alleged mishaps of the Provisional Occupation Authority under Ambassador L. Paul Bremer, especially his decision to disband the Iraqi army (Barton and Crocker 2003; Coughlin 2006; Lehman 2006; Phillips 2005, 113–154). In a detailed and balanced study, Gordon and Trainor (2006, 497–507) incorporated these and other factors to provide a five part-inventory of failure, including the "Bush administration disdain for nation building." In his book *State of Denial*, Bob Woodward (2006,), noted that the administration ignored urgent pleas for more American soldiers to stabilize the country.

Without dismissing technical blunders, the opposing school of thought took a more intrinsic view of the problem. These observers pointed out that Iraq was unfit for a democratic experiment as it was plagued by a history of sectarian and political violence. Specifically, with "opposing subnational groups divided along ethnic and sectarian lines" it was hardly a fertile ground for adopting a democratic system that required legitimizing a national authority system, respect for law, and a sense of fair play. One exasperated commentator questioned whether "Saddam Hussein was the way he was" because "Iraq is a congenitally fractured society that could only be held together by a murderous thug" (Friedman 2004, 28).

More systematic efforts to assess the prospect of democracy in Iraq and the Middle East have been equally discouraging. An index quantifying Arab democracy found that, with the exception of the free elections in Lebanon and Iraq, good governance, free speech, and other democratic staples were sorely missing. The author of the index blamed Arab education with its strong emphasis on obedience and memorization and absence of critical thinking as major deterrents to the development of a democratic political culture (Sarsar 2006).

Complicating matters, in January 2006, Hamas, an officially recognized terrorist organization, came to power in a free election in the Palestinian Authority. In spite of some initial optimism that Hamas would moderate its way when confronted with the challenge of governance, the group refused to recognize Israel and renounce terrorism, a precondition for international aid. On the contrary, Hamas has continued to engage in acts of terror, triggering Israeli retaliation. Hezbollah, another terrorist organization, which won a number of seats in the free electrons to the Lebanese parliament, chose to pursue its armed struggle with Israel by kidnapping two Israeli soldiers in July 2006. In the ensuing war, parts of the south and the Shiite neighborhoods in Beirut were destroyed along with much of the Lebanese infrastructure.

In spite of considerable suffering, Hamas and Hezbollah retained their popularity at home and increased their following in the region. Both have supported an Islamic theocracy, a sentiment that has gained strength in the Middle East. The Muslim Brotherhood showed unexpected vitality in the November 2005 election to the Egyptian parliament, taking one-fifth of the seats (Guindy 2006). Commenting on these developments, Barry Rubin (2006a, 2006b), the author of a comprehensive study on the struggle for democracy in the Middle East, wrote that "democracy movement is close to death," unable to compete with "the passion and demagoguery" that produced the "poisons mix of nationalism, religious sentiments, and hatred of Israel and the West."

Perhaps most discouraging was the fact that Hezbollah and Hamas were described as pioneers of he "ballot and the bullet" model of "democracy" in the Middle East. While seeking democratic legitimacy through elections and playing a major role in the governmental process, both groups have operated a flourishing paramilitary force (Feldman 2006a) That the "ballot and bullet" model was adopted by the two major Shiite parties in the Iraqi parliament has been a most unwelcome development for the supporters of the Democratic Project. In addition to the sectarian clashes between the Shiites and Sunnis, the power struggle between Moktadah al-Sadr and Abdul Aziz al-Hakim, the head of the Supreme Council for the Islamic Revolution in Iraq, has occasionally turned into full-fledged violence.

The resilience of Iran and Syria was an equally unwelcome development from the point of view of the Bush doctrine. Far from "falling like dominoes," Iran has proceeded with its nuclear program in defiance of the United States and the international community. Both Iran and Syria have fomented sectarian tensions in Iraq and used Hezbollah to reignite the conflict with Israel.

As discouraging as these setbacks have been, some democracy advocates have pleaded for a longer-time perspective. Participants in a Middle *East Quarterly* roundtable suggested that in Europe the process of democratization was slow and arduous, taking hundreds of years to accomplish (Debate: 2006). Stressing the virtue of patience, another assessment noted that the United States should "outwait" negative developments in the hope that, as democratic principles take root, more stable forms of democracy would emerge in the region (Craner 2006). Speaking of future prospects rather than present realities, Boot (2006) advised the skeptics that democratic transition cannot occur overnight and that, like the cold war, change is bound to be gradual and generational. In his book *The Foreinger's Gift: The Americans, the Arabs, and the Iraqis in Iraq,* Fouad Ajami (2006, xi) likewise argued that "it is too soon" to write off the Iraqi experiment.

The slow, "organic" democratic transition, with an emphasis on fundamental changes in the educational system and a healthy growth of civil society may ultimately prove correct. However, the sectarian carnage in Iraq has led to increasing attacks on the Bush doctrine from a number of quarters. Claiming vindication, both Realists and Liberal Internationalists suggested that "the budgetary, political and diplomatic realities" had caught up with the unrealistic vision of the first Bush administration (Gordon 2006). The Coalition for a Realistic Foreign Policy went further, stating that the war was fought on behalf of Israel as part of a larger neoconservative plan of "creative destruction" to promote anarchy that would sweep away regimes hostile to the Jewish state (Bipartisan Disaster 2006). Mearsheimer and Walt (2006) created a firestorm by accusing the Jewish lobby of having an undue influence on American policy in the Middle East. Brzezinski (2006, 63) called the influence of the Jewish lobby "a dangerous exception," adding that, over time, U.S. policy in the Middle East had shifted from "relative impartiality" to "essentially adopting an Israeli point of view on the Arab-Israeli conflict."

Traditional conservatives and Republican realists took to denouncing the Democratic Project as a "spectacular misnamed radicalism" (Will 2006). They were joined by some disenchanted neoconservatives who conceded that "Iraq unified under a democratic system is nothing more than a mirage." Much to the dismay of hard-core neoconservatives, these and other critics were ready to back the idea of a tripartite division of Iraq as a "second best" option (Podhoretz 2006).

Fueled by mid-term elections, the question of whether the "Bush doctrine is dead" has dominated the foreign policy discourse in 2006. Although Norman Podhoretz (2006), a leading neoconservative, proclaimed that the reports on its death were "premature," others rushed to offer alternatives ranging from classical realism to liberal universalism, with such hybrids as "principled realism," "realistic Wilsonianism," or "principled engagement" thrown into the mix.

Replacing the Bush Doctrine: Using the Past to Look at the Future

As will be recalled from the theoretical discussion, American foreign policy has been driven by assumptions about political changes that are underpinned by notions of what constitutes a legitimate political order. While the initial debate on Kantian peace was confined to the academy, the specter of rogue regimes colluding with Islamic fundamentalists bent on a "clash of civilizations," convinced an important segment of the discursive community that democratic change was not only a public good in its own right, but also an urgent security imperative. Rejecting the MESA paradigm that blamed the Arab-Israeli conflict for Arab exceptionalism, the Bush doctrine called for regime change as an alternative way to affect democratic progress in the Middle East.

The setback in Iraq has encouraged a new look at some of the old foreign policy models, notably Liberal Internationalism and Realism. True to form, the former has contended that the United States should contain rather than change rogue states, using the tactics developed to handle the Soviet Union. Combined with positive incentives, including a better appreciation of the security concerns of rogue regime, such policies have been expected to manage the threat of WMD. Stanley Hoffmann (2006), a prominent Harvard scholar noted, that "all kinds of arms control agreements . . . were worked out in the later phases of the Cold War with the Soviet Union." To assuage the "plausible fear of attack provoked by their neighbors and the U.S," Hoffman urged American security guarantees for nuclear proliferators. Graham Allison (2005) another prominent Harvard scholar, asserted that, with judicious

U.S. and international management, nuclear terrorism is the "ultimately avoidable catastrophe."

Truman doctrine style containment has been at the center of Peter Beinart (2004) effort to fashion a post-Iraq liberal foreign policy. Beinart, a disenchanted war supporter, contended that a carefully calibrated mix of sanctions, oversight, and positive incentives would defeat Islamic fascism. Something of a neodevelopmentalist, Beinart has put much faith in economic development, advocating an updated Marshall Plan for the Middle East. Still further to the left, in a reflection of the resurgent McGovern-Carter vision, many Democrats have demanded a return to "muscular internationalism." In the words of Gary Hart (2004, 157–158), the author of "principled engagements," this new internationalism "should be based on historic American principles of liberal democracy, tolerance of diversity, respect for difference of culture," and "economic growth and justice." Nye (2001), the long-standing advocate of "soft power," argued that his formula represents the "means to success in world politics."

Realism, the preferred mode of traditional Republicans and leading IR scholars, permeated the thinking of the Iraq Study Group, co-chaired by James Baker and Lee Hamilton. Released in December 2006, the Group's report suggested a New Diplomatic Offensive in which the United States was urged to "engage constructively" with Iran and Syria to stabilize Iraq. Although there was an acknowledgment that the Iranian and Syrian regimes have an interest in fomenting unrest in Iraq, the ISG put its faith in the diplomatic give-and-take to change the behavior of such rogues.

Not incidentally, the newly popular Liberal Internationalist and Realist models have signaled a return to the MESA view that the Arab-Israeli conflict is at the heart of the Middle East problems. Beinart's forecast of a Middle East flourishing with the help of Marshall-style economic plan was borrowed from the "New Middle East" vision of Shimon Peres, the architect of the failed Oslo peace imitative. The ISG argument that the way to reform the Middle East leads through Jerusalem was more direct. Accordingly, "U.S. cannot achieve its goals in the Middle East unless it deals directly with the Arab-Israeli conflict." Seven out of the more than seventy recommendations of the report dealt with the Arab-Israeli conflict.

To the extent that all foreign policy approaches contain a predictive element, the lessons of American history of trying to change Saddam Hussein' regime against the background of a rising Islamist movement should be of major interest. As the concluding chapter makes clear, the Iraqi case is a somber reminder of the predictive predicaments of whatever formula that is adopted.

7

Reflections on the Iraqi Predictive Predicament

Efforts to understand the politics of American intelligence in Iraq have preoccupied scholars, foreign policy practitioners, and intelligence officials. Complicating the task is the fact that the forecasts leading to Operation Iraqi Freedom have been subject to an intense and divisive scrutiny. While the number of studies has increased exponentially, this book is the first attempt to present a longitudinal, integrated chronological-thematic analysis of the highly complex process that shaped American views of the Iraqi regime, the various attempts to modify its behavior and ultimately to depose the regime.

With this task accomplished, it remains the burden of the concluding chapter to sum up the predictive predicament that Iraq has posed by recalling the paradigmatic foreign policy and intelligence dimensions of the problem. This analytic scheme allows for reducing the highly synergistic predictive process to manageable categories. Equally important, to the extent that problems of forecasting are comparable, this format can provide an insight into future predictive predicaments.

Paradigmatic Level Predicament: Peaceful Coexistence or "Clash of Civilizations"?

The theoretical chapter in this work makes it clear that political change, whether revolutionary or incremental, is rooted in changing norms of legitimacy underlying the collective belief system of a society. Ideally, any successful effort to predict change involves an attentive reading of the legitimacy discourse. However, this is virtually impossible in closed societies, where citizens practice preference falsification to avoid the punitive wrath of their rulers.

In the absence of empirical evidence, observers have relied on political science models of change, which, at their core, reflect legitimacy norms of the discursive community of scholars and lay practitioners. Built on different ontological and epistemic assumptions about societal realities as well as divergent views of human nature, rival epistmetic communities have offered diametrically opposite paradigms of change.

As noted, the developmental paradigm, with its built-in assumptions of linearity, saw the Middle East moving in the direction of a Western-style polity and market economy. The contending neo-Marxist paradigm postulated a secular, socialist, postcolonial/postimperialist era. Though the fundamentalist revolution in Iran confounded both predictions, many of the neo-Marxist precepts were included in the orientalist critique of Edward Said and Eqbal Ahmad that inspired a new generation of MESA scholar-activists.

While the merging of scholarship and left-wing activism was, of course, a triumph for the Gramscian vision of the social sciences, this trend exacted a high cost on the understanding of the Middle East in America. Ideally, scientific discourse should allow the testing of various paradigmatic assumptions. However, the hegemony of MESA, buttressed by peer review practices, precluded fruitful intellectual exchange. Excluded from virtually all official venues, dissenting scholars moved on to establish their own discursive network and push their contending views of change in the Middle East.

Going beyond MESA scholarship, the predominantly secular and liberal academy has left substantial sectors of the population—traditional conservatives, neoconservatives, and evangelical Christians—with a sense of alienation epitomized by the experience of George W. Bush at Yale. Years later when Bush won what many liberal considered a flawed election, the division between the two camps turned into a chasm. Well before the war in Iraq, some respected professors urged their colleagues and students to organize "mainstream dissent" against the president. A leading presidential historian Robert Dallek described George W. Bush as "the stupidest man ever to sit in the Oval Office" (quoted in Kelley 2004, 611).

Under normal circumstances intramural battles are confided to the academy. However, the interlocking issues of Arab exceptionalism, Pan-Islamic terrorism, and WMD proliferation brought these debates to the forefront of the national discourse in the 1990s. The MESA epistemic community contended that the absence of democracy in the Middle East should be blamed on the Arab-Israeli conflict. To the extent that Islamic terrorism was acknowledged, MESA professors called for a "root cause" analysis with a special emphasis on poverty, inequality, and capitalist globalization. MESA's rivals emphasized an antithetical causal structure: they suggested that the authoritarian regimes in the region had perpetuated the Arab-Israeli conflict to cover up a severe legitimacy deficit. As for Islamic terrorism, Bernard Lewis pointed out that it was a harbinger of a wave of radical Islamism bent on a "clash of civilizations" with the Judeo-Christian West.

In the bitter public exchanges between the epistemic rivals in the 1990s, the MESA paradigm seemed to hold the upper hand. MESA scholars scorned the "terrorolgists" and charged that the discussion of Islamic terrorism was little more than a cover for "fearmongering" intended to delegitimize Islam, an argument echoed in liberal circles. Even Huntington's widely publicized recasting of Lewis' "clash of civilizations" did little to raise the level of alarm about a megaterrorist attack on American soil. As demonstrated, most of Huntington's IR colleagues were ill equipped to discern the Islamist challenge. Three factors in particular undermined the contribution of assorted IR models to the analysis of the complex nexus of Islamic terrorism, WMD, and rogue states.

First, the state-centered view of international relations failed to consider the impact of substate actors such as al Qaeda. It is entirely plausible that Mearsheimer's (2001) ambitious effort to chart the trajectory of change for the twenty-first century would have been less deeply flawed, had it included some references to bin Laden. Second, with few exceptions, IR theorists have failed to incorporate American experience in the Middle East into their universe of case studies and illustrations. Assumptions of robust universality notwithstanding, the heavy use of European history and cold war case studies is puzzling, given the fact that studies in international anthropology, including the pioneering work of Edward Hall, have long shown considerable variance in stock concepts of rationality and deterrence. The paucity of culturally appropriate examples reflects poorly on IR; more than a quarter century after the start of the Iran-Iraq War, the field of Arab military history and Arab and Islamist strategic thought are underdeveloped and mired in polemics. Unlike the organic relation between IR scholarship and European history, attempts to incorporate Middle East case studies into contemporary international theory have been few and far between.

Third, and probably most important, the structure of incentives in IR rewards smart formulations and catchy generalities rather than empirical relevance or predictive acumen. Though many IR formulations have ended up in the proverbial "dustbin of history," their authors invariably go on to enjoy the status of "leading experts." Completely wrong conclusion have not discredited academics because, in the words of one observer, it is not "necessarily one of the criteria used with respect to judging scholarship in the academic community" (Horowitz 1980, 180). In spite of dismissing the threat of al Qaeda, Robert Jervis (2006) would later criticize the various post–September 11 commissions for not following "good social science practices." It is ironical but not surprising that Jervis has served on high-profile panels investigating intelligence failures.

With both MESA and IR scholarship either ignoring or underplaying the lethal potential of radical Islam, terrorist studies in general and Islamic terrorism in particular, were limited to a small cadre of experts and think tanks. In the wave of post–September "soul searching," one observer lamented that, before the attack, terrorist studies were an "academic backwater;" and another added that a "principle interest in terrorism virtually guarantees exclusion from . . . academic positions" (Byman 2003, 140–141). Recognized by Schelling as a contributing factor to the "poverty of expectations" phenomenon, such omissions hampered the predictive capacity of the United States. To recall, scholars who participated in the 2000 National Intelligence Council survey ranked terrorism scarcely above the dangers of overpopulation. Further down the intellectual food chain, Paul Pillar and other intelligence followers of John Esposito failed to incorporate a megaterrorist attack into their prognostication.

9/11 discredited the MESA paradigm and the epistemic community formed around it. In the Kuhnian sequence, MESA rivals could now claim victory in the predictive game, thus legitimizing their own position in the national discourse. At the applied level, this somewhat disparate coalition of traditional hard-liners, neoconservatives, and Christian evangelicals turned their own paradigmatic assumptions into a foreign policy blueprint for Iraq.

Foreign Policy Level: Containment versus Preemption

There was nothing in the initial contacts between Saddam Hussein and the United States to indicate that Iraq would emerge as a testing ground for a number of novel foreign policy experiments. As detailed in chapter 2, the outgoing Carter administration and its Republican successor entertained the modest hope that Hussein could be persuaded to replace the shah of Iran as the new Twin Pillar. The decline of the Soviet Union and the unexpected resilience of the fundamentalist regime in Iran forced Washington to fashion a more coherent policy of behavior modification for Baghdad. With many in the scholarly community vouching for Hussein's newly found moderation, administrations of both Reagan and Bush Senior offered Iraq a range of political and economic incentives in exchange for joining the "community of nations."

Iraq's surprise invasion of Kuwait posed a challenge for the cautiously realistic foreign policy team of the older Bush. The subsequent policy of containing Iraq turned into a real ordeal for the domestically oriented and scandal-plagued Clinton administration. Most significantly, Baghdad was taxing the Liberal Internationalist creed, which the Carter-era appointees had fashioned. For the administration to succeed in containing Baghdad, a number of assumptions had to come true. Foremost was the belief that an effective multilateral effort led by the United Nations would keep the lid on Saddam Hussein's troublesome behavior.

However, by the end of Clinton's first term, this new exercise in behavior modification had run into a number of contradictions. First, the high level of international cooperation needed to sustain the sanction regime evaporated in the rush to strike deals with oil-rich Baghdad. Second, the United Nations, the lynchpin of "objective multilateralism," turned into an arena of anti-American challenges by France and other Iraqi allies. To make matters worse, the corruption-riddled Oil for Food program administered by the United Nations, bolstered rather than undermined Hussein's rule. Third, Baghdad's successful public relations campaign, amplified by a large assortment of leftists NGOs and antiglobalization advocates, painted the United States as a bully who starved Iraqi children. In the second Clinton administration, the high cost of "keeping Hussein in the box" was, as noted, bemoaned by Madeline Albright and other exasperated foreign policy officials. All this when the deterrent part of containment had eroded so badly that Baghdad faced few repercussions for expelling the UNSCOM inspectors.

With so much riding on the issue of deterrence, the behavior of the Iraqi dictator and, most specifically, the question of his rationality had turned into a cottage industry, replete with contentious but ultimately inconclusive debates. As indicated, part of the problem stemmed from the different ways in which rationality is defined in political science, not to mention clinical psychology. However, the question whether Hussein was rational and thus deterrable was also a dispute about the capacity of the Liberal Internationalist protocols to contain rogue states. Predictably, liberals were confident that the Iraqi dictator was rational enough to be deterred, a view that was vehemently challenged by their critics (Seliktar and Dutter 2006).

For the latter, the case of Iraq represented all that was wrong with Clinton's multilateralism, including his attempts to manage rogues and their terrorist protégés through the United Nations As noted, the House Republican Task Force compiled a record of alleged contacts between Iraq and al Qaeda to shame the Clinton administration. The Heritage Foundation list of sanction busting was yet another effort to expose the alleged bankruptcy of his Iraqi policy. To these critics, the mainstream media's scant attention to such reports was indicative of the willful disregard of reality in the service of Liberal Internationalism.

September 11 not only discredited much of the liberal international creed but also focused attention on the hitherto theoretical link between Islamist terrorists, WMD, and state sponsors. Although "smoking gun" evidence was scarce, the unexpectedly advanced state of al Qaeda's *al Zabadi* program and the anthrax attacks in the fall of 2001, combined with the widespread assumption about Iraq's capabilities, prompted George W. Bush to argue for a preemptive attack as a prelude for regime change.

Articulated in the National Security Directive of September 2002 and subsequently elaborated by administration officials, there were two parts to this argument. First, containing a rogue such as Saddam Hussein was a costly and ultimately futile gamble, given his craftiness and the willingness of the international community to break UN resolutions. The administration pointed out that "coercive containment" and "intrusive inspections" were short-term remedies executed only after the United States threatened an invasion. Hussein's ability to outwit and manipulate restrictions without abandoning his goals or belligerence was seen as proof that sustained and highly punitive containment was not a viable option. Second, as links between a WMD-equipped rogues and terrorist organization were inherently murky, with the margin for error in assessments virtually nonexistent, administration held that preempting the threat was the only way to safeguard the United States.

This so called one percent doctrine was part of a broader strategy of dealing with emerging threats long advocated by strategic theorists such as Thomas Schelling and Albert and Roberta Wohlstetter. By acknowledging the narrow margin for error, the National Security Directive had also legitimized a more subjective way of intelligence analysis.

INTELLIGENCE LEVEL: OBJECTIVE VERSUS SUBJECTIVE

Historically, the CIA was mandated to provide objective and impartial intelligence to Washington policymakers. To recall, Sherman Kent, the architect of the Directorate of Intelligence reflecting the then strong positivist belief in a "rational" political universe, decreed that experts could analyze reality in an objective and detached way. To avoid "contamination," Kent demanded a separation between the operational and analytic branches, a policy enforced well into the 1990s. For their part, through the Church committee, the Carter-Turner reform, and the Clinton-Deutch "reformation," Democrats tried to ensure that the CIA would uphold the high ethical standards of undercover operations deemed essential for a democratic society. Combined with a zeal for Kentian analytical objectivism, this so-called liddism, that is, keeping the lid on intelligence, preoccupied academic experts and intelligence practitioners right up to the al Qaeda attack (Gill 2004).

That the DI and the DO could not maintain such high standards should have been clear from their failure to predict the fundamentalist revolution in Iran. The Carter reform, which all but eliminated HUMINT (human intelligence) in favor of the ethically "clean" SIGINT, greatly hindered the understanding of the complex and murky world of Islamism. The collapse of the Soviet Union was a reminder that "objective" and "quantifiable" data used in the Soviet estimate ignored the underlying economic pathologies. Reflecting what one observer called a "culture of exactitude," the CIA had continued to use GNP and other statistical tools, even when it became clear that the Soviet Union's endemic corruption and mismanagement made a mockery of rational economic measurements (Seliktar 2004, 186–192, 215).

Overshadowed by the headline-grabbing demands to turn the CIA into a branch of the Library of Congress, efforts to study the Agency's failed analytical traditions were few and far between. A number of issues, including the politicization of the DI as epitomized in the Soviet estimate, the dispute over the use of émigrés and dissident informants, the handling of murky data, and the ontological and epistemic problems of dealing with the resulting uncertainty, needed urgent attention. To tackle these issues, the CIA established the Sherman Kent Center for Intelligence Analysis, but the results were meager.

Acknowledging that intelligence officials are creatures of the paradigms they favor would have put an end to the myth of an "objective and dispassionate analyst." Though Donald Rumsfeld, Paul Wolfowitz, and other disciples of Wohlstetter and Schelling took up the problem of built-in biases and uncertainty management, their efforts were dismissed as partisan posturing akin to the Team B exercise. The Commission to Assess the Ballistic Missile Threat to the United States that analyzed high-impact, low-probability events and warned analysts "not too quickly dismiss dangers simply because of a lack of hard evidence or clear precedent" was harshly assailed by liberals. In their view, such second-guessing of intelligence analysis was driven by "suspicion of experts, who, through adherence to inductive reasoning and academic methodologies, claim to provide objective research and analysis" (Davis 2003; Foer 2004, 17–18).

Much of the same disagreement pertained to the use of regime opponents. Historically, CIA was suspicious of émigrés and dissidents on account of their political bias, a decision that contributed to the erroneous Soviet estimate. The fact that William Casey made extensive use of émigrés in his quest to undermine the Soviet regime, made them even less popular with the Soviet division in the Directorate of Intelligence (SOVA) , where dislike of Casey and his deputy Robert Gates was running high (Seliktar 2004, 215, 218). In the Iraqi case, the CIA and DoD engaged in a bitter quarrel over the respective merits of Iyad Alawi's INF as opposed to Ahmed Chalabi's INC. This was not entirely surprising because, as already detailed, the "Chalabi issue" was a proxy for the larger Agency debate on the wisdom of regime change. September 11 presented the Wolhstetterians with an opportunity to challenge some of the Kentian analytical practices. To recall, Rumsfeld, Wolfowitz, and Shulsky, all believed that doctrinal emphasis on objective analysis coupled with insistence on "smoking gun" evidence was the root cause of predictive failures. Seasoned observers of the SOVA battles and veterans of Team B exercise, they were ready to publicly admit that intelligence officers fall short of the ideal of absolute objectivity. The Wolhstetterians have also emphasized that data on the terrorist-rogue state nexus is complex, ambiguous, and subject to intentional deception and bona fide misinterpretation. Accordingly, filling such "unknowns" required a creative and more subjective reading of data. Since analysts could not be expected to deal with the resulting uncertainty, an interface between intelligence and policymakers was, in this view, crucial. Efforts to change the intelligence analysis, however, proved to be an uphill task. As described, serious centers of opposition to intelligence on Iraqi nuclear program and its ties with al Qaeda emerged within the CIA and the State Department. To complicate matters, tensions within individual agencies escalated into rival interagency quarrels, at times paralyzing the estimative effort altogether.

Whatever the merits of the subjective approach, the Iraqi debacle has discredited its architects. Academic intelligence experts dismissed the innovations introduced by the DoD group as a "method, tested and tried by the right" to challenge the CIA on "political ground" (Ryan 2006, 286). Another aggressive intelligence effort, Terrorism Information Awareness renamed Total Information Awareness (TIA), was described by critics as a "wet dream for Big Brother" and subsequently abolished by Congress (Gill 2004, 476).

The backlash against aggressive methods of data gathering and analysis has surfaced at all levels. Schelling and Wohlstetter were described as "blind oracles" and critics railed against the use of torture to extract actionable evidence (Kuklick 2006). Much to the relief of Goodman (2003) and other advocates of intelligence oversight, calls to stop the "politicization of intelligence" and demands to give the State Department a larger role in intelligence analysis have been on the increase. Sensing an opportunity, some Liberal Internationalists renewed their calls for a truly international intelligence-gathering operation attached to the United Nations. Anthony Kennedy (2006, 246–273) the Yale professor made famous by his "decline theory," went so far as to advocate the establishment of a Directorate of Intelligence operated by the UN bureaucracy.

Nowhere has been the return to the "culture of exactitude" more pronounced than among critics of risk-rating system for homeland security. The U.S. General Accounting Office (GAO) recommended that public warning on threats should include "specific, consistent, accurate and clear information on the nature of the threat, location, and . . . time frames." The prominent British authority on security, Lawrence Freedman noted that GAO did not specify how such high-grade information can be obtained (Freedman 2005, 380).

Because intelligence collection and analysis have emerged as major election issues, this backlash is neither surprising nor avoidable. In the intensely partisan atmosphere of the discourse, the structural reform that created the post of the National Director of Intelligence represents the limit of the consensus on avoiding surprise attack in the future. However, as this book indicates, structural reforms are only modestly effective in guarding against future threats because factors in predictive failure are paradigmatic in nature. The more low-key analytical remedy of creating a "devil's advocates" and/or "thinking outside the box" unit, known in the CIA as the "red cell," is not a guarantee for success either. When information is imperfect and uncertainty prevails, the ideological battles among intelligence officials tend to intensify. Under such circumstances, the amount of exactitude required in analytical products turns into one more skirmish in the internal struggle.

That intelligence analysts and outside experts were split on an array of issues pertaining to Pan-Islamic terrorism, unconventional weapons in Iraq, and its ties to al Qaeda has been made abundantly clear in this work. Yet in the postmortem recriminations, there was great reluctance to probe the fragmentation of the intelligence community and its open partisanship. Nor has there been much appetite to study why intelligence officials could recall dramatically different versions of similar events or change their account because of an altered structure of incentive (Levitt and Dubner 2005, 92).

Instead, the revisionist view holds that the administration's arm-twisting compelled the intelligence community, conveniently depicted as a unitary actor, to sign off on information that would justify Operation Iraqi Freedom. Whatever the merit of this argument, an emphasis on division, doubt, and uncertainly, which George Tenet candidly acknowledges in his memoir, would have detracted from the normative belief in Kentian intelligence. To make matters more complicated, learning from past intelligence failures is not a panacea for avoiding pitfalls in the future. Lesson from the past "can be confounded by paradigmatic disagreements prompting different observers to learn different lessons" (Headly 2005). In cases of terrorism where even *post factum* "smoking gun" evidence is difficult to obtain, dramatically different conclusions can emerge.

The continuous debate about bin Laden operations in East Asia is a case in point. A number of books supportive of the George W. Bush administration's contention that al Qaeda operated an extensive network in the region received a negative review from an expert who noted that "sourced academic judgment gives way to conclusions . . . that bear surprisingly resemblance to US foreign policy statements" (Brown 2006, 156, 161). Like other academic purists, this particular reviewer worried that a failure "to engage critically with . . . sources" and extensive reliance "on anonymous sources . . . [that] cannot be independently checked or verified" may altogether prevent a definitive reconstruction of past events pertaining to terrorist networks. As a result, "tentative allegations are transmitted, through a kind of process of academic Chinese whisper into established fact." How to "engage critically" with murky terrorist sources was left unexplained.

Ironically, reliance on sources whose identity, reliability, and political motivation are difficult to verify is common in the public discourse, especially as intelligence has been "privatized" by journalists, Web sites, and critics who use anonymous sources or sensationalized known ones. When al Libi, claiming torture, recanted his testimony linking Iraq to al Qaeda's chemical production, the new version was routinely used by critics to denounce the administration. An Internet search reveals that the number of references to al Libi far exceeds that to *al Zabadi*. Privatized intelligence is especially harmful because it tends to legitimize one version over another through sheer repetition. Tenet's (2007, 243) comments that "we just don't know" when al Libi spoke the truth is a sober reminder that in complex deception systems, truth can be elusive.

Politicized or sensationalized use of intelligence sources is a poor substitute for the more demanding debate on the difficulties of obtaining and verifying information on terrorist networks and rogue states. As noted, the Unites States relied on a wide variety of sources, including friendly intelligence services in the West and the Middle East, the IAEA, and UNSCOM (Iraqi National Congress, and Iraqi National Accord) to monitor the Iraqi regime and track its WMD programs in the 1990s. Informed by their respective intelligence services, King Hussein, King Fahd, Prince Bandar, and President Mubarak believed that Saddam Hussein would not invade Kuwait; the KGB conveyed the same message to James Baker through the then Soviet foreign minister Eduard Shevardnadze. The IAEA under Hans Blix found no evidence of lethal programs, a view fully reflected in the CIA assessment.

The role of foreign intelligence in the run-up to Operation Iraqi Freedom shows the same pattern. Richard Butler, the last UNSCOM head, along with virtually all foreign intelligence agencies, was convinced that Iraq possessed a lethal arsenal. Iraq's alleged efforts to buy yellow cake in Niger were brought to the attention of the CIA by Britain's MI6. According to the subsequent inquiry of the House of Commons led by Lord Butler (2004), the

Rome forgery aside, there was credible evidence from multiple sources to suspect that Iraq was considering the purchase of the uranium ore. Although Curveball proved to be unreliable, according to Lord Butler (2004, 127), his testimony was in line with UNSCOM's information that Iraq was planning to manufacture biological agents in "mobile production centers." Before his change of heart, Scott Ritter (1999, 202) considered Chalabi's sources to be reliable, writing that "he has a network of well placed informants in Iraq" who provided "some information" that "proved to be of considerable value to UNSCOM's work."

In spite of the continuous preoccupation with Curveball, the larger issue of relations with foreign intelligence services and their assets has hardly been discussed. Jennifer Sims (2006), a former liaison with foreign intelligence agencies, warned that such cooperation can end up to be a "deal with the devil." Besides stating the obvious, there is little in her article to provide a better understanding of this complex issue. Along the same lines, there is a need for a debate on the merits of working with dissidents and refugees beyond the de rigueur reviling of Chalabi and Curveball. Historically, such sources have a mixed record, but in spite of the risk, there are few alternatives for penetrating highly denied regimes.

It would be impossible to conclude the discussion of the sensationalization and politicization of intelligence without pointing out the role of Congress. Congressional intelligence committees were set up to provide an objective oversight of the community. However, evidence presented here demonstrates that partisanship built into the oversight process has harmed the predictive endeavor. Leaks, a weapon of choice in Washington, have been used, sometimes with far-reaching consequences, as the Guatemala-"Deutch scrub" illustrates. Open dissent with regard to particular intelligence product poses another problem. The House Task Force on Terrorism was born out of Republican frustration with the perceived slow pace of CIA's inquiry into Islamist terrorism. How to keep oversight from partisan uses, let alone inflamed political passions, has eluded experts and practitioners alike.

Still, a more dispassionate analysis is essential not just for those who would probe the predictive predicament of September 11 and Operation Iraqi Freedom. The dimensions that make up forecasting—the paradigmatic, policy, and intelligence—harbor numerous potential pitfalls. The fractured academic community, the deep division among the foreign policy elite, and the politicized intelligence community could exacerbate these problems as the United States faces an uncertain intelligence future.

Understanding the "Great Unknown": Islamic Terrorism, Rogue States, and WMD—Round Two

It is customary in the concluding chapter of a work such as this to offer some suggestions about avoiding a predictive predicament in the future. With the ongoing challenge of Pan-Islamic terrorism, WMD, and enigmatic dictatorships such as that of North Korea with possible links to Syria and fundamentalist Iran, the difficulties are as daunting as ever.

To the extent that this study offers more general insights into prediction of terrorist networks, rogue states, and closed societies, its implications are sobering. To be successful, intelligence warnings have to be issued early enough to alert the administration and enable it to intervene effectively to avert a crisis or seize an opportunity. However, none of the problems highlighted in the Iraqi case are easy to resolve.

At the paradigmatic level, the question about the sources of Arab discontent and exceptionalism and the way in which to remedy them has been left unanswered. There is little doubt that much of Iraqi behavior was driven by Saddam Hussein's pathology rather than any particular "Arabism." At the same time, an argument can be made that his sultantist regime could only be sustained because of the peculiar tribalism and ethnoreligiosity of the Iraqi political culture. Because of the inconclusive nature of the Iraqi case, the debate between those who see the Arab-Israeli conflict as the major problem in the Middle East and those who blame Islamist nationalism fueled by Iran, has continued unabated. In a heuristically interesting exercise of "what if" Josef Joffe (2005) the editor of *The Zeit,* argued that in a "world without Israel," stagnant and corrupt Arab regimes would still be the norm. Joffe's article prompted Juan Cole (2005) to assert that without the 1948 War, there would have been a liberal Egypt and Lebanon and "authoritarian governance would be much less prevalent." However, Ajami (2005, 63–65, 2007) found Cole's writing to be a reflection of the habit of "the Arab intellectual class...to "assign Israel a large place in its autopsy of what ails them."

Although ostensibly focused on Israel, the stakes in this exchange are much higher. Since 9/11 made it hard to maintain that radical Islamism is a figment of imagination of those seeking to create a new bogeyman, MESA scholars and their epistemic allies have mobilized to push the view that al Qaeda and, by implication, Hezbollah, Hamas, and Iran, are quite rational and limited in their demands. Accordingly, the United States could go a long way to assuage their concern by curtailing its pro-Israeli policy and withdrawing its troops from the Middle East. Jimmy Carter's *Peace Not Apartheid* is a popular reflection of this movement. The effort to adopt the MESA paradigm to IR has been led, as indicated, by Mearsheimer and Walt. A 2007 survey of IR professors found that this strategy has been successful. A large majority believes that the Arab-Israeli conflict is to blame for Middle East ills and 66 percent agrees that Israeli lobby has too much influence on American foreign policy (Maliniak et al. 2007).

If, on the other hand, the anti-Israeli animus is just a "rational" fig leaf to cover an apocalyptical struggle for world domination, as the "clash of civilizations" theory holds, "the struggle becomes existential" and there is little hope that "changing U.S. policy would decrease support for al Qaeda" (Byman 2003, 143, 147; Paz 2007). By drawing on doctrinal pronouncement and actual behavior, Efraim Karsh (2006, 207), a leading Middle East scholar, has concluded that Islamists are planning to revive the Islamic empire. According to their vision, Israel's existence in the Middle East is just a short-lived aberration in the unfolding historical process that would culminate in the Islamic triumph in the region and beyond. The Hizb ut Tahrir, a growing pan-Islamic movement advocating the revival of the Islamic Caliphate could be construed as supportive of this argument.

At the foreign policy level, the divisions are equally daunting. Both Liberal Internationalists and Realists have pushed for negotiations with North Korea and Iran. The former believe that conflict, a rarely acceptable form of action, can be settled within the extant international framework, including sanctions and inspections (Lopez and Cortright 2004). The latter are predisposed to a universalistic notion that WMD have a deterrent logic of their own that flows from the destructive nature of the weapons. Both use assumed rationality-cum- unitary actor approach when evaluating the behavior of exotic dictatorships. In a testimony to the enduring appeal of such heuristics, the Iraq Study Group has consistently referred to "Iran" rather than to its controversial president Mahmoud Ahmadinejad or other actors.

Critics of the ISG have argued that, as in Iraq, the rationality of dictators cannot be taken for granted. According to this view, culture, religion, or personal idiosyncrasy can trump the assumed logic of deterrence and trigger a regional or global conflagration. To illustrate this point, they suggest that Ahmadinejad's behavior—threats to eliminate Israel, Holocaust denial, and determination to continue with the nuclear program in spite of the presumed cost to Iran—are deviations from unitary actor rationality. These and other analysts have suggested that Iran has a long history of manipulating the West and negotiating in bad faith. Not incidentally, scientists from the Sensor System Division at the Pentagon-funded Lincoln Laboratory have included deception and insincere negotiations in their inventory of asymmetrical threats to the United States (Primmerman 2006). Violations of sanctions by Russia and France should make it clear that mendacity is not limited to rogues.

Syrian and Iranian support for Islamic terrorism poses an equally difficult quandary. In the immediate aftermath of 9/11, even the liberal Brookings Institution acknowledged that identifying state sponsorships of translational terrorist networks is difficult. Brookings and U.S. Institute of Peace scholars argue that denying terrorist organizations sanctuary and support by "any and all countries" will disrupt and cripple them. However, there is no evidence that their preferred method, the so-called shrewd sanctions have dissuaded either Syria or Iran from sponsoring a wide array of Islamist terrorist groups.

By far, the intelligence level predicament is the most challenging. Robert Gates, who replaced Donald Rumsfeld as secretary of defense in 2006, announced that any future United States actions would be based on high evidentiary standards of intelligence. How to obtain such quality information in the notoriously fuzzy world of Islamist terrorism that may be linked to shadowy state sponsors, is far from clear. Calls to develop "analytical frameworks" to incorporate the "increased complexity" stemming from "religiously motivated terrorism" have produced few results.

The debate on the role of Iran in fueling the Iraqi insurgency is a case in point. Intelligence showing that Teheran supplied weapons to Shiite groups to target Americans has been challenged by an array of Democratic critics and self-appointed media watchers. In a sign of heightened sensitivity to such scrutiny, the Bush administration was forced to admit that a direct link to the Iranian leadership cannot be proved beyond reasonable doubt. Plans by the administration to declare the Iranian Revolutionary Guards a terrorist organization have met with a mixed response.

Predicting a large-scale terrorist attack on the United States could be even more daunting, given a return to a culture of analytical exactitudes and human rights concerns about methods of information gathering. Complicating matters, pre-9/11-style divisions among observes have emerged again.

Intelligence officials and academic experts on terrorism have asserted that al Qaeda and/or other Islamist groups are intent on carrying out a WMD assault on America. Tenet (2007, 273–274) speculated that Ayman al Zawahiri called off a planned cyanide attack on the New York subway in early 2003 because the device, the "mobtaker," could not deliver a spectacular enough result. These experts estimate that the range of possible weapons to be used in a lethal attack has actually expanded since 9/11 to include nuclear devices, radiological bombs, chemical agents, and bioterrorism. The last is said to have become very attractive due to recent advances in molecular biology, which makes manufacturing and weaponizing biological agents easy (Hellmich and Redig 2007). To deal with the shadowy nature of state sponsorship, the intelligence community and the Department of Defense have worked on the so-called nuclear attribution problems (Sanger and Shanker 2007). As for timing of a catastrophic attack, intelligence experts emphasize that al Qaeda is known to be very patient, a pattern demonstrated in its previous actions. On the basis of these and other estimates, one influential observer has painted a chilling picture of Islam and terror in the Second Nuclear Age (Feldman 2006b).

Many IR and Middle East scholars have rejected the catastrophic terrorism scenario. In a *Foreign Affairs* article Mueller (2006) argues that the absence of a major attack means that al Qaeda "must not be trying very hard, or must be far less dedicated, diabolic, and competent than the common image would assume." The article implies that bin Laden might have abandoned catastrophic terrorism altogether because of concerns about public opinion in the Muslim word. Mueller notes that "although some Arab and Muslims took pleasure" in the suffering inflicted by 9/11, the "common response among jihadists and religious nationalists was a vehement rejection of al Qaeda strategy." Lustick (2006, 71, 173) warns that America is psychologically trapped in an "abstract and far reaching war on terror" reminiscent of the cold war scare. He urges "clear thinking" to reconceptualize the problem and accuses some experts, including Graham Allison, of "framing" the terrorist threat through selectively quoting of Abu Ghait and other Islamists. Lustick's book is long on reference to other "clear thinkers" in the academic community, but short on specifics such as al Qaeda's efforts to develop a second generation of *al Zabadi* products.

Divisions have also plagued the assessment of the Iranian nuclear program, raising a broader question about the ability of intelligence services to discern the precise status of enemy weapons system. On occasion, this notoriously difficult estimate has been colored by partisanship. In one public display, a Republican on the House Intelligence Committee accused the CIA of downplaying the pace of Iran's nuclear development. Such charges have intensified after Democrats regained control of Congress in 2007.

That the intelligence process should retreat, at least partially, to a pre-9/11 mode is understandable. Just as it has undertaken other "course corrections," the CIA now looks to the past to better understand the future. But, as this work makes clear, some of these corrections may carry a high predictive cost and, if Wohlstetter and Schelling are right, they contain the seeds of the next surprise attack. Acknowledgment of such problems is essential for improving forecasting, and therein lie challenges for future studies.

Bibliography

Abdo, Geneive 2001. Re-thinking the Islamic Republic: A Conversation with Ayatollah Hossein Ali Montazeri. *Middle East Journal* 55: 9–24.

Aburish, Said K. 1985. *Payoff: Wheeling and Dealing in the Arab World*. London: Andre Deutsch.

———. 2000. *Saddam Hussein: The Politics of Revenge*. New York: Bloomsburg Press.

Ackerman, Spencer, and John B. Judis. 2003. The Operator: George Tenet Undermines the CIA. *New Republic,* September 12.

Adelman, Kenneth. 2002. Desert Storm II Would Be a Walk in the Park. *London Times,* August 29.

———. 2003. The Threat of Terror. In *The Next American Century,* ed. Jeffrey T. Bergner, 143–150. Lanham: Rowan & Littlefield.

Ahmad, Eqbal. 1991. Portents of a New Century. In *Beyond the Storm,* ed. Phyllis Bennis and Michael Moushabeck. New York: Olive Branch Press. 7–21.

———. 1998. After the Winter Bombs. *Dawn,* December 20.

———. 2000. *Confronting Empire: Interviews with David Barsamian*. Cambridge, MA: South End Press.

Ahmed, Nafeez Mossaddeq. 2005. *The War on Truth. 9/11, Disinformation and the Anatomy of Terrorism*. Northampton, MA: Olive Branch Press.

Ajami, Fouad. 1981. *The Arab Predicament. Arab Political Thought and Practice since 1967.* Cambridge: Cambridge University Press.

———. 2003a. The Anti-Americans. *Wall Street Journal,* July 3.

———. 2003b. Iraq and the Arab Future. *Foreign Affairs* 82 (January–February): 2–18.

———. 2004. Best Intentions. *New Republic,* January 28.

———. 2005. A Bold Experiment. *Foreign Policy* 147 (March–April): 63–64.

———. 2006. *The Foreigner's Gift: The American, the Arabs, and the Iraqis in Iraq*. New York: Free Press.

———. 2007. The American Iraq. *Wall Street Journal,* January 30.

Albright, Madeleine. 2003. *Madam Secretary: A Memoir*. New York: Miramax Books.

———. 2006. *Mighty and Almighty: Reflection on America, God, and World Affairs*. New York: HarperCollins.

Albright, David, and Khidhir Hamza. 1998. Iraq's Reconstitution of Its Nuclear Program. *Arms Control Today* 28: 9–15.

Algosaibi, Ghazi A. 1993. *The Gulf Crisis: An Attempt to Understand*. London: Kegan Paul International.

al Jabri, Mohammed A. 1982. *Arab Political Discourse*. Beirut: Center for Arab Unity Studies.

al-Khalil, Samir. 1989. *Republic of Fear: The Inside Story of Saddam's Iraq*. New York: Pantheon Books.

Allison, Graham. 2005. *Nuclear Terrorism: The Ultimate Preventable Disaster.* New York: An Owl Book.

Almond, Gabriel. 1990. *A Discipline Divided: Scholars and Sects in Political Science.* Newbury Park, CA: Sage.

———. 1996. Political Theory and Political Science. *The American Political Science Review* 60: 869–879.

Almond, Gabriel, and Sidney Verba. 1965. *The Civic Culture.* Boston: Little, Brown.

Alterman, Eric. 1991. No. Hussein Was One of Kind. *New York Times,* March 4.

Amin, Samir. 1982. *The Arab Economy Today.* London: Zed Press.

Amirie, Abbas, and Hamilton A. Twitchell. 1978. Synthesis, In *Iran in the 1980s,* ed. Abbas Amirie and Hamilton A. Twitchell. Teheran: Institute for International Political and Economic Studies.

Anderson, Myrolene. 1986. Cultural Concatenation of Deceit and Secrecy. In *Deception: Perspective on Human and Nonhuman Deceit,* ed. Robert W. Mitchell and Nicholas S. Thomson. Albany: State of New York Press. 323–340.

Arend, Anthony Clark. 2003. International Law and Preemptive Use of Military Force. *Washington Quarterly* 26: 89–103.

Arkin, William M. 1996. Calculated Ambiguity: Nuclear Weapons and the Gulf War. *The Washington Quarterly* 19: 3–18.

———. 2002. The Secret War. *Los Angeles Times,* October 27.

Arnove, Anthony. 2000. Iraq under Siege. *Monthly Review,* December 7: 14–25.

Ash, Timothy G. 2004. *Free World. America, Europe, and the Surprising Future of the West.* New York: Random House.

Aswad, Barbara C. 1993. Arab Americans: Those Who Followed Columbus. *MESA Bulletin* 27: 14–17.

Auster, Bruse B. 1998. An Inside Look at Terror, Inc. *US News and World Report,* October 19.

Axelgard, Frederick W. 1986a. *Iraq in Transition: A Political, Economic, and Strategic Perspective.* Boulder: Westview Press.

———. 1986b. War and Oil: Implications for Iraq's Postwar Role in Gulf Security. In *Iraq in Transition: A Political, Economic, and Strategic Perspective,* ed. Frederick W. Axelgard. Boulder: Westview Press. 1–20

———. 1988. *A New Iraq: The Gulf War and Implications for U.S. Policy.* New York: Praeger.

———. 1989. Iraq. The Postwar Political Setting. *American-Arab ffairs* 28: 30–37.

Babbin, Jed. 2004. *Inside the Asylum. Why the United Nations and Old Europe Are Worse than You Think.* Washington, DC: Regnery.

Bacevich, Andrew J. 1993. Strategic Studies: In from the Cold. *SAIS Review* 13: 11–23.

———. 2001. Terrorizing the Truth. *Foreign Policy* (July–August): 74–75.

Baer, Robert. 2002. *See No Evil: The True Story of a Ground Soldier in the CIA's War on Terrorism.* New York: Crown Publishers.

———. 2003. *Sleeping with the Devil: How Washington Sold Our Soul for Saudi Crude.* New York: Three Rivers Press.

Baker, James A. 1995. *The Politics of Diplomacy: Revolution, War, and Peace: 1989–1992 with Thomas M. Defrank.* New York: G.P. Putnam's and Sons.

———. 2000. Iraq: Ten Years Later: Sanctions Weaken Saddam's Threat. *American Legion Magazine* 149: 12–17.

Baker, Peter. 2000. *The Breach: Inside the Impeachment and Trial of William Jefferson Clinton.* New York: Scribner's Sons.

Baker, Peter, and Susan Baker. 2005. *Kremlin Rising: Vladimir Putin's Russia and the End of the Revolution*. New York: A Lisa Drew Book/Scribner's Sons.
Baldwin, David. A. 1999–2000. The Sanctions Debate and the Logic of Choice. *International Security* 24: 80–107.
Bamford, James. 2001. *Body of Secrets. Anatomy of the Ultra-secret National Security Agency*. New York: Doubleday.
———. 2004. *A Pretext for War: 9/11, Iraq, and the Abuse of America's Intelligence Services*. New York: Doubleday.
Baram, Amazia. 1980. Saddam Hussein: A Political Biography. *Jerusalem Quarterly* 17: 115–144.
———. 1991. *Culture, History, and Ideology in the Formation, of the Ba'athist Iraq*. New York: St. Martin's Press.
———. 1995. The Regime #2 Defects. *Middle East Quarterly* 2: 15–22.
———. 2000. The Effect of Iraqi Sanctions: Statistical Pitfalls and Responsibility. *Middle East Journal* 54: 194–223.
———. 2002. The Iraqi Invasion of Kuwait. In *The Saddam Hussein Reader*, ed. Turie Munthe. New York: Thunder's Mouth Press. 251–287.
Barber, Benjamin R. 1995. *Jihad vs. McWorld*. New York: Times Books.
———. 1997–98. Fantasy of Fear. Huntington and the West versus the Rest. *Harvard International Review* 22: 66–71.
Barnett, Michael N. 1998. *Dialogues in Arab Politics*. New York: Columbia University Press.
Barnett, Thomas P.M. 2003. The Pentagon's New Map. *Esquire*, March.
Barton, Frederick D., and Bathsheba Crocker. 2003. Winning the Peace in Iraq. *Washington Quarterly* 26: 7–22.
Battle, Joyce, and Thomas Blanton. 2007. Ed. *Top Secret Polo Step*. Washington: National Security Archive Electronic Briefing Book no. 214. February 14. www.gwu.edu/~nsarchiv/NSAEBB/NSA Ebb2114/index.htm-45-(accessed September 20, 2007).
Beinart, Peter. 2004. State of Mind. *The New Republic*, April 12.
Beinin, Joel. 1988. Israel: The Political Economy of a Garrison State and Its Future. In *The Next Arab Decade. Alternative Futures*, ed. Hisham Sharabi. Boulder: Westview Press.
———. 2003. Middle East Studies after September 11, 2001. *MESA Bulletin* 37: 2–19.
Beitz, Charles R. 1999. International Liberalism and Distributive Justice. *World Politics* 51: 269–296.
Bengio, Ofra. 1998. *Saddam's World: The Political Discourse in Iraq*. Oxford: Oxford University Press.
———. 2002. Saddam Husayan's Novel of Fear. *Middle East Quarterly* 9 (Winter): 9–18.
Benjamin, Daniel, and Steven Simon. 2003. *The Age of Sacred Terror: Radical Islam's War against America*. New York: Freedom House.
———. 2005. *The Next Attack: The Failure of the War on Terror and a Strategy of Getting It Right*. New York: Henry Holt.
Bennet, Brian, and Vivienne Walt. 2004. Field of Jihad. *Time*, February 23.
Bennis, Phyllis. 1991. False Consensus: George Bush's United Nations. In *Beyond the Storm*, ed. Phyllis Bennis and Michael Moushabeck. New York: Olive Branch Press. 112–125.
———. 1996. *Calling the Shots: How Washington Dominates Today's UN*. New York: Olive Branch Press.

Bennis, Phyllis. 2000. The Lift the Sanctions Resolution that Doesn't. IPS Release. Washington: Institute for Policy Studies. January 12.

———. 2002. Talking Points. IPS Release, Washington: Institute for Policy Studies, February 14.

Berger, Samuel. 2000. A Foreign Policy for the Global Age. *Foreign Affairs* 79: 22–39.

———. 2002. *Senate Armed Services Committee Testimony,* September 25.

Berkowitz, Bruce. 2002. Intelligence and the War on Terrorism. *Orbis* 45: 289–332.

Betts, Richard K. 1997. Should Strategic Studies Survive? *World Politics* 50: 7–33.

———. 1998. The New Threat of Mass Destruction. *Foreign Affairs* 77: 26–41.

———. 2002. Fixing Intelligence. *Foreign Affairs* 81: 43–59.

Bhatia, Shyam, and Daniel McGrory. 2000. *Brighter than the Sun: Saddam's Hussein Threat to the United States.* Washington, DC: Regnery.

Bialer, Seweryn. 1986. The Question of Legitimacy. In *States and Societies,* ed. David Held, 418–430. Oxford: Basil Blackwell.

Binder, Leonard. 1966. Preface. *Politics of Lebanon,* ed. Leonard Binder. New York: John Wiley.

Binder, Leonard, James S. Coleman, Joseph LaPalombara, Lucian W. Pye, Sidney Verba, and Myron Weiner. 1971. Eds. *Crisis and Sequence in Political Development.* Princeton: Princeton University Press.

Bipartisan Disaster. 2006. Article published in *Prospect.* London: Prospect Publishing.

Bitzinger, Richard A. 1994. The Globalization of the Arms Industry. *International Interaction* 19: 170–198.

Blaustein, Susan. 2002. Editorial. *Washington Post,* August 4.

Blix. Hans. 2004. *Disarming Iraq.* New York: Pantheon Books.

Blumenthal, Sidney. 2003. *The Clinton Wars.* New York: Farrar, Straus, and Giroux.

Bodansky, Yossef. 1999. *Bin Laden: The Man Who Declared War on America.* Rocklin, CA: Forum.

Bolton, John R. 2001. Clandestine War in Indonesia. *International Journal of Intelligence and Counterintelligence* 14: 121–127.

Boot, Max. 2002. Look Who Likes Deterrence Now: The Left's New Love Affair with Containment. *Weekly Standard,* November 11.

———. 2006. It's Not Over Yet. *Time,* September 11.

Borger, Julian. 2002. Inside Story; The Anthrax Hunter. *The Guardian,* April 10.

Boroujerdi, Mehrzad. 1996. *Iranian Intellectuals and the West: The Tormented Triumph of Nativism.* Syracuse, NY: Syracuse University Press.

Boyer, Peter J. 2004. The Believer. *New Yorker,* November 1.

Bracken, Paul. 2003. The Structure of the Second Nuclear Age. *Orbis* 47(3): 399–413.

Bratton, Michael, and Nicolas Van De Valle. 1994. Neopatrimonial Regimes and Political Transitions in Africa. *World Politics* 46: 453–489.

Bremer, L. Paul. 1995. Seizing the Initiative: The US Role in Combating Global Terrorism. *Harvard International Review* 17: 76–78.

———. 2000. *Countering the Changing Threat of International Terrorism.* Washington: Report of the National Committee on Terrorism.

Brzezinski, Zbigniew. 2004. Lowered Vision. *New Republic,* June 7 and 14.

———. 2006. A Dangerous Exception. Why Should the Israeli Lobby Be Immune from Criticism. *Foreign Policy,* July–August. 63–64.

Brooks, David. 2004. *The Republican Noise Machine: Right Wing Media and How It Corrupts Democracy*. New York: Crown Publishers.

Brown, Graham. 2006. The Perils of Terrorism: Chinese Whispers, Kevin Bacon, and Al Qaeda in South East Asia. *Intelligence and National Security* 21: 150–162.

Brown, Michael B. 1985. *Models in Political Economy: A Guide to the Argument*. Boulder: Lynne Rienner.

Buchanan, Patrick J. 1999. *A Republic, Not an Empire: Reclaiming American Destiny*. Washington DC: Regnery.

Bulliet, Richard W. 1993. The Future of the Islamic Movement. *Foreign Affairs* 72: 38–44.

———. 1994. Rhetoric, Discourse, and the Future of Hope. In *Under Siege. Islam and Democracy*, ed. Richard W. Bulliet. New York: Middle East Institute of Columbia University., 1–13.

Bulloch, John, and Harvey Morris. 1991. *Saddam's War: The Origins of the Kuwait Conflict and the International Response*. London: Faber and Faber.

Burnell, Gibson, and Gareth Morgan. 1985. *Sociological Paradigms and Organizational Analysis. Elements of the Sociology of Corporate Life*. London: Heinemann.

Bush, George, and Brent Scowcroft. 1998. *A World Transformed*. New York: Alfred A. Knopf.

Butler, Lord. 2004. *Review of Intelligence on Weapons of Mass Destruction*. Report of a Committee of Privy Councilors. London: House of Commons, July 14. www. butlerreivew .org. uk/-6k (accessed September 20, 2007).

Butler, Richard 2000a. *The Greatest Threat: Iraq, Weapons of Mass Destruction, and the Growing Crisis of Global Security*. New York: Public Affairs Press.

———.2000b. Why Saddam Loves the Bomb. *Middle East Quarterly* 7: 65–75.

Buzby, Tonya Ugoretz. 1995. Saddam's Dysfunctional Family. *Middle East Quarterly* 2: 23–30.

Byman, Daniel l. 1999. Proceed with Caution: U.S. Support for the Iraqi Opposition. *Washington Quarterly* 22: 23–37.

———. 2003. Al-Qaeda as an Adversary. Do We Understand Our Enemy? *World Politics* 56: 139–163.

Byman, Daniel, Kenneth Pollack, and Gideon Rose. 1999. The Pullback Fantasy. *Foreign Affairs* 78: 24–41.

Callinicos. Alex. 2003. *The New Mandarins of American Power: The Bush Administration's Plans for the World*. Cambridge: U.K. Polity.

Callum, Robert. 2001. The Case for Cultural Diversity in the Intelligence Community. *International Journal of Intelligence and Counterintelligence* 14: 25–49.

Campbell, Joseph F. 1971. *The Foreign Affairs Fudge Factory*. New York: Basic Books.

Cardoso, Fernando, and Enzo Faletto. 1979. *Dependency and Development in Latin America*. Berkeley: University of California Press.

Carluci, Frank, Robert Hunter, and Zalmay Khalilzad. 2000. Taking Charge: A Bipartisan Report to the President Elect on Foreign Policy and National Security. Discussion Paper. Santa Monica: RAND.

Carothers, Thomas. 1999. *Aiding Democracy Abroad: The Learning Curve*. Washington: Carnegie Endowment for International Policy.

Carpenter, Ted Galen. 1994. The Balkan Crisis and the Faulty 1930s Analogy. *Mediterranean Quarterly* 5: 17–29.

Carpenter, Ted Galen. 1999–2000. Think Again: Civil Society. *Foreign Policy* 117 (Winter): 18–29.

Carter, Jimmy. 2005. *Our Endangered Values. America's Moral Crisis.* New York: Simon & Schuster.

Carus, W. Seth. 1989. A Threatening New Superpower. *Moment,* December: 50–57.

Chalabi, Ahmad. 1991. Iraq: The Past a Prologue? *Foreign Policy* 83: 20–29.

Chan, Stephen, and Andrew J. Williams. 1994. *Renegade States: The Evolution of Revolutionary Foreign Policy.* Manchester: Manchester University Press.

Chandler, Robert W., and Ronald J. Trees. 1996. *Tomorrow's War, Today's Decisions: Iraqi Weapons of Mass Destruction.* McLean, VA: Amcoda Press.

Chapman, Robert D. 2001. Dealing with Fanatics. *International Journal of Intelligence and Counterintelligence* 14: 127–133.

Charen, Mona. 2003. *Useful Idiots. How Liberals Got It All Wrong in the Cold War and Still Blame America First.* Washington, DC: Regnery.

Christopher, Warren. 1998. *In the Stream of History: Shaping Foreign Policy for a New Era.* Stanford: Stanford University Press.

Claire, Rodger William. 2004. *Raid on the Sun: Inside Israel's Secret Campaign That Denied Saddam the Bomb.* New York: Broadway Press.

Clark, Mark T. 1997. Deterrence in the Second Nuclear Age. *Orbis* (Winter): 130.

———. 1998. Emerging Security Threats. *Orbis* 42: 121–129.

Clarke, Richard A. 2004. *Against All Enemies: Inside America's War on Terror.* New York: Free Press.

———. 2006a. The Dark Side. *PBS Documentary,* June 20.

———. 2006b. Questions Surround Alleged al Qaeda Plot. *ABC News Website,* June 31.

Clarridge, Duane R. with Digby Diehl. 1997. *A Spy for All Seasons: My Life in the CIA.* New York: Scribner's Sons.

Clinton, Bill. 2004. *My Life.* New York: Alfred A. Knopf.

Clinton, William J. 1999. Memorandum on Assistance to Iraqi Democratic Opposition Organization. *Weekly Compilation of Presidential Documents,* February 8.

Cockburn, Alexander, and Ken Silverstein. 1996. *Washington Babylon.* London: Verso.

Cockburn, Andrew, and Patrick Cockburn. 2002. *Saddam Hussein: An American Obsession.* London: Verso.

Cohen, Eliot A. 2000. Defending America in the Twenty-First Century. *Foreign Affairs* 79: 40–56.

Cole, Juan. 2005. An Alternate Alternative History. *Foreign Policy* 147 (March–April): 61–62.

Coll, Steve. 2004. *Ghost Wars: The Secret History of the CIA, Afghanistan, and Bin Laden, from the Soviet Invasion to September 10, 2001.* New York: Penguin Press.

Cooley, John K. 1991. *Payback: America's Long Way in the Middle East.* Washington, DC: Brassey's.

Cordesman, Anthony H. 1987. *The Iranian-Iraq War and Western Security 1984–87: Strategic Implications and Policy Options.* London: Jane's Publishing.

———. 1999. *Iraq and the War of Sanctions. Conventional Threats and Weapons of Mass Destruction.* Westport, CT: Praeger.

Cordesman, Anthony H., and Ahmed S. Hashim. 1997. *Iraq Sanctions and Beyond.* Boulder: Westview Press.

Cortright, David. 2001. A Hard Look at Iraq Sanctions. *Nation*, December 3.
Cortright, David, and George A. Lopez. 2000. *The Sanctions Decade: UN Strategies in the 1990s*. Boulder: Lynne Rienner.
Coughlin, Con. 2002. *Saddam: King of Terror*. New York: Ecco Books.
———. 2006. *American Ally. Tony Blair and the War on Terror*. New York: Ecco Books.
Coulter, Ann. 2003. *Treason: Liberal Treachery for the Cold War to the War on Terrorism*. New York: Crown Forum.
Cox, Harvey. 1965. *The Secular City*. New York: Macmillan.
Craner, Lorne. 2006. Will U.S. Democratization Policy Work?
Democracy in the Middle East 13:3 (Summer). www.meforum.or/article/942-39k (accessed September 19, 2007).
Crawford, Beverly. 1996. Explaining Defection from International Cooperation. *World Politics* 48: 482–521.
Croddy, Eric. 2002. Dealing with Al Shifu: Intelligence and Counterproliferation. *International Journal of Intelligence and Counterintelligence* 15: 52–60.
Crossette, Barbara. 2000. U.S. Monitor Argues Iraqis Have Little to Conceal. *New York Times,* July 3.
Crowley, Michael. 2002. What Had Turned the Hawkish Iraq Inspector into a Dove? *Slate,* September 25.
Cupitt, Richard T. 2001. Hearing. U.S. Senate Committee on Banking, Housing and Urban Affairs. February 7.
Dabelko, David D., and Geoffrey D. Dabelko. 1993. The International Environment and the U.S. Intelligence Community. *International Journal of Intelligence and Counterintelligence* 6: 21–42.
Dan, Uri. 2003. Loose Lips. *JP,* December 18.
Daniel, Donald C., and Katherine L. Herbig. 1981. Propositions on Military Deception. In *Strategic Military Deception,* ed. Donald C. Daniel and Katherine L. Herbig. New York: Pergamon Press.
Darwish, Adel with Gregory Alexander. 1991. *Unholy Babylon: The Secret History of Saddam's War*. New York: St. Martin's Press.
Davis, Jack. 2003. *Strategic Warning: If Surprise Is Inevitable: What Role for Analysis?* Occasional Paper Washington: Sherman Kent Center for Intelligence Analysis, Central Intelligence Agency, January.
Dawisha, Adeed I. 1980–81. Iraq: The West's Opportunity. *Foreign Policy* 41: 134–153.
———. 1992. The United States and the Middle East: The Gulf War and Its Aftermath. *Current History* 91: 1–5.
———. 2000. Arab Nationalism and Islamism. *International Studies Review* 2: 79–90.
Dean, John. 2004. *Worse than Watergate: The Secret Presidency of George W. Bush*. New York: Little Brown.
De Atkine, Norvell B. 1994. Middle East Scholars Strike Out in Washington. *Middle East Quarterly* 1: 3–12.
Debate: 2006. "Democracy Is about More than Elections: Democracy in the Middle East." *Middle East Quarterly* (Summer) 14: 3. www. meforum.org/article/983-40k (accessed September 19, 2007).
de Borchgrave, Arnaud. 2005. Iraqi Palmistry. *Washington Times,* February 3.
Decter, Midge. 1990. Arab Rage, Islamic Fury, and the Culture of Violence. *Midstream* 36: 4–7.

Decter, Midge. 2003. *Rumsfeld. A Personal Portrait.* New York: Harper Paperbacks.

de Marenches, Alexandre, and David A. Andelman. 1992. *The Fourth War. Diplomacy and Espionage in the Age of Terror.* New York: William Morrow.

Denitch, Bogdan D. 1979. Legitimating and the Social Order. In *Legitimating of Regimes,* ed. Bogdan Denitch. Beverley Hills, CA: Sage. 5–22.

DeParle, Jason. 1995. Bob (Torricelli) and Bianca (Yes, That One) to the Rescue. *New York Times Magazine,* June 4: 32–35.

Deutsch. Karl W. 1953. *Nationalism and Social Communication: An Inquiry into the Foundation of Nationality.* Cambridge, MA: MIT Press.

———. 1963. *The Nerves of Government: Models of Political Communication and Control.* New York: Free Press.

DeYoung. Karen. 2006. *Soldier. The Life of Colin Powell.* New York: Alfred A. Knopf.

de Wijk, Rob. 2002. The Limits of Military Power. *Washington Quarterly* 25: 75–92.

Diamond, Larry. 2004. What Went Wrong with Iraq. *Foreign Affair* 83 (July–August): 34–56.

Dickey, Christopher, Gregory L. Vistica, and Russell Watson. 1999. Saddam+Bin Laden? *Newsweek,* January 9.

Dionne Jr., E. J. 2003. Democracy at Home and Abroad. *Commonweal,* November 21.

Dobson, Christopher, and Ronald Payne. 1986. *War without End: The Terrorists: An Intelligence Dossier.* London: Harrop.

Dolnik, Adam. 2001. America's Worst Nightmare? Osama bin Laden and Weapons of Mass Destruction. Center for Policy Studies in Russia, PIR Center, September 12.

Donaldson, Gary A. 1996. *America at War since 1945: Politics and Diplomacy in Korea, Vietnam, and the Gulf War.* Westport, CT: Praeger.

Douglass, Joseph D. Jr., and Neil C. Livingstone. 1987. *America the Vulnerable: The Threat of Chemical Biological Warfare.* Lexington, MA: Lexington Books.

Douglas, Mary. 1992. *Risk and Blame: Essays in Cultural Theory.* London: Routledge.

Dovi, Suzanne. 2001. Evil Enemies. Stigmatizing Our Opponents or Legitimizing Our Wars? *Peace Research* 31: 101–112.

Doyle, Michael W. 1983. Kant, Liberal Legacies, and Foreign Affairs. *Philosophy and Public Affairs* 12: 323–353.

Dror, Yehezkel. 1971. *Crazy States: A Counterconventional Strategic Problem.* Lexington, MA: Heath Lexington Books.

Drumheller, Tyler. 2006. *On the Brink: An Insider's Account of How the White House Compromised American Intelligence.* New York: Carroll & Graff.

Dubose, Lou, and Jack Bernstein. 2006. *Vice. Dick Cheney and the Hijacking of the American Presidency.* New York: Random House.

Easton, David. 1953. *The Political System.* New York: Alfred Knopf.

———. 1965. *Systems Analysis of Political Life.* Chicago: Chicago University Press.

———. 1969. The New Revolution in Political Science. *American Political Science Review* 63: 1051–1061.

Ehrenreich, Barbara. 1999. The Bimbo Bombing. *In These Times,* February 7.

Eickelman, Dale F. 1988. Inside the Islamic Reformation. *Wilson Quarterly* 22: 82.

———. 1992. The Re-imagination of the Middle East: Political and Academic Frontiers. *Middle East Studies Association Bulletin* 26: 3–12.

———. 1993. Islamic Liberalism Strikes Back. *MESA Bulletin* 27: 167.

Eilts, Hermann Frederick. 1990. Islamic Fundamentalism. *Mediterranean Quarterly* 1: 27–45.

Eisenstadt, Michael. 1990. *The Sword of the Arabs: Iraq's Strategic Weapons.* The Washington Institute Policy Papers. Washington, DC: The Washington Institute for Near East Policy.

———. 2001. Iraq's Weapons of Mass Destruction (WMD): An Emerging Challenge for the Bush Administration. *Policy Watch.* Washington: Washington Institute for Near East Policy.

Ekeus, Rolf. 1996. Dismantling Saddam's Arsenal, an Interview. *Middle East Quarterly* 3: 71–79.

Elliott, Kimberly Ann. 1998. The Sanctions Glass: Half Full or Completely Empty? *International Security* 23: 50–65.

Elliott, Michael. 2003. So, What Went Wrong? *Time,* October 6.

Elshtain, Jean Bethke, 2003. *Just War against Terror: The Burden of American Power in a Violent World.* New York: Basic Books.

Emerson, Steven. 1991. Capture of a Terrorist. *New York Magazine,* April 21: 30–69.

———. 1997. Get Ready for Twenty Trade Center Bombings. *The Middle East Quarterly* 6: 71–82

———. 2001. Unholy War. *New Republic,* September 14 and 21.

Emerson, Steven, and Daniel Pipes. 2001. Terrorism on Trial, *Wall Street Journal,* May 31.

Erdman, Andrew P.N. 1999. The U.S. Presumption of Quick Costless Wars. *Orbis* 43: 363–382.

Esposito, John L. 1990. Presidential Address 1989: The Study of Islam: Challenges and Prospects. *Middle East Studies Association Bulletin* 24: 1–12.

———. 1992. *The Islamic Threat: Myth or Reality?* New York: Oxford University Press.

———. 1994. Political Islam: Beyond the Green Menace. *Current History* 93: 19–24.

———. 1995. *The Islamic Threat: Myth or Reality?* Rev. ed. New York: Oxford University Press.

———. 1997. Claiming the Center: Political Islam in Transition. *Harvard International Review* 19: 8–11, 60–63.

———. 2002. *Unholy War. Terror in the Name of Jihad.* Oxford: Oxford University Press.

Esty, Daniel C., Jack Goldstone, Ted Robert Gurr, Pamela T. Surko, and Alan N. Unger. 1995. *Working Papers: State Failure Task Force Report.* McLean, VA: Science Applications International Corporation.

Etzioni-Halevy, Eva. 1985. *The Knowledge Elite and the Failure of Prophecy.* London: George Allen and Unwin.

Euben, Roxanne L. 2002. Jihad and Political Violence. *Current History* 101: 365–376.

Evan, Michael. 2002. Baghdad Using Syrian Rail Link to Smuggling in Military Hardware. *London Times,* June 10.

Evans, Peter B. 1979. *Dependent Development: The Alliance of Multinational, State, and Local Capital in Brazil.* Princeton: Princeton University Press.

Everest, Larry. 2004. *Oil Power and Empire: Iraq and the U.S. Global Agenda.* Monroe, ME: Common Courage Press.

Falk, Richard. 1976. *Future Worlds.* New York: Foreign Policy Association.

Fagan, Richard. 1978. A Funny Thing Happened on the Way to the Market; Thoughts on Extending Dependency Ideas. *International Organization* 32: 287–300.

Farah, Douglas, and Colum Lynch. 2002. Hussein Said to Exploit Oil forFood. *Washington Post,* September 18.

Feder, Stanley A. 2002. Forecasting for Policy Making in the Post-colonial Period. *Annual Review of Political Science* 5: 111–125.

Fedora. 2004. What Wilson Didn't Say about Africa. *Free Republic,* October, 25. www. freerepublic.com/focus/fnews/1256475/posts?q=1&& Page+1-39K-(accessed September 18, 2007).

Fein, Leonard. 2005. More Lucky than Prescient? The War's Place in History. *Jewish Exponent,* March 17.

Feldman, Noah. 2006a. Ballots and Bullets. *New York Times,* July 21.

———. 2006b. Islam, Terror and the Second Nuclear Age. *New York Times Magazine,* October 24.

Feldman, Shai. 1982. The Bombing of Osiray—Revisited. *International Security* 7: 114–142.

Ferreira, Anton. 2003. Wolfowitz Defends Murky Evidence. *Philadelphia Inquirer,* July 28.

Feyerabend, Paul. 1975. *Against Method: Outline of an Anarchistic Theory of Knowledge.* London: New Left Books.

Filkins, Dexter. 2006. Where Plan A Left Ahmad Chalabi. *New York Times,* November, 5.

Finnie, David H. 1992. *Shifting Lines in the Sand: Kuwait's Elusive Frontier with Iraq.* Cambridge: Harvard University Press.

Foer, Franklin. 2004. The Closing of the Presidential Mind. *New Republic,* July 5 and 12.

Francona, Rick. 2005. *A Personal Note on the Execution of Saddam Hussein.* Hardblogger, December 29.

Franks, Tommy. 2004. *American Soldier.* New York: Regan Books.

Freedman, Lawrence. 2005. The Politics of Warning: Terrorism and Risk Communication. *Intelligence and National Security* 20: 379–418.

Freedman, Lawrence, and Efraim Karsh. 1993. *The Gulf Conflict, 1990–1991: Diplomacy and the War in the World Order.* Princeton: Princeton University Press.

Freeh, Louis J. 2005. *My FBI: Bringing Down the Mafia, Investigating Bill Clinton, and Fighting the War on Terror.* New York: St. Martin's Press.

Frelick, Barry. 1992. State Terror and the Degradation of Politics in Iraq. *Middle East Report* 22 (May–June): 15–21.

Friedman, Alan. 1993. *Spider's Web: The Secret History of How the White House Illegally Armed Iraq.* New York: Bantam Books.

Friedman, Thomas L. 2004. People Power. *National Republic,* June 28.

Frisch, Hillel. 2002. Explaining Third World Security Structures. *The Journal of Strategic Studies* 25: 161–190.

Frum, David, and Richard Perle. 2003. *An End to Evil: How to Win the War on Terror.* New York: Random House.

Fukuyama, Francis. 2006. *America at the Crossroad. Democracy, Power, and the Neoconservative Legacy.* New Haven: Yale University Press.

Gaba, Egon G. 1990. The Alternative Paradigm Dialogue. In *The Paradigm Dialogue,* ed. Egon G. Gaba. Newbury Park, CA: Sage.

Gaddis, John Lewis. 2002. A Grand Strategy. *Foreign Policy* (November– December): 50–57.

Galbraith, John K. 1967. *The New Industrial State.* Boston: Houghton Mifflin.

Galbraith, Peter W. 2006. *The End of Iraq: How American Incompetence Created a War without End.* New York: Simon & Schuster.

Galston, William A. 1980. *Justice and the Human Good.* Chicago: University of Chicago Press.

Galtung, Johan. 1971. A Structural Theory of Imperialism. *Journal of Peace Research* 8: 81–117.

———. 1976. Toward New Indicators of Development. *Futures* 8: 261–265.

Ganon, John C. 2001. Challenge to National Security. National Intelligence Council. www.cia.gov/cia/public-24 affairs/speeches 2001/ganon_Speeches_0124001. html-33 (accessed October 2, 2007).

Garrett, Laurie. 2001. The Nightmare of Bioterrorism. *Foreign Affairs* 80 (1): 76–89.

Gates, Robert M. 1996. *From the Shadows: The Ultimate Insider's Story of Five Presidents and How They Won the Cold War.* New York: Simon & Schuster.

Gause III, Gregory F. 1994. The Illogic of Dual Containment. *Foreign Affairs* 73: 56–66.

———. 1999. Getting It Backward in Iraq. *Foreign Affairs* 78: 53–65.

———. 2002. Who Lost Middle East Studies. *Foreign Affairs* 81: 164–169.

Gelb, Leslie H. 1991. Yes or No to Mr. Gates. *New York Times,* October 2.

George, Alexander L. 1993. *Bridging the Gap: Theory and Practice in Foreign Policy.* Washington, DC: United States Institute of Peace Press.

Gerecht, Reuel Mark. 2000. The Counterterrorism Myth. *Atlantic Online,* July–August.

———. 2001. The Terrorist Encyclopedia. *Middle East Quarterly* 8: 73–85.

Gertz, Bill. 1999. *Betrayal: How the Clinton Administration Undermined American Security.* Washington, DC: Regnery.

Ghabra, Sahfeeq N. 2001. Iraq's Culture of Violence. *Middle East Quarterly* 8: 39–50.

Ghalyoun, Burhan. 1985. *Assassination of Reason.* Beirut: Arab Institute for Research and Publishing.

Ghibbs, David N. 2001. Social Science as Propaganda? International Relations and the Question of Bias. *International Studies Perspectives* 2: 417–427.

Gibbs, Nancy, and Michael Ware. 2003. Chasing a Mirage. *Time,* October 6.

Gill, Peter. 2004. Securing the Globe: Intelligence and Post-9/11 Shift from "Liddism to Drainism." *Intelligence and National Security* 19: 487–489.

Gilmore, Inigo, and Charles Laurence. 2003. Iraqis Tried to Bribe Scott Ritter with Gold. *Daily Telegraph,* May 4.

Gitlin, Todd. 2002. Blaming America First. *Mother Jones,* January–February.

Gold, Dore. 2004. Tower of Babel: How the United Nations Fueled Global Chaos. New York: Crown Forum.

Goldberg, Jeffrey. 2003. The Unknown. *New Yorker,* February 10.

Goodman, Melvin A. 1997. Ending the CIA's Cold War Legacy. *Foreign Policy* 106: 128–143.

———. 2003. 9/11: The Failure of Strategic Intelligence. *Intelligence and National Security* (December): 59–71.

Gordon, Michael R. 2006. Military Charts Movement of Conflict in Iraq toward Chaos. *New York Times,* November 1.

Gordon, Michael R., and General Bernard E. Trainor. 1995. *The General's War: The Inside Story of the Gulf Conflict in the Gulf.* Boston: Little Brown.

———. 2006. *Cobra II: The Inside Story of the Invasion and Occupation of Iraq.* New York: Pantheon Books.

Gordon, Philip H., and Michael E. O'Hanlon. 2002. *Should the War on Terrorism Target Iraq? Implementing a Bush Doctrine on Deterrence.* Global Politics Policy Brief no. 93. Washington, DC: Brookings Institution Press.

Gormley, Denis M. 2004. On Not Confusing the Unfamiliar with the Improbable. Low-Technology Means of Delivery of Weapons of Mass Destruction. The Weapons of Mass Destruction Commission. October 24. wmdc.org (accessed October 20, 2006).

Graham, Bob with Jeff Nussbaum. 2004. *Intelligence Matters. The CIA, the FBI, Saudi Arabia, and the Failure of America's War on Terror.* New York: Random House.

Graham-Brown, Sarah. 1999. *Sanctioning Saddam. The Politics of Intervention in Iraq.* London: I.B. Tauris Publishers.

Gray, Colin S. 1999. Second Nuclear Age. Boulder: Lynne Rienner.

Greenberger, Robert S. 1992. Islamic Fundamentalism's Rise in Sudan Sparks Concern over Movement's Spread. *Wall Street Journal,* March 16.

Gries, David. 1995. A New Look for Intelligence. *Intelligence and National Security* 10: 180–182.

Gross, Netty C. 2005. A Grand Old Party. *Jerusalem Post,* April 1.

Guindy, Adel. 2006. The Islamization of Egypt. *MERIA* 10:3 (September). meria.idc.ac.il/journal/2006/issues3/jv/10no3a7.html-64k (accessed September 19, 2007).

Guitta, Oliver. 2005. The Chirac Doctrine. *Middle East Quarterly* (Fall): 12:3. online books.library.upenn.edu-webbin/serial?id=mequarter-3k (accessed September 26, 2007).

Gunter, Michael M. 1992. *The Kurds of Iraq: Tragedy and Hope.* New York: St. Martin's Press.

———. 1999a. The Iraqi Opposition and the Failure of U.S. Intelligence. *International Journal of Intelligence and Counterintelligence* 12: 135–167.

———. 1999b. *The Kurdish Predicament in Iraq: A Political Analysis.* New York: St. Martin's Press.

Gup, Ted. 2002. Clueless in Langley. *Mother Jones,* January–February.

Haar, Lisa. 1995. Institute Professor John Deutsch Heads CIA. What Next? *The Thistle* 9.

Haass, Richard N. 1991. Friendly Tyrants: A Policy Primer. In *Friendly Tyrants: An American Dilemma,* ed. Adam Garfinkle and Daniel Pipes. New York: St. Martin's Press. 507–519.

———. 1998. Ed. *Economic Sanctions and American Diplomacy.* New York: Council on Foreign Relations.

———. 2003. Toward Greater Democracy. *Washington Quarterly* 26: 137–148.

Haass, Richard, N., and Megan L. O'Sullivan. 2000. *Honey and Vinegar: Incentives, Sanctions, and Foreign Policy.* Washington, DC: Brookings Institution Press.

Habermas, Jurgen. 1975. *Legitimation Crisis.* Boston: Beacon Press.

Hadar, Leon T. 1996. Meddling in the Middle East: Europe Challenges U.S. Hegemony in the Region. *Mediterranean Quarterly* 7: 40–54.

Haddad, Yvonne Y. 1991. Middle East Area Studies: Current Concerns and Future Directions (1990 Presidential Address). *MESA Bulletin* 25: 1–2.

Halevy, Efraim. 2006. *Man in the Shadows: Inside the Middle East Crisis with a Man Who Led the Mossad.* New York: St. Martin's Press.

Hall, Edward T. 1977. *Beyond Culture.* Garden City, NY: Anchor Books.

Hall, Mimi, and Toni Locy. 2004. Ashcroft Says Clinton's Rules "Handcuffed" Anti-terrorism. *USA Today,* April 14.

Halliday, Denis J. 1999. Iraq and the UN's Weapons of Mass Destruction. *Current History* 98: 65–68.

Halliday, Fred. 1979. *Iran: Dictatorship and Development.* Harmondsworth, UK: Penguin Books.

Halperin, Morton H. 2002. Testimony on Iraq. Senate Foreign Relations Committee, July 31. http//www.cfr.org/pub4698/morton.h.halperin (accessed September 17, 2007).

———. 2003. A Case for Containment. Washington Post, February 3.

Halperin, Morton, Jerry Berman, Robert Borosage, and Christine Marwick. 1976. Lawless State. New York: Penguin Books.

Halpern, Manfred. 1963. *The Politics of Social Change in the Middle East North Africa.* Princeton: Princeton University Press.

Hamza, Khidir. 2000. *Saddam's Bombmaker. The Terrifying Inside of the Iraqi Nuclear and Biological Weapons Agenda.* New York: Scribner's Sons.

Hamzawy, Amr. 2005. Is the Arab Modernization Wave Real? *Bitterlemons* 3, March 31.

Hannity, Sean. 2004. *Deliver Us from Evil: Defeating Terrorism, Despotism, and Liberalism.* New York: Regan Books.

Hanson, Victor Davis. 2003a. War Folklore. *National Review Online,* July 25.

———. 2003b. The Western Disease. *National Review Online,* December 30.

———. 2004. Do We Have Enough Troops in Iraq? *Commentary,* June.

———. 2005. The Bush Doctrine Next Test. *Commentary,* May.

Hard, Michael, and Antonio Negri. 2000. *Empire.* Cambridge: Harvard University Press.

Harris, John F. 2005. *The Survivor: Bill Clinton in the White House.* New York: Random House.

Hart, Gary. 2004. *The Fourth Power. Grand Strategy for the United States in the Twenty-First Century.* New York: Oxford University Press.

Hart, Roderick. 1999. *Seducing America: How Television Charms the Modern Voter.* Rev. ed. Thousand Oaks, CA: Sage.

Hashim, Ahmed. 2003. Saddam Husuan and Civil-Military Relations. *Middle East Journal* 57: 9–41.

Haslam, Jonathan. 2002. *No Virtue like Necessity. Realist Thought in International Relations since Machiavelli.* New York: Yale University Press.

Hawthorn, Amy. 2003. Political Reform in the Arab World. A New Era. *Daily Star,* July 7.

Hayes, Stephan F. 2002. The Baghdad Democrats: David Bonior and Jim McDermott Create a Headache for Their Party. *Weekly Standard,* October 14.

———. 2003a. Case Closed. *Weekly Standard,* November 24.

———. 2003b. The Clinton View of Iraq-al Qaeda Ties. *Weekly Standard,* December 19.

———. 2004. *The Connection: How al Qaeda's Collaboration with Saddam Hussein Has Endangered America.* New York: HarperCollins.

Hazelton, Fran. 1994. *Iraq since the Gulf War: Prospects for Democracy.* London: Zed Books.

Headly, John. 2005. Learning from Intelligence Failures. *International Journal of Intelligence and Counterintelligence* 18: 435–450.

Hedges, Chris. 1994. In Sudan, Islamic Leader Talks of Tolerance. *New York Times,* December 6.

Heikal, Mohamed. 1992. *Illusions of Triumph: An Arab View of the Gulf War.* New York: HarperCollins.

Heilbrunn, Jacob. 1997. The Great Equivocator. *The New Republic,* March 24.
Hellmich, Christian, and Amanda J. Redig. 2007. The Question Is When: The Ideology of Al Qaeda and the Reality of Bioterrorism. *Studies in Conflict and Terrorism* 30 (5): 375–396.
Helmer, Olaf. 1986. The Future Relationship between the Superpowers. *Futures* 18: 493–507.
Helms, Christine Moss. 1984. *Iraq. Eastern Flank of the Arab World.* Washington, DC: Brookings Institution Press.
Henderson, Errol A., and Richard Tucker. 2001. Clear and Present Strangers: The Clash of Civilizations and International Conflict. *International Studies Quarterly* 45: 317–338.
Henderson, Simon. 1991. *Instant Empire: Saddam Hussein's Ambition for Iraq.* San Francisco: Mercury House.
Hendrickson, Ryan C. 2002. *The Clinton Wars: The Constitution, Congress, and War Powers Act.* Nashville: Vanderbilt University Press.
Henriksen, Thomas H. 2002. The Blowback Myth: How Bad History Makes Bad Policy. *Weekly Standard,* October 15.
Heo, Uk, and Alexander C. Tan. 2001. Democracy and Economic Growth: A Causal Analysis. *Comparative Politics* 33: 463–474.
Hermann, Margaret G. 2003. Saddam Hussein's Leadership Style. In *The Psychological Assessment of Political Leaders: With Profiles of Saddam Hussein and Bill Clinton,* ed. Jerold M Post, 375–386. Ann Arbor: University of Michigan Press.
Hersh, Seymour M. 2001. What Went Wrong. *New Yorker* October, 8.
———. 2004. Chain of Command. The Road from 9/11 to Abu Ghraib. New York: HarperCollins.
———. 2005. The Coming Wars, What the Pentagon Can Now Do in Secret. *New Yorker,* January 24 and 31.
Herzig, Christopher. 1983. Director of the Division of External Relations at the International Atomic Energy Agency. *International Security* 7: 195–199.
Hilsman, Roger. 1992. *George Bush vs. Saddam Hussein: Military Success! Political Failure?* Novato, CA: Lyford Press.
———. 1995. Does the CIA Still Have a Role? *Foreign Affairs* 74: 104–116.
Hiro, Dilip. 1991. *The Longest War: The Iran-Iraq Military Conflict.* New York: Routledge.
———. 2002. *Iraq: In the Eye of the Storm.* New York: Thunder's Mouth Press.
———. 2003. *Neighbors, Not Friends: Iraq and Iran after the Gulf Wars.* London: Routledge.
Hitz, Frederick P. 2000. The Future of American Espionage. *International Journal of Intelligence and Counterintelligence* 13: 1–20.
Hoffman, Bruce. 1996. Intelligence and Terrorism: Emerging Threats and New Security Challenges. *Intelligence and National Security* 11: 207–223.
———. 1998. *Inside Terrorism.* New York: Columbia University Press.
———. 2001. Combating Terrorism: In Search of a National Strategy. Testimony before Subcommittee on National Security, Veterans Affairs, and International Relations. House Committee on Government Reform. March 27.
Hoffmann, Stanley. 1990. Correspondence. *International Security.*15: 191–199.
———. 2006. The Foreign Policy the US Needs. *New York Review of Books,* August 10.
Holsti, K.J. 1978. A New International Politics? Diplomacy in Complex Interdependence. *International Organization* 32: 513–530.

Holsti, Ole R. 1962. The Belief System and National Image: A Case Study. *Journal of Conflict Resolution* 6: 244–252.

Homer-Dixon. 2002. The Rise of Complex Terrorism. *Foreign Policy* 128: 52–63.

Hooker, Gregory. 2005. *Shaping the Plan for Operation Iraqi Freedom: The Role of Military Intelligence Assessment.* Rev. ed. Washington, DC: Washington Institute for Near East Studies.

Horowitz, David L. 1980. Discussion. In *Intelligence Requirements for the 1990s. Analysis and Estimates*, ed. Roy Godson, 180. Washington, DC: National Strategy Information Center.

———. 2003. *Left Illusion. An Intellectual Odyssey.* Dallas: Spence Publishing.

———. 2004. *Unholy Alliance. Radical Islam and the American Left.* Washington, DC: Regnery.

Hotaling. 2001. Ed. *Islam without Illusions. Its Past, Its Present and Its Challenges for the Future.* Syracuse: Syracuse University Press.

Howard, Michael. 2002. What's in a Name? *Foreign Affairs* 81(1): 8–13.

Hoyt, Paul D. 2000. "Rogue States" and International Relations Theory. *Journal of Conflict Studies* 20:1. www.lib.unb.ca/texts/JCB/bin/get7.cg? directory=fall1000/ 8filename=hoyt.htm_41k (accessed September 17, 2007).

Hudson, Michael C. 1977. *Arab Politics: The Search for Legitimacy.* New Haven: Yale University Press.

———. 1987. *From Lebanon to "Irangate": A Review of Recent American Middle East Policy.* Washington, DC: Center for Contemporary Arab Studies, Georgetown University.

Hulnick, Arthur S. 1999. *Fixing the Spy Machine: Preparing American Intelligence for the Twenty-First Century.* Westport, CT: Praeger.

———. 2004. Espionage. Does It Have a Future in the 21st Century? *Brown Journal of World Affairs* 11: 165–173.

Hunter, Shireen T. 1992. Persian Gulf Security: Lessons of the Past and the Need for New Thinking. *SAIS Review* 12: 155–166.

———. 1998. *Is Iranian Perestroika Possible without Fundamental Change? The Washington Quarterly* 21: 23–42.

Huntington, Samuel P. 1993. The Clash of Civilizations. *Foreign Affairs* 72: 22–49.

———. 1996. *The Clash of Civilizations and the Remaking of World Order.* New York: Simon & Schuster.

Hussein, Saddam. 1979. *Social and Foreign Affairs.* Trans. Khalid Kishtainy. London: Croom Helm.

Ignatieff, Michael. 2001. Bush's First Strike. *New York Review of Books,* March 29.

Ijaz, Mansoor. 2004. Politicized Intelligence. *National Review Online,* April 15.

Ikenberry, G. John. 2002. America's Imperial Tradition. *Foreign Affairs* 81 (September–October): 44–60.

Inman, Bobby R. 2001. Spying. *New York Times*, October 9.

Isenberg, David. 1999. *Imperial Overreach. Washington's Dubious Strategy to Overthrow Saddam Hussein. Policy Analysis* no. 360. New York: Cato Institute.

Iskander, Amir. 1980. *Saddam Hussein: The Fighter, the Thinker, and the Man.* Trans. Hassan Selim. Paris: Hathette Realités.

Israeli, Raphael. 1997. Islamikaze and Their Significance. *Terrorism and Political Violence* 9: 96–121.

James, Carolyn C. 2000. Iran and Iraq as Rational Crisis Actors. *Journal of Strategic Studies* 23: 52–73.

Jasper, William. 2001. The Power behind bin Laden. *New American,* December 31.

Jehl, Douglas. 1993. It Takes a Good Host to Run a Spy Agency. *New York Times,* April 5.

———. 2004. C. I. A. Shakeup Continues as 2 Senior Officials Quit. *New York Times,* November 15.

Jentleson, Bruce W. 1994. *With Friends like These: Reagan, Bush and Saddam 1982–1990.* New York: W.W. Norton.

———.2000. *Coercive Prevention. Normative, Political, and Policy Dilemmas.* Washington, DC: United States Institute of Peace.

Jervis, Robert. L. 2001. Weapons without Purpose? Nuclear Strategy in the Post–Cold War Era. *Foreign Affairs* 80: 143–149.

———. 2002a. An Interim Assessment of September 11: What Has Changed and What Has Not. *Political Science Quarterly* 117: 37–54.

———. 2002b. The Dustbin of History: Mutual Assured Destruction *Foreign Policy* 133: 40–42.

———. 2003a. The Compulsive Empire. *Foreign Policy* 137: 82–87.

———. 2003b. The Confrontation between Iraq and the US: Implications for the Theory and Practice of Deterrence. *European Journal of International Relations* 9: 315–337.

———. 2003c. Understanding the Bush Doctrine. *Political Science Quarterly* 118: 365–389.

———. 2006. Reports, Politics, and Intelligence Failure: The Case of Iraq. *Journal of Strategic Studies* 29: 1(February): 3–52.

Joffe, Josef. 2005. A World without Israel. *Foreign Policy* 144 (January–February): 44–46.

Johnson, Ben. 2004. Teresa Heinz Kerry. Bag Lady for the Radical Left. *Frontpage Magazine*, February 13.

Johnson, Chalmers. 2000. *Blowback: The Cost and Consequences of American Empire.* New York: Metropolitan Books.

Johnson, Larry C. 2001. The Declining Terrorist Threat. *New York Times,* July 10.

Johnson, Loch K. 1989. Strategic Intelligence: An American Perspective. *International Journal of Intelligence and Counterintelligence* 3: 299–332.

———. 1992–93. Smart Intelligence. *Foreign Policy* 89: 53–69.

———. 1996a. Analysis for a New Age. *Intelligence and National Security* 11: 657–671.

———. 1996b. *Secret Agencies: U.S. Intelligence in a Hostile World.* New Haven: Yale University Press.

———. 2003–04. Preface to a Theory of Strategic Intelligence. *International Journal of Intelligence and Counterintelligence 16*: 638– 663.

Johnson, Peter, and Judith Tucker. 1975. Middle East Network in the United States. *MERIP Report* 38: 3–20.

Jones, Christopher M. 2001. The CIA under Clinton: Continuity and Change. *Intelligence and Counterintelligence* 14: 503–528.

Jones, Garrett. 2006. Welcome to the CIA. *Foreign Policy Research Institute Enotes,* June 12. www. fpri.og/enotes/20060608.americanwar. Jones.welcomecia. htm/-20k (accessed September 16, 2007).

Judis, John B. 2004. *The Folly of Empire. What George Bush Could Learn from Theodore Roosevelt and Woodrow Wilson.* New York: Scribner's Sons.

Juster, Kenneth I. 1994. The Myth of Iraqgate. *Foreign Policy* 94: 105–119.

Kadushin, Charles. 1974. *The American Intellectual Elite.* Boston: Little Brown.

Kalugin, Oleg. 2004. Terrorism and Human Intelligence: The Soviet Experience. *Brown Journal of World Affairs* 11: 183–188.

Kam, Efraim. 2004. Exceeding the Boundaries, the Parliamentary Report on Israel's Intelligence System: Strategic Assessment. *JCSS* 7: 2 (August): 4–10.

Kann, Peter R. 1991. The Pundits Lose the War with Reality. *Wall Street Journal*, February 28.

Kaplan, Robert D. 1992. Tales from the Bazaar. *Atlantic Monthly*, August.

———. 2006. Old States. New Threats. *Washington Post*, April 23.

Karabell, Zachary. 1996–97. Fundamental Misconception: Islamic Foreign Policy. *Foreign Policy* 105: 77–90.

Karmon, Ely. 2005. *Coalition between Terrorist Organizations, Revolutionaries, Nationalists and Islamists*. Leiden, the Netherlands: Martinu Nijhoff. Karsh, Efraim. 2002. Politics as a Lethal Game. In *Inside Iraq. The History, the People, and the Modern Conflicts of the World's Least Understood Lands*, ed. John Miller and Aaron Kenedi, 237–254. New York: Marlow.

———. 2006. *Islamic Imperialism. A History*. New Haven: Yale University Press.

Karsh, Efraim, and Inari Rautsi. 1991. *Saddam Hussein: A Political Biography*. London: Brassey's.

Kashkett, Steven B. 1982. Iraq and the Pursuit of Nonalignment. *Orbis* 26: 477–495.

Katzman, Kenneth. 2001. *Terrorism: Near Eastern Groups and State Sponsors*. Washington, DC: Congressional Research Service. September 10.

Kean, Thomas H., and Lee H. Hamilton. 2004. *The 9/11 Report. The National Commission on Terrorist Attacks upon the United States*. New York: St. Martin's Press.

Keddie, Nikki R. 1972. The Roots of the Ulama's Power in Modern Iran. In *Scholars, Saints and Sufis: Muslim Religious Institutions in the Middle East since 1500*, ed. Nikki R. Keddie. Berkeley: University of California Press. 211–231.

Keegan, John. 2004. *The Iraq War*. New York: Alfred A Knopf.

Kelley, Kitty. 2004. *The Family: The Real Story of the Bush Dynasty*. New York: Doubleday.

Kelly, Michael. 2002. Mob Town. In *Inside Iraq: The History, the People, and the Modern Conflicts of the World's Least Understood Lands*, ed. John Miller and Aaron Kenedi, 77–123. New York: Marlow.

Kengor, Paul. 2004. *God and George W. Bush*. Washington, DC: Regnery.

Kennedy, Paul. 2006. *The Parliament of Men: The Past, Present and Future of the United Nations*. New York: Random House.

Kessler, Donald. 2004. *A Matter of Character. Inside the White House of George W. Bush*. New York: Sentinel Press.

Kessler, Ron. 2003. *The CIA at War: Inside the Secret Campaign against Terror*. New York: St. Martin's Press.

Khalef, Roula. 2002. US Raises Pressure on Iraq Oil Revenue. *Financial Times*, July 29.

Khalidi, Rashid. 1995. Is There a Future for Middle East Studies? *MESA Bulletin* 29: 1–6.

Khan, M.A. Muqtedar. 1997. Policy Entrepreneurs: The Third Dimension in American Foreign Policy Culture. *Middle East Policy* 5: 3 (September). www.campus watch.org/article/ied597-75k (accessed September 26, 2007).

Kholi, Atul, Peter B. Evans, Peter J. Katzenstein, and Adam Przeworki. 1995. The Role of Theory in Comparative Politics. A Symposium. *World Politics* 48: 1–49.

Khoury, Phillip S. 1999. Lessons from the Eastern Shore. 1998 Presidential Address. *MESA Bulletin* 33.

Kimche, David. 1991. *The Last Option after Nasser, Arafat, and Saddam Hussein: The Quest for Peace in the Middle East.* New York: Scribner's Sons.

Kincade, William H. 1995. *Nuclear Proliferation: Diminishing Threat?* Institute for National Security Studies. Colorado Springs, CO: U.S. Air Force Academy.

Kirk, Roger, and Mircea Raceanu. 1994. Dealing with Dictatorship: Lesson from Ceausescu's Romania. *Mediterranean Quarterly* 5: 25–36.

Kissinger, Henry A. 1981. *For the Record: Selected Statements, 1977–1980.* Boston: Little Brown.

Klare, Michael T. 1998. Clinton and Saddam Hussein: Brothers in Arms. *The Progressive,* February 2.

———. 2000a. Resource Competition and World Politics in the Twenty-First Century. *Current History,* 99: 403–407.

———. 2000b. The Strategic Obsolescence of the "Rogue Doctrine" *Harvard International Review* 22: 46–51.

Klein, Peter. 2006. Beyond Top Secret. *History Channel,* November 27.

Knott, Stephen F. 2000. The Great Republican Transformation on Oversight. *International Journal of Intelligence and Counterintelligence* 13: 49–63.

Knowlton, Brian. 2007. The Reach of War: Rice Rebuts Tenet's Assertion That '01 Warning Ignored. *New York Times,* April 30.

Kolko, Gabriel. 1997. Privatizing Communism. *World Policy Journal* 14: 23–34.

———. 2002. *Another Century of Warfare?* New York: The New Press.

Korany, Baghat. 1986. *How Foreign Policy Decisions Are Made in the Third World.* Boulder: Westview Press.

Kramer, Martin. 1997. Ballots and Bullets: Islamist and the Relentless Drive for Power. *Harvard International Review* 19: 16–19.

———. 2001. *Ivory Towers on Sand: The Failure of Middle Eastern Studies in America.* Washington, DC: Washington Institute for Near East Policy.

———. 2002a. Middle East Studies in America: A Briefing. *Middle East Forum,* March 14.

———. 2002b. MESA Culpa. *Middle East Quarterly* 9:4 www.meforum. org/articles/ 500-47k (accessed August 6, 2006).

———. 2003a. Coming to Terrorism. Fundamentalist or Islamists? *Middle East Quarterly* 10: 65–77.

———. 2003b. Congress Probes Middle Eastern Studies. *Campus Watch,* June 23.

Krepon, Michael. 2001. Moving away from MAD. Survival 43: 81–95.

Kristol, William, and Robert Kagan. 1996a. A Great Victory for Iraq. *Washington Post,* February 26.

———. 1996b. Toward a Neo-Reaganite Foreign Policy. *Foreign Affairs* 75: 18–32.

Krueger, Alan B., and Jitka Maleckova. 2004. Does Poverty Cause Terrorism? *New Republic,* June 24.

Kuhn, Thomas S. 1970. *The Structure of Scientific Revolution.* 2nd ed. Chicago: University of Chicago Press.

Kuklick, Bruce. 2006. *Blind Oracles: Intellectuals and War from Kennan to Kissinger.* Princeton: Princeton University Press.

Kupchan, Charles A. 1999. Life after Pax Americana. *World Policy Journal* 16: 20–27.

Kurlantzick, Joshua. 2004. The Left and the Islamists. *Commentary,* December.

Kuznetz, Simon. 1955. Economic Growth and Inequality. *American Economic Review* 45: 1–28.
Lake, Anthony. 1994. Confronting Backlash States. *Foreign Affairs* 73: 45–55.
Lake, Eli J. 2001. Recruiting an Iraqi Opposition: Is General Khazraji the Right Man to Liberate Baghdad? *Weekly Standard*, December 24.
Laqueur, Walter. 1996. Postmodern Terrorism. *Foreign Affairs* 75 (September–October): 24–36.
Larson, Deborah. 1985. *Origins of Containment: A Psychological Explanation.* Princeton: Princeton University Press.
Lebanon, Michelle, and Jurle Crocker. 2000. Why the "Foreign" Matters in Foreign Affairs. *Harvard International Review* 22: 54–59.
Ledeen, Michael A. 1996. *Freedom Betrayed: How America Led a Global Democratic Revolution, Won the Cold War, and Walked Away.* Washington, DC: AEI Press.
Leebaert, Derek. 2002. *The Fifty-Year Wound: The True Price of America's Cold War Victory.* Boston: Little Brown.
Lehman, John F. 2004. America after 9/11. *Foreign Policy Research Institute.* www.fpri.org/fpriwire/1203.200412.lehman.america after911.html-30k (accessed June 3, 2006).
———. 2006. Despite Some Notable Achievements New Thinking Is Needed on the Home Front and Abroad. *Washington Post*, August 31.
Leitenberg, Milton. 2000. *Deadly Unknowns about Iraq's Biological Weapons Programs.* College Park, MD: Institute for Science and International Security, University of Maryland.
Lenczowski, George. 1978. Political Process and Institutions in Iran: The Second Pahlavi Kingship. In *Iran under the Pahlavis,* ed. George Lenczowski. Stanford: Stanford University Hoover Institute Press. 433–476.
Lerner, Daniel. 1958. *The Passing of Traditional Society: Modernizing the Middle East.* Glencoe, IL: Free Press.
Lesch, Ann M. 2002.Osama bin Laden's "Business" in Sudan. *Current History* 101: 202–209.
Lesser, Ian O. Bruce Hoffman, John Arquilla, David Ronfeld, and Michael Zanini. 1999. Eds. *Countering the New Terrorism.* Santa Monica: RAND.
Levitt, Steven D., and Stephen J. Dubner. 2005. *Freakonomics: A Rogue Economist Explores the Hidden Side of Everything.* New York: William Morrow.
Lewis, Bernard. 1976. The Return of Islam. *Commentary,* January.
———. 1982. The Question of Orientalism. *New York Review of Books,* June 24.
———. 1990. The Roots of Muslim Rage. *Atlantic Monthly,* September: 47–60.
———. 1993. *Islam and the West.* New York: Oxford University Press.
———. 1998. License to Kill. *Foreign Affairs* 77(6):14–19.
———. 2002. *What Went Wrong? Western Impact and Middle East Response.* Oxford: Oxford University Press.
———. 2003. *The Crisis of Islam. Holy War and Unholy Terror.* New York: Modern Library.
———. 2004. *From Babel to Dragomans. Interpreting the Middle East.* Oxford: Oxford University Press.
———. 2005. Freedom and Justice in the Modern Middle East. *Foreign Affairs* 84 (May–June): 36–51.
Lewis, William H. 1996. Algeria at 35: The Politics of Violence. *Washington Quarterly* 19: 3–18.
Lieber, Robert J. 2003. The Folly of Containment. *Commentary,* April.

Lijphart, Arendt. 1968. *The Politics of Accommodation*. Berkeley: University of California Press.
Linton, Ralph. 1945. *The Cultural Background of Personality*. New York:
D. Appleton-Century.
Lipset, Seymour M. 1979. The New Class and the Professorate. In *The New Class?* ed. Bruce-Briggs. New Brunswick, NJ: Transaction Books. 67–88.
Lipsky, Seth. 2001. Ned Walker's Wrong Turn. *Wall Street Journal*, November 28.
Little, David. 1998. Religion and Global Affairs: Religion and U.S. Foreign Policy. *SAIS Review* 18: 25–31.
Litwak, Robert S. 2000a. "Rogue State" Label Was a Bad Fit. *Los Angeles Times*, June 28.
———. 2000b. Rogue States and U.S. Foreign Policy: Containment after the Cold War. Baltimore: Johns Hopkins University Press.
———. 2002–03. The New Calculus of Preemption. *Survival* 44:53–79.
Lochman, Zachary. 2004. *Contending Visions of the Middle East: The History and Politics of Orientalism*. Cambridge: Cambridge University Press.
Looney, Robert E. 1977. *Iran at the End of the Century: A Hegelian Forecast*. Lexington, MA: Lexington Books.
Lopez, George A. 2001. U. S. *Secretary of State Creates a New Momentum*. Policy Brief no. 5. Joan B. Krock Institute for International Peace Studies: Notre Dame Press.
Lopez, George A., and David Cortright. 2000. *The Sanctions Decade: Assessing U.S. Strategic Sanctions in the 1990s*. Boulder: Lynn Rienner.
———. 2004. Containing Iraq: Sanctions Worked. *Foreign Affairs* 83 (July–August): 90–103.
Lopez, Kathryn Jean. 2003. Interview with Richard Miniter. *NRO*, September 11.
Losman, Donald L. 1997. Pain without Gain: The Sanctions Saga. *The Mediterranean Quarterly* 8: 36–59.
Lowry, Rich. 2003. *Legacy: Paying the Price for the Clinton Years*. Washington, DC: Regnery.
Lukitz, Liora. 1995. *Iraq: The Search for National Identity*. London: Frank Cass.
Lund, Michael S. 1996. *Preventing Violent Conflict: A Strategy for Preventive Diplomacy*. Washington, DC: United States Institute of Peace.
Lustick, Ian. 2002. Neo-conservative "Cabal" & US/Iraq. Middle East Policy Council, October 1, 2002. www.campus-watch. org/articles/id/442-12k (accessed September 17, 2007).
———. 2006. *Trapped in the War on Terror*. Philadelphia: University of Pennsylvania Press.
Lynch, Colum. 2000. *Ex-UN Inspector Ritter to Tour Iraq. Make Documentary. Washington Post*, July 27.
Mackey, Sandra. 2002. *The Reckoning: Iraq and the Legacy of Saddam Hussein*. New York: W.W. Norton.
MacLeod, Scott. 1996. The Paladin of Jihad. *Time*, May 6.
Mahle, Melissa Boyle. 2004. *Denial and Deception: An Insider's View of the CIA from Iran-Contra to 9/11*. New York: Nation Books.
Majone, Giandomenico. 1989. *Evidence, Argument and Persuasion in the Policy Process*. New Haven: Yale University Press.
Makiya, Kanan. 1993. *Cruelty and Silence: Way, Tyranny, Uprising, and the Arab World*. New York: W.W. Norton.

Maliniak, Daniel, Amy Oakes, Susan Peterson, and Michael J. Tierney. 2007. Inside the Ivory Tower. *Foreign Policy* 159 (March–April): 62–69.
Mandel, Daniel. 2005. The Churchill Doctrine. *FrontPage Magazine*, January 26.
Mann, James. 2004. *Rise of the Vulcans: The History of Bush's War Cabinet.* New York: Viking.
Mansfield, Edward. 1995. International Institutions and Economic Sanctions. *World Politics* 47: 575–606.
Mansfield, Peter. 1982. Saddam Hussein's Political Thinking: The Comparison with Nasser. In *Iraq: The Contemporary State*, ed. Tim Niblock. New York: St. Martin's Press. 62–73
Mantius, Peter. 1995. *Shell Game: A True Story of Banking, Spies, Lies, Politics.* New York: St. Martin's Press.
Marr, Phebe. 1985. *The Modern History of Iraq.* Boulder: Westview Press.
———. 2004. *The Modern History of Iraq.* 2nd ed. Boulder: Westview Press.
Marshall, Joshua M. 2002. Bomb Saddam? In *The Saddam Reader*, ed. Turie Munthe. New York: Thunder's Mouth Press. 405–416.
Marty, Martin E., and R. Scott Appleby. 1991. *Fundamentalism Observed.* Chicago: University of Chicago Press.
Masoud, Tarek E. 1998. Misreading Iran. Current History 97 (January): 38–43.
Matar, Fouad. 1981. *Saddam Hussein, the Man, the Cause, and the Future.* London: Third World Center.
Maynes, Charles William. 1989. Coping with the '90s. *Foreign Affairs* 74: 42–62.
———. 1993–94. A Workable Clinton Doctrine. *Foreign Policy* 93: 3–21.
Mazetti, Mark, 2007. CIA Lays out Errors Made before September 11. *New York Times*, August 22.
McCuen, Garry E.1999. *Biological Terrorism and Weapons of Mass Destruction.* Hudson, WI: G.E. McCuen Publications.
McGrath, Alister E. 2004. *The Twilight of Atheism. The Rise and Fall of Disbelief in Modern World.* New York: Doubleday.
McInerney, Thomas, and Paul Vallely. 2004. *Endgame.* Washington, DC: Regnery.
Mead, Walter Russell. 2006. God's Country. *Foreign Affairs* 85 (September–October): 24–44.
Mearsheimer, John J. 1990a. Back to the Future: Instability in Europe after the Cold War. *International Security* 15: 5–56.
———. 1990b. Why We Would Soon Miss the Cold War. *The Atlantic Monthly*, August.
———. 1992. Disorder Restored. In *Rethinking America's Security: Beyond Cold War to New Word Order*, ed. Graham Allison and Gregory F. Treverton. New York: W.W. Norton. 213–237.
———. 2001. *The Tragedy of Great Power Politics.* New York: W.W. Norton.
———. 2002. Hearts and Minds. *National Interest* 69 (Fall): 13–16.
Mearsheimer, John J., and Stephen M. Walt. 2002. Can Saddam Be Contained? History Says Yes. Cambridge, MA: Occasional Paper. Belfer Center for Science and International Affairs. Harvard University, November 12.
———. 2003. An Unnecessary War. *Foreign Policy* 134 (January–February): 51–59.
———. 2006. The Israel Lobby and U.S. Foreign Policy. *London Review of Books*, March 23.
Mellinger, Phillip. 2001. A Matter of Precision. *Foreign Policy* 123 (March-April): 78–79.
Meyer, Karl E. 1999. Enforcing Human Rights. *World Policy Journal* 16: 45–50.

Milhollin, Gary, and Kelly Motz. 2001. Shopping with Saddam Hussein. *Commentary*, July–August.

Miller, Abraham H. 1997. How the CIA Fell Victim to Myth Posing as Journalism. *International Journal of Intelligence and Counterintelligence* 10: 257–268.

Miller, Anita, Jordan Miller, and Sigalit Zetouni. 2002. *Sharon: Israel's Warrior-Politician*. Chicago: Academy Publishers.

Miller, Judith. 1996. *God Has Ninety Nine Names*. New York: Simon &Schuster

———. 2004. Panel Pegs Illicit Iraq Earnings at $21.3 Billion. *New York Times*, November 16.

Miller, Judith, and Eric Lipton. 2004. Report Cites U.S. Profit in Sale of Iraqi Oil under Hussein. *New York Times*, October 9.

Miller, Judith, and Laurie Mylroie. 1990. *Saddam Hussein and the Crisis in the Gulf*. New York: Times Books.

Miller, Judith, Stephen Eghleberg, and William Broad. 2002. *Biological Weapons and America's Secret Wars*. New York: Touchstone Books.

Miller, Judith, and Warren Hogue. 2004. Inquiry on Food-for-Oil Plan. *New York Times*, February 4.

Miller, Steven E. 2002. The End of Unilateralism or Unilateralism Redux? *Washington Quarterly* 25: 15–30.

Miller, Tamar, and Tamar Morad. 2002. Inspecting Saddam: An Israeli Historian Helps Diagnose the Dictator. *Boston Globe*, October 27.

Miniter, Richard. 2003. *Losing Bin Laden: How Bill Clinton's Failure Unleashed Global Terror*. Washington, DC: Regnery.

Mishra, Rajesh Kumar. 2003. *Clear and Present Danger to Nonproliferation*. South Asia Analysis Group. February 7.

Mitchell, Robert W., and Nicholas S. Thompson. 1986. *Deception: Perspectives on Human and Nonhuman Deceit*. Albany: State University of New York Press.

Moghadam, Val. 1991. The Neopatriarchal State in the Middle East: Development, Authoritarianism and Crisis. In *The Gulf War and the New World Order*, ed. Haim Bresheeth and Nira Yuval-Davis. London: Zed Books. 199–210.

Moore, James 2004. *Bush's War for Reelection, Iraq, the White House and the People*. New York: John Wiley.

Morris, Dick. 2003. *Off with Their Heads. Traitors, Crooks, and Obstructionists in American Politics, Media, and Business*. New York: Regan Books.

Mosmoudi, Radwan. 2001. Struggles behind Words. *SAIS Review* 21 (Summer–Fall): 19–24.

Moynihan, Daniel Patrick. 1988. *Came the Revolution: Argument in the Reagan Era*. San Diego: Harcourt, Brace Iovanovich.

Mueller, John. 2006. Is There Still a Terrorist Threat? The Myth of the Omipresent Enemy. *Foreign Affairs* 85 (September–October): 2–8.

Mueller, John, and Karl Mueller. 1999. Sanctions of Mass Destruction. *Foreign Affairs* 78: 54–65.

Mufson, Steve. 2000. A "Rogue" Is a "Rogue" Is a "State of Concern." *Washington Post*, June 20.

Muravchik, Joshua. 2003. The Neoconservative Cabal. *Commentary* September.

Murphy, Craig. 2001. Presidential Address. *International Studies Perspectives* 3: 340–370.

Mylroie, Laurie. 1987. Appeasing the Ayatollah. *Orbis* 31: 141–144.

———. 1988. The Baghdad Alternative. *Orbis* 32: 339–354.

———. Mylroie. 1989. Iraq's Changing Role in the Persian Gulf. *Current History* 88: 89–92.
———. 1991. *The Future of Iraq*. Washington, DC: Washington Institute for Near East Policy.
———. 1995–96. The World Trade Center Bomb: Who Is Ramzi Yousef? And Why It Matters. *The National Interest*, Winter. www.fas.org/irp/world/Iraq/956-tni.htm-51k (accessed October 14, 2007).
———. 2000. *Study in Revenge: Saddam Hussein's Unfinished War against America*. Washington, DC: American Enterprise Institute.
———. 2001. *Study of Revenge: The First World Trade Center and Saddam Hussein's War against America*. Washington, DC: AEI Press.
———. 2003. *Bush vs. Beltmey: How the CIA and the State Department Tried to Stop the War on Terror*. New York: HarperCollins.
———. 2004a. Mishandling Terrorism. *National Review Online*, January 23.
———. 2004b. The Saddam-9/11 Link Confirmed. *FrontPage Magazine*, May 11.
Mylroie, Laurie, and Daniel Pipes. 1987. Back Iraq: It's Time for a US Tilt. *New Republic*, April 27: 14–15.
Nafisi, Azar. 2003. They the People. *New Republic*, March 3.
Nelson, Bruce W. 1990. Who Lost Kuwait? *Time*, October 1.
Netanyahu, Benjamin. 1995. *Fighting Terrorism: How Democracies Can Defeat Domestic and International Terrorism*. New York: Farrar, Strauss and Giroux.
Newbury, Michael C. 1983. Colonialism, Ethnicity, and Rural Political Protest in Rwanda and Zanzibar in Comparative Perspective. *Comparative Politics* 15: 253–280.
Nisan, Mordechai. 2004. The Ethos of Islam. *Jerusalem Post*, April 12.
Nolan, Cynthia M. 1999. Seymour Hersh's Impact on the CIA. *International Journal of Intelligence and Counterintelligence* 12: 18–34.
Nordlinger, Eric A. 1995. *Isolationism Reconfigured: An American Foreign Policy for a New Century*. Princeton: Princeton University Press.
Norton, Augustus Richard. 1993. The Future of Civil Society in the Middle East. *Middle East Journal* 47: 205–216.
Norton, Augustus Richard, and Robin Wright. 1994–95. The Post-peace Crisis in the Middle East. *Survival* 36: 7–20.
Novak, Robert. 2004. Is CIA at War with Bush? *Chicago Sun-Times*, September 27.
No War for Israel. com. 2003. nowarfor Israel.com/Bush's%20 israeli%20 advisers%20%20america%20into%war.htm-23k-(accessed September 19, 2007).
Nye, Joseph S. Jr. 1990. *Bound to Lead: The Changing Nature of American Power*. New York: Basic Books.
———. 2001. Military Deglobalization. *Foreign Policy* 122 (January–February): 82–83.
O'Hanlon, Michael. 2001. Come Partly Home: How to Downsize U.S. Deployment Abroad. *Foreign Affairs* 80 (March–April): 2–8.
O'Neill, Barry. 2001. Risk Aversion in International Relation Theory. *International Studies Quarterly* 45: 617–640.
O'Rourke, P.J. 2004. *Peace Kills*. New York: Atlantic Monthly Press.
O'Toole, Tara, and Donald A. Henderson 2001. A Clearly Present Danger: Confronting the Threat of Bioterrorism. *Harvard International Review* 23 (Fall): 49–59.

Ottaway, Marina, and Thomas Carothers, 2004. Democracy in the Middle East. *Foreign Policy* 145 (November–December): 22–28.

Ottaway, Marina, Thomas Carothers, Amy Hawthorne, and Daniel Brumbery. 2002. *Domestic Mirage in the Middle East.* Policy Brief no. 20. Washington, DC: Carnegie Endowment for International Peace.

Owen, J. Judd. 2004. The Task of Liberal Theory after September 11. *Perspectives on Politics* 2: 325–330.

Packenham, Robert A. 1992. *The Development Movement: Scholarship and Politics in Development Studies.* Cambridge: Harvard University Press.

Pape, Robert A. 1998. Why Economic Sanctions Still Do Not Work. *International Security* 23: 66–77.

Parenti, Michael. 1995. *Against Empire.* San Francisco: City Lights Books.

Parmelee, Jennifer. 1992. Sudan Denies "Khartoum-Teheran Axis" to Promote Islamic Regimes in Africa. *Washington Post,* March 12.

Parmet, Herbert S. 1997. *George Bush: The Life of a Lone Star Yankee.* New York: Scribner's Sons.

Parsons, Talcott. 1951. *The Social System.* Glencoe, IL: Free Press.

Paseman, Floyd L. 2004. *A Spy's Journey.* St. Paul, MN: Zenith.

Patai, Raphael. 1983. *The Arab Mind.* New York: Scribner's Sons.

Paul, Ron. 2003. Neo-conned. Address to U.S. House of Representatives. July 10. http//www. thelibertycommitee.org/neo-conned. htm (accessed September 17, 2007).

Payne, Anthony. 1984. Introduction: Dependency Theory and the Commonwealth Caribbean. In *Dependency Under Challenge: The Political Economy of Commonwealth Caribbean,* ed. Anthony Payne and Paul Sutton. Manchester: Manchester University Press.

Payne, Keith B. 1996. *Deterrence in the Second Nuclear Age.* Lexington, KY: University Press of Kentucky.

Paz, Reuven. 2007. The 2006 Lebanon War's Effect on Global Jihad Groups. *MERIA* 11: 1 (March). www. meria. Idc. Ac.il/journal/2007/issue 1/jvl/no.1a3 html-19k (accessed September 21, 2007).

PeaceWatch Briefing. 1998. Terrorism, Afghanistan and Regional Instability Washington, DC: United States Institute of Peace, August 26.

Peck, Edward L. 1998. Dealing with Saddam. *Mediterranean Quarterly* 9: 11–24.

Pekel, Kent. 1998. The Need for Improvement: Integrity, Ethics, and the CIA. *Studies in Intelligence,* Spring.

Pelletiere, Stephen C., Douglas Johnson II, and Leif R. Rosenberg. 1990. *Iraqi Power and U.S. Security in the Middle East.* Carlisle Barracks, PA: Strategic Studies Institute.

Peretz, Martin. 2002. Regrets. *National Republic,* April 22: 50.

Perl, Raphael F. 2001. *National Commission on Terrorism Report: Background and Issue for Congress.* Washington, DC: Congressional Research Service, February 2.

Perle, Richard. 1990a. Op-ed. *Wall Street Journal,* August 22, 1990.

———. 1990b. Op-ed. *New York Times,* September 23.

Perry, Mark. 1992. *Eclipse. The Last Days of CIA.* New York: William Morrow.

Perry, William J. 2001. Preparing for the Next Attack. *Foreign Affairs* 8 (November–December): 31–45.

Persico, Joseph E. 1990. *Casey: The Lives and Secrets of William J. Casey from the OSS to the CIA.* New York: Viking.

Pettman, Ralph. 1975. *Human Behavior and World Politics.* New York: St.Martin's Press.
Phillips, David L. 2005. *Losing Iraq. Postwar Reconstruction Fiasco.* New York: Basic Books.
Phillips, Kevin 2004. *American Dynasty. Aristocracy, Fortune, and the Politics of Deceit in the House of Bush.* New York: Viking.
Pillar, Paul R. 2001. *Terrorism and Foreign Policy.* Washington, DC: Brookings Institution Press.
———. 2006. Intelligence, Policy, and the War in Iraq. *Foreign Affairs* 86 (March–April): 15–19.
Pipes, Daniel. 1983. *In the Path of God. Islam and Political Power.* New York: Basic Books.
———. 1991. Let the Iraqis Get Rid of Saddam. *Washington Post,* December 22.
———. 1994. An Islamic International? *Forward,* July 22.
———.1995a. Testimony to the United States Senate. Subcommittee on the Near East and South East Asia. March 2, 1995. Danielpipes.org (accessed September 9, 2007).
———. 1995b. There Are No Moderates: Dealing with Fundamentalism. *National Interest* 41: 48–57.
———. 1996. *The Hidden Hand: Middle East Fear of Conspiracy.* New York: St. Martin's.
———. 1997a. On Arab Rejectionism. *Commentary,* December.
———. 1997b. *Conspiracy: How the Paranoid Style Flourishes and Where It Comes From.* New York: Free Press.
———. 1999. How Dare You Define Islam. *Commentary,* November.
———. 2003a. Islam's Image Problem. *New York Post,* July 29.
———. 2003b. Where Are Iraq's Weapons. *Jerusalem Post,* October 8.
Pitt, William Rivers, and Scott Ritter. 2003. *War on Iraq: What Team Bush Doesn't Want You to Know.* New York: Context Books.
Podhoretz, Norman. 2006. Is the Bush Doctrine Dead? *Commentary,* September.
Pollack, Kenneth M. 2002a. The Threatening Storm. The Cause for Invading Iraq. New York: Random House.
———. 2002b. Why Invade Can't Be Deterred. *New York Times,* September 26.
———. 2004. *The Persian Puzzle: The Conflict between Iran and America.* New York: Random House.
Popper, Karl R. 1963. *The Poverty of Historicism.* London: Routledge and Kegan Paul.
Posner, Gerald. 2003. *Why America Slept: The Failure to Prevent 9/11.* New York: Random House.
Post, Jerrold M. 1990. A Political Personality Profile of Saddam Hussein. Testimony to House Foreign Affairs Committee, December.
———. 2003a. Saddam Hussein of Iraq. A Political Psychological Profile. In *The Psychological Assessment of Political Leaders: With Profiles of Saddam Hussein and Bill Clinton,* ed. Jerrold M. Post. Ann Arbor: University of Michigan Press. 335–366.
———. 2003b. Saddam Hussein of Iraq. A Political Psychological Profile. www.case.edu/saddamtrial/documents/saddam_Hussein_political_psychology_profile.pdf (accessed September 24, 2007).
Post, Jerrold M., and Amazia Baram. 2002. Saddam Is Iraq: Iraq Is Saddam. In *Know Thy Enemy: Profiles of Adversary Leaders and their Strategic Culture,* ed. Barry R. Schneider and Jerrold M. Post. Maxwell Air Base: Alabama. Air University Press. 163–220.

Preston, Richard. 2000. Updating the Smallpox Vaccine. *New Yorker*, January 17.
Primakov, Yevgeny. 1991. The Inside Story of Moscow's Quest for a Deal. *Time*, March 4.
Primmerman, C.A. 2006. *Thoughts on the Meaning of "Asymmetric Threats."* Lexington, MA: MIT Lincoln Laboratory. March 8. www. comw.org/ma/full text/asymmetric.html. 61k (accessed September 21, 2007).
Prothero, P. Mitchell. 2003. Top White House Anti-terror Boss Resigns. *United Press, International*, March 19.
Pryce-Jones, David. 1989. *The Closed Circle: An Interpretation of the Arab*. New York: Harper and Row.
Pucker, George. 2003. *The Fight Is for Democracy: New Liberal Unorthodoxies*. New York: Perenial/HarperCollins.
Pugh, Deborah.1990. Crisis in the Gulf: Sudan May Have Chemical Arms. *Guardian*, August 13.
Punditwatch 2003. March 2, punditwatch.blogspot.com/-55k (accessed June 3, 2006).
Radu, Michael. 2002. The Futile Search for "Root Causes" of Terrorism. *Foreign Policy Research Institute Enotes*. www. fpri/org/research/Terrorism/publications. htm/-9k (accessed September 9, 2007).
Ramphal, Shridath. 1992. Globalism and Meaningful Peace: A New World Order Rooted in International Community. *Mediterranean Quarterly* 3: 8–16.
Randal, Jonathan. 2004. *Osama: The Making of a Terrorist*. New York: Alfred A. Knopf.
Ranstorp, Magnus. 1996. Terrorism in the Name of Religion. *Journal of International Affairs* 50: 41–62.
Rapoport, David C. 2001. The Fourth Wave: September 11 in the History of Terrorism. *Current History* 100: 403–650.
Record, Jeffrey. 1993. *Hollow Victory: A Contrary View of the Gulf War*. Washington, DC: Brassey's.
———. 2004. *Dark Victory. America's Second War against Iraq*. Annapolis, MD: Naval Institute Press.
Reeve, Simon. 2002. *The New Jackals*. Boston: Northwestern University Press.
Reuter, Christoph. 2004. *My Life as a Weapon: A Modern History of Suicide Bombing*. Trans. Helana Ragg-Kirbky. Princeton: Princeton University Press.
Rice, Condoleezza. 2000. Promoting the National Interest. *Foreign Affairs* 79 (January–February): 45–62.
Richelson, Jeffrey T. 2001. *The Wizards of Langley*. Boulder: Westview Press.
———. 2006. *Spying on the Bomb. American Nuclear Intelligence from Nazi Germany to Iran and North Korea*. New York: W.W. Norton.
Ricks, Thomas E. 2006. *Fiasco: The American Military Adventure in Iraq*. New York: Penguin Press.
Ricks, Thomas M. 1980. Iran and Imperialism: Academics in the Service of the People or the Shah? *Arab Studies Quarterly* 2: 265–277.
Risen, James. 2006. *State of War: The Secret History of the CIA and the Bush Administration*. New York: Free Press.
Ritter, Scott. 1999. *Endgame: Solving the Iraq Problem—Once and for All*. New York: Simon & Schuster.
———. 2000. The Case for Iraq's Qualitative Disarmament. *Arms Control Today* 30 (June): 8–14.
———. 2001. The Saddam Trap. *Harvard International Review* 22: 28–32.

———. 2005. *Iraq Confidential: The Untold Story of the Intelligence Conspiracy to Undermine the UN and Overthrow Saddam Hussein.* New York: Nation Books.

Rizvi, Yaseen. 1991. *The Renegade: A Narration of the Mother of All Retreats.* Lahore: Point Point.

Robb, Charles S., and Laurence H. Silberman. 2005. Report to the President. Commission on the Intelligence Capabilities of the United States regarding Weapons of Mass Destruction. www.wmd. gov/about. html-12k (accessed September, 19. 2007).

Roberts II, John B. 2004. White House-CIA Breach. *Washington Times,* October 1.

Roberts, Paul William. 1997. *The Demonic Comedy: Some Detours in the Baghdad of Saddam Hussein.* New York: Farmer, Straus, and Giroux.

Robins, Robert S., and Jerrold M. Post. 1997. *Political Paranoia: The Psychopolitics of Hatred.* New Haven: Yale University Press.

Robinson, Adam. 2001. *Bin Laden: Behind the Mask of the Terrorist.* New York: Arcade Publishing.

Rodman, Peter. 1994. Co-opt or Confront Fundamentalist Islam? *Middle East Quarterly* 1: 61–64.

Rosenbaum, Ron. 1998. *Explaining Hitler: The Search for the Origins of Evil.* New York: Random House.

Rostow, Walt W. 1964. *The Stages of Economic Growth: A Non-Communist Manifesto.* Cambridge: Cambridge University Press.

Rotberg, Robert I. 2000. The New Wave of Nation-State Failures. *Washington Quarterly* 25: 85–46.

Roth, Kenneth, 1993. Ed. *Campaign against the Kurds. Middle East Watch Report.* New York: Human Rights Watch.

Rothestein, Robert L. 1972. *Planning, Prediction, and Policymaking in Foreign Affairs: Theory and Practice.* Boston: Little Brown.

Rothmell, Andrew 2002. Toward Post-modern Intelligence. *Intelligence and National Security* 17: 87–104.

Roxborough, Ian. 2001. The Hart-Rudman Commission and the Homeland Defense. Report commissioned by the U.S. Army War College External Research Associates Program. Strategic Studies Institute, U.S. Army War College. Carlisile Barracks, PA.

Rubin, Barry. 1982. United States-Iraq Relations: A Spring Thaw? In *Iraq: The Contemporary State,* ed. Tim Niblock. New York: St. Martin Press. 109–124.

———. 2006a. *The Long War for Freedom: The Arab Struggle for Democracy in the Middle East*. Hoboken, NJ: John Wiley.

———. 2006b. The Region: Opiate of the Arab World. *Jerusalem Post,* January 26.

Rubin, Michael. 2000. Afghanistan: as Bad as Its Reputation. *Middle East Quarterly* 7: 3 (September), www. meforum.org/article/72-45k (accessed September 20, 2007).

———. 2001. Sanctions Have Helped Northern Iraq. Middle. *Middle East Forum,* July 10.

———. 2002. How to Free Iraq. *Middle East Quarterly* 9 (Winter): 3–8.

———. 2004. Web of Conspiracies *National Review Online,* May 18.

Rummel, Rudolph J. 1991. *The Conflict Helix: Principles and Practices of Interpersonal, Social, and International Conflict and Cooperation.* New Brunswick: Transaction Books.

Russett, Bruce M. 1990–91. Correspondence. *International Security* 15: 216–222.

Ryan, Maria. 2006. Filling the "Unknowns": Hypothesis-Based Intelligence and the Rumsfeld Commission. *Intelligence and National Security* 21: 286–315.

Sachedina. Abdul aziz. 1998. Religion and Global Affairs: Islamic Religion and Political Order. *SAIS Review* 18 (Summer–Fall): 59–64.

Sachs, Susan, and Judith Miller. 2004. Under Eye of U.N. in Billions for Hussein in Oil. *New York Times,* August 13.

Sada, Georges with Jim Nelson Black. 2006. *Saddam's Secrets: How an Iraqi General Defied and Survived Saddam Hussein.* Brentwood, TN: Integrity Publishers.

Sadiki, Larbi. 2000. Popular Uprising and Arab Democratization. *International Journal of Middle East Studies* 32: 71–95.

Safi, Louay M. 1994. *The Challenge of Modernity: The Quest for Authenticity in the Arab World.* Lanham, MD: University Press of America.

Sageman, Marc. 2004. *Understanding Terror Networks.* Philadelphia: University of Pennsylvania Press.

Said, Edward W. 1978. *Orientalism.* New York: Pantheon Books.

———. 1979. *The Question of Palestine.* New York: Times Books.

———. 1981. *Covering Islam: How the Media and the Experts Determine How We See the Rest of the World.* New York: Pantheon Books.

———. 1985. Orientalism Reconsidered. *Race and Class* 27: 1–15.

———. 1991a. The Gulf War. *London Review of Books,* March 7.

———. 1991b. Thoughts on a War: Ignorant Armies Clash by Night. In *Beyond the Storm,* ed. Phyllis Bennis and Michael Moushabeck. New York: Oliver Branch Press. 5–6.

———. 1993. *Culture and Imperialism.* New York: Knopf.

———. 1994. *The Politics of Dispossession: The Struggle for Palestinian Self-determination, 1969–1994.* New York: Pantheon Books.

———. 1997. Iraq: Apocalypse New. *Al Ahram* English Edition January. www.zmag.org/crisisCurEvt/Iraq/saidiraq. htm.15k (accessed September 7, 2007).

———. 2000a. "A Devil Theory" of Islam. *Nation,* July 25.

———. 2002a. The Clash of Ignorance. In *A Just Response: The Nation on Terrorism, Democracy, and September 11, 2001,* ed. Katrina Vanden Heuvel. New York: Thunder's Mouth Press/Nation Books. 233–239.

———. 2002b. Israel, Iraq, and the United States. *Counterpunch,* October 19.

———. 2005. *From Oslo to Iraq and the Road Map.* New York: Vintage Books.

Salame, Ghasan. 1993. Islam and the West. *Foreign Policy* 90: 3–21.

Salinger, Pierre, and Eric Laurent. 1991. *Secret Dossier: The Hidden Agenda behind the Gulf War.* Trans. Howard Curtis. New York: Penguin Press.

Salmoni, Barak A. 2004. America's Iraq's Strategy; Domestic Chimera, Regional Realities. *Current History* 103 (January): 17–20.

Sanger, David E., and Thom Shanker. 2007. U.S. Debates Deterrence for Nuclear Terrorism. *New York Times,* May 8.

Sariolghalam, Mahmoud. 1994. The Determinants of Iraqi Foreign Policy Behavior in the 1980s. In *Renegade States,* ed. Stephen Chan and Andrew J. Williams. Manchester: Manchester University Press. 185–198.

Sarsar, Saliba. 2006. Quantifying Arab Democracy in the Middle East. *Middle East Quarterly* (Summer): 13: 3. www.meforum.org/meq/issues/summer 200606-13k (accessed September, 20, 2007).

Sasson. Jean. 2003. *Mayada. Daughter of Iraq.* New York: Dutton.

Satterlee. Carrie 2003. *Facts on Who Benefited from Keeping Saddam in Power.* Washington, DC: The Heritage Foundation, WebMemo No. 217, February 28.

Schaar, Stuart. 1979. Orientalism at the Service of Imperialism. *Race and Class*, 21: 67–80.

Scheuer, Michael. 2002. *Through Our Enemies Eyes: Osama Laden, Radical Islam and Future of America*. Washington, DC: Brassey's. Originally published anonymously.

———. 2004. *Imperial Hubris: Why the West Is Losing the War on Terrorism*. Washington, DC: Brassey's. Originally published anonymously.

———. 2006. New York Subway Plot and al Qaeda's WMD Strategy. *Terrorism Focus*, June 20.

Schmid. Alex P. 2000. Terrorism and the Use of Weapons of Mass Destruction. In *The Future of Terrorism*, ed. Max Taylor and John Horgan. London: Frank Cass. 106–132.

Schoenfeld, Gabriel. 2003. The Terror Ahead. *Commentary*, November: 17–25.

———. 2005. What Became of the CIA. *Commentary*, March: 44–51.

Schultz, Kenneth A. 2005. The Politics of Risking Peace: Do Hawks or Doves Deliver the Olive Branch? *International Organization* 59: 1–38.

Schweitzer, Peter. 2005. *Do as I Say (Not as I Do). Profiles in Liberal Hypocrisy*. New York: Random House.

Schweitzer, Peter, and Rochelle Schweitzer. 2004. *The Bushes: Portrait of a Dynasty*. New York: Doubleday.

Sciolino, Elaine. 1991. *The Outlaw State: Saddam Hussein's Quest for Power and the Gulf Crisis*. New York: John Wiley.

———. 2001. Is Baghdad's Tiger a Literary Lion? *New York Times*, May 25.

Sciolino, Elaine, and Patrick E. Taylor. 2001. A Nation Challenged: Saddam Hussein. *New York Times*, October 12.

Seliktar, Ofira.1986. Identifying a Society's Belief System. In *Political Psychology*, ed. Margaret G. Hermann. San Francisco: Jossey-Bass Publishers. 320–350.

———. 2000. *Failing the Crystal Ball Test: The Carter Administration and the Fundamentalist Revolution in Iraq.*, CT: Praeger.

———. 2004. *Politics, Paradigms, and Intelligence Failures: Why So Few Predicted the Collapse of the Soviet Union*. Armonk, NY: M.E. Sharpe.

Seliktar, Ofira, and Lee E. Dutter. 2006. Assessing the Rationality of Dictators: The Puzzling Case of Saddam Hussein. Paper presented at the annual meeting of International Studies Association-South, Birmingham, Alamaba, October, and also at the Regional International Studies Association meeting.

Shafer, Michael D. 1988. *Deadly Paradigms. The Failure of U.S. Counterinsurgency Policy*. Princeton: Princeton University Press.

Shain, Yossi. 1994. Marketing the Democratic Creed Abroad. US Diasporic Politics in the Era of Multiculturalism. *Diaspora* 3: 85–111.

Shamir, Yitzhak. 1994. *Summing Up. Sadam Autobiography*. Boston: Little Brown.

Shane, Scott. 2006. In Video, Hussein Uses Slingshots and Bows to Rally Iraqis for War. *New York Times*, November 24.

Shanker, Thom. 2004. Iraqis, Seeking of Saudis, Contacted bin Laden, File Says. *New York Times*, June 25.

Shapiro, Ian. 2003. *The State of Democratic Theory*. Princeton: Princeton University Press.

Sharabi, Hisham. 1988. *Neopatriarchy: A Theory of Distorted Change in Arab Society*. New York: Oxford University Press.

Sharansky, Natan. 2004. *The Case for Democracy. The Power of Freedom to Overcome Tyranny and Terror*. New York: Public Affairs.

Sharon, Moshe. 1990. The Saddam Hussein Show. *Jerusalem Post*, December 15.

Shepard, William E. 2003. Sayyid Qutb's Doctrine of Jahiliyya. *International Journal of Middle East Studies* 35: 521–546.

Shimko, Keith L. 1993. The Prince of Darkness and the Evil Empire: Richard Perle, the Soviet Union, and the U.S. Arms Control Policy. *International Interaction* 18: 283–308.

Shirley, Edward G. 1998. Can't Anybody Here Play the Game? *Atlantic Monthly*, February.

Shore, Zachary. 2003. Three Faces of Realism. *Orbis* 47: 349–358.

Shulsky, Abram. 1993. *Silent Warfare. Understanding the World of Intelligence.* Washington, DC: Brassey's.

Shulsky, Abram, and Gary Schmitt. 1996. *The Future of U.S. Intelligence Report Prepared for the Working Group on Intelligence Reform.* Washington: Consortium for the Study of Intelligence.

Sicherman, Harvey. 1981. Reflections on Iran and Iran at War. *Orbis* 24: 1981.

Silverstein, Ken. 2006. Six Questions for Dr. Emil A. Nakhleh on the CIA and the Iraqi War. *Harper's Magazine*, June 30.

Silvert, Kalman H. 1964. Ed. *Discussion at Bellagio: The Political Alternative of Development.* New York: American Universities Field Staff.

Simon, Merril. 1984. *Jerry Falwell and the Jews.* Middle Village, NY: Jonathan David.

Simons, Geoff L. 2003. *Targeting Iraq. Sanctions and Bombing in U.S. Policy.* London: Saqi Books.

Simpson, William. 2006. *The Prince: The Secret Story of the World's Most Intriguing Royal. Prince Bandar bin Sultan.* New York: Regan/HarperCollins.

Sims, Jennifer. 2006. Foreign Intelligence Liaison: Devils, Deals, and Details. *International Journal of Intelligence and Counterintelligence* 19: 195–217.

Sivan, Emmanuel. 1990. The Islamic Resurgence: Civil Society Strikes Back. *The Journal of Contemporary History*, May/June: 353–64.

———. 1998. The Holy Tradition in Islam. *Orbis* 42: 171–194.

Smist, Frank J. Jr. 1994. *Congress Oversees the United States Intelligence Community 1947–1994.* Knoxville: University of Tennessee Press.

Smith, G. Davidson. 1993. Sources of Terrorist Weaponry and Major Methods of Obtaining Weapons and Technology. *Terrorism and Political Violence* 5: 123–129.

Smith, James A. 1993. *Strategic Calling: The Center for Strategic and International Studies 1962–1992.* Washington, DC: The Center for Strategic and International Studies.

Smith, Sally Bedell. 2004. *Grace and Power. The Private World of the Kennedy White House.* New York: Random House.

Smyth, Frank. 1998. Culture Clash: Bin Laden, Khartoum, and the War against the West. *Jane's Intelligence Review* 10: 22–25.

Snyder, Robert S. 1999. The U.S. and Third World Revolutionary States: Understanding the Breakdown in Relations. *International Studies Quarterly* 43: 265–290.

Sofaer, Abraham D. 2003. On the Necessity of Pre-emption. *European Journal of International Law* 14: 209–226.

Sopko, John F. 1996–97. The Changing Proliferation Treaty. *Foreign Policy* 105: 3–20.

Spector, Leonard S. 1985. Silent Spread. *Foreign Policy* 58: 53–78.

Sperzel, Richard. 2003. No Smoking Gun. *National Review Online*, January 13.

Sprinzak, Ehud. 1998. The Great Superterrorism Scare. *Foreign Policy* 112 (Fall): 110–124.

SSCI. 2004. *Report on the U.S. Intelligence Community's Prewar Intelligence Assessment on Iraq*. Senate Select Committee on Intelligence, July 7. www. fas. org/irp/congress/2004_rpt/ssci_iraq.pdf (accessed September 25, 2007).

———. 2006. *Report of the Select Committee on Postwar Findings about WMD Program and Links to Terrorism and How They Compare with Prewar Assessments*, Senate Select Committee on Intelligence, September 8. www. fas.org/irp/congress/2006-rpt/sept 109-331.pdf (accessed September 25, 2007).

Staniland, Martin. 1991. *American Intellectuals and African Nationalism 1955–1970*. New Haven: Yale University Press.

Stark, Rodney, and Charles Y. Glock. 1968. *American Piety: The Nature of Religious Commitment*. Berkeley: University of California Press.

Steele, Robert David, 2000. Possible Presidential Intelligence Initiatives. *International Journal of Intelligence and Counterintelligence* 13: 409–423.

———. 2002. Crafting Intelligence in the Aftermath of Disaster. *International Journal of Intelligence and Counterintelligence* 15: 161–178.

Steinberg, Gerald M. 1990. Can Iraq's Gambler/Maniac Be Deterred? *Jerusalem Post*, August 18.

Steinberg, Jeffrey. 2005. Larry Franklin Case: AIPAC Leaders Snared. *Executive Intelligence Review*, August 12.

Steinberg, Michele. 2001. "Wolfowitz Cabal" Is an Enemy within U.S. *Executive Intelligence Review*, October 26.

Steinbruner, John D. 1997–98. Biological Weapons: A Plague upon All Houses. *Foreign Policy* 109: 85–96.

Sterling, Claire. 1981. *The Terror Network: The Secret War of International Terrorism*. New York: Berkeley Books.

Stern, Jessica Eve. 1999. *The Ultimate Terrorist*. Cambridge: Harvard University Press.

———. 2003. *Terror in the Name of God: Why Religious Militants Kill*. New York: Ecco Books.

Stern, Yoav. 2007. Report: Missing Iranian Officials Can Prove Teheran-Terror Link. *Haaretz*, March 9.

Sterner, Michael. 1997. Closing the Gate: The Persian Gulf War Revisited. *Current History* 96: 13–19.

Steury, Donald P. 1994. *Sherman Kent and Board of National Estimates. Collected Essays*. Washington, DC: Center for the Study of Intelligence.

Stewart, James B. 1996. *Blood Press: The President and His Advisers*. New York: Simon & Schuster.

Stoessinger, John G. 1985. *Crusaders and Pragmatics: Movers of Modern American Policy*. 2nd ed. New York: W.W. Norton.

Stout, David. 2007. Senate Panel Debates Iraq Intelligence. *New York Times*, February, 9.

Strasser, Steven. 2004. *The 9/11 Investigations*. New York: Public Affairs.

Strauss, Mark. 2000. Rogue by Any Other Name. *Chronicles of Higher Education*, December, 15.

———. 2002. Attacking Iraq. *Foreign Policy*, March–April: 14–19.

Strother, Roger. 2006. *Post Saddam Iraq: The War Game*. National Security Archive Electronic Briefing Book no. 207, November 4. www.gwu.ed/~narchive/NSAEBB/NSAEBB2007/index.htm_25k (accessed September 22, 2007).

Suedfeld, Peter 2003. Saddam Hussein's Integrative Complexity under Stress. In *The Psychological Assessment of Political Leaders: With Profiles of Saddam Hussein and Bill Clinton,* ed. Jerrold M. Post, 391–398. Ann Arbor: University of Michigan Press.

Suskind, Ron. 2004. *The Price of Loyalty. George W. Bush, the White House, and the Education of Paul O'Neill.* New York: Simon & Schuster.

———. 2006. *The One Percent Doctrine. Deep inside America's Pursuit of Its Enemies since 9/11.* New York: Simon & Schuster.

Szamuely, George. W's Oil Warriors. 2000. *New York Press,* August 1.

Taheri, Amir. 2004a. Islam and Democracy: The Impossible Union. *The Sunday Times,* UK, May 23.

———. 2004b. Radicals for Freedom. *New York Post,* June 18.

Talbott, Strobe. 1990. The Search for Supervillain. *Time,* September 3.

Tamir, Avraham. 1988. *A Soldier in Search of Peace: An Inside Look at Israel's Strategy.* New York: Harper and Row.

Tanner, Henry. 1982. Mideast Balance Held Endangered. *New York Times Magazine,* May 16.

Tanter, Raymond. 1998. *Rogue Regimes: Terrorism and Proliferation.* New York: St. Martin's Press.

Tanter, Raymond, and Richard H. Ullman. 1972. *Theory and Policy in International Relations.* Princeton: Princeton University Press.

Taubman, Philip. 1982. Iraq, Iran, and the US. *New York Times Magazine,* July 14.

Taubman, William. 1974. The Change to Change in Communist Systems: Modernization, Postmodernization and Soviet Politics. In *Soviet Politics and Society in the 1970s,* ed. Henry W. Morton and Rudolf L. Tokes, New York: Free Press. 369–395.

Teicher, Howard, and Gayle Radley Teicher. 1993. *Twin Pillars to Desert Storm: America's Flawed Vision in the Middle East from Nixon to Bush.* New York: William Morrow.

Tenet, George. 2007. *At the Center of the Storm: My Years at the CIA* New York: HarperCollins.

Tessler, Mark. 2002. Islam and Democracy in the Middle East: The Impact of Religious Orientations on Attitudes toward Democracy. *Comparative Politics* 34: 337–354.

Thatcher, Margaret. 1995. *The Path to Power.* London: HarperCollins.

Thomas, Stafford T. 1999–2000. The CIA's Bureaucratic Dimension. *International Journal of Intelligence and Counterintelligence* 12: 399–413.

Timmerman, Kenneth R. 1990. *The Poison Gas Connection Special Report.* Los Angles: Simon Wiesenthal Center.

———. 1991. *The Death Lobby: How the West Armed Iraq.* Boston: Houghton Mifflin.

———. 1997. The Murky Depth of Anthony Lake. *American Spectator.* April.

Tobin, Jonathan. 2005. Still Blaming the Jews? *Jewish Exponent,* June 25.

Trainor, Bernard E. 1987. U.S. Experts Still Puzzled about Future of Gulf War. *New York Times,* January 25.

Traves, Russell E. 1997. A New Millennium and a Strategic Breathing Space. *Washington Quarterly* 20: 97–114.

Trevan, Tim. 1994. Ongoing Monitoring and Verification in Iraq. *Arms Control Today* 24: 11–15.

———. 1999. *Saddam's Secrets: The Hunt for Iraq's Hidden Weapons.* New York: HarperCollins.

Triplett II, William C. 2004. *Rogue State. How a Nuclear North Korea Threatens America.* Washington, DC: Regnery.

Tripp, Charles. 2000. *A History of Iraq.* Cambridge: Cambridge University Press.

Tuathail, Gearoid O. 1999. Understanding Critical Geopolitics. *Journal of Strategic Studies* 22: 107–124.

Tucker, David. 2001. What is New about the New Terrorism and How Dangerous Is It? *Terrorism and Political Violence* 13: 1–14.

Tucker, Jonathan B. 1999. Lessons of Iraq's Biological Warfare Program. *Arms Control* 14: 229–271.

Turner, Stansfield. 1991. Purge the CIA of KGB Types. *New York Times,* October 2.

Twing, Stephen W. 1998. *Myths, Models and U.S. Foreign Policy. The Cultural Shaping of Three Cold Warriors.* Boulder: Lynne Rienner.

Unger, Craig. 2004. *House of Bush, House of Saud: The Secret Relationship between the World's Two Most Powerful Dynasties.* New York: Scribner's Sons.

Vance, Cyrus R. 1983. *Hard Choices: Critical Years in American Foreign Policy.* New York: Simon & Schuster.

Van Hollen, Christopher. 1981. Don't Engulf the Gulf. *Foreign Affairs* 59: 1004–1078.

Venter, Al J. 1999. New-Era Threat: Iraq's Biological Weapons. *Middle East Policy* 6: 104–117.

Voll, John Obert. 1994. The End of Civilization Is Not So Bad. *MESA Bulletin* 29: 1–8.

Voll, John Obert, and John L. Esposito. 1994. Islam's Democratic Essence. *Middle East Quarterly* 1: 3–11.

Walker, Tony, and Andrew Gowers. 2003. *Arafat: The Biography.* London: Virgin Books.

Waller, Douglas. 1996. Master of the Game. *Time,* May 6.

Wallerstein, Immanuel. 1997. The Unintended Consequences of Cold War Area Studies. In *The Cold War and the University: Toward an Intellectual History of the Postwar Years,* ed. Noam Chomsky. New York: New Press. 195–231.

Walt, Stephen M. 1997. Building Up New Bogeymen. *Foreign Policy* 106: 177–189.

———. 2001a. Commentary on the Terrorist Attacks against the United States. *Boston Globe,* September 30.

———. 2001b. Fragile: Package with Care. *Boston Globe,* September 30.

———. 2002. Keeping the World Off Balance. Self Restraint and U.S. Foreign Policy. In *America Unravel: The Future of the Balance of Power,* ed. G. John Ikenberry, 121–154. Ithaca, NY. Cornell University Press.

Waltz, Kenneth. 1990. Realistic Thought and Neorealist Theory. *Journal of International Affairs* 44: 21–37.

Waltzer, Michael. 2002. Can There Be a Decent Left. *Dissident.* Spring. dissentmazine.org/article?/article-598-28k (accessed September 18, 2007).

Wantchekon, Leonard. 2004. The Paradox of "Warlord" Democracy: A Theoretical Investigation. *APSR* 98: 17–34.

Warren, Stephen. 1979. Theoretical Barriers to the Understanding of Evangelical Christianity. *Sociological Analysis* 40: 1–9.

Warrick, Joby. 2006. Warnings on WMD "Fabricator" Were Ignored. *Washington Post,* June 25.

Warrick, Joby, and Joe Stephens. 2001. Before Attack, US Expected Different Hit: Chemical, Germ Agents Focus of Preparation. *Washington Post,* October 2.

Washington Files. 2000. U.S. Commentary. International Information Program, U.S. Information Agency, State Department, May 1. http://usembassy.cz/puas/uscom/com 00-6.htm (accessed September 18, 2007).

Weiner, Tim. 1995. Nominee for CIA Vows to Clear Out Cold War Culture. *New York Times,* April 27.

Weiss, Murray. 2003. *The Man Who Warned America: The Life and Death of John O'Neill, the FBI's Embattled Counterterror Warrior.* New York: Regan Books.

Weitman, Ezer. 1981. *Battle for Peace.* Toronto: Bantam Books.

White, Mary Jo. 2001. Prosecuting Terrorism in New York. *Middle East Quarterly* 8: 11–18.

Will, George F. 2006. Transformation's Tall. *Washington Post,* July 18.

Williams, Paul L.2006. The Dunces of Doomsday. Nashville, TN: A WND Book.

Wills, Garry. 1999. Bully of the Free World. *Foreign Affairs* 78 (March–April): 50–59.

Wilson, Joseph. C. 2002. War with Iraq: A Cost Benefit Analysis. Symposium. *Middle East Policy Council,* October 9.

———. 2003. Republic or Empire. *Nation,* March 3.

———. 2004. *The Politics of Truth: Inside the Lies That Led to War and Betrayed My Wife's CIA Identity. A Diplomat's Memoir.* New York: Caroll & Graf Publishers.

Wirtz, James J. 1991. Miscalculation, Surprise and American Intelligence after the Cold War. *International Journal of Intelligence and Counterintelligence* 5: 8–13.

Wise, David. 1996. Another CIA Disaster. *New York Times,* September 13.

Wohlstetter, Roberta. 1962. *Pearl Harbor: Warning and Decision.* Stanford: Stanford University Press.

Wolfowitz, Paul D. 1990–91. Remarks on the Conclusion of the Gulf War. *Arab-American Relations* 35: 1–10.

———. 1994a. Clinton's First Year. *Foreign Affairs* 73: 28–43.

———. 1994b. Crusade: The Untold Story of the Gulf War. *National Interest* 35 (Spring). Findarticles.com/p/articles'mi_m2751/is_n35/ai-15353291-28k (accessed October 12, 2007).

———. 1998. Statement to the House National Security Committee Hearings on Iraq, September 16. http://www.fas.org/spp/starmers/congress/ (accessed July 7, 2006).

———. 2003. News Transcript. US Department of Defense, May 9. www.defenselink.mil/transcript.aspx? transcriptid=2594-161k (accessed September 9, 2007).

Woods, Kevin, James Lacey, and William Murray. 2006. Saddam's Delusion: The View from Inside. *Foreign Affairs* 85 (May–June): 2–26.

Woodward, Bob. 1991. *The Commanders.* New York: Simon & Schuster.

———. 2004. *Plan of Attack.* New York: Simon & Schuster.

———. 2006. *State of Denial.* New York: Simon & Schuster.

Woolsey R. James, 2001. The Iraqi Connection: Blood Baath. *New Republic,* September 24.

———. 2004. Decisive, Resolute and Wrong. *Financial Times,* April 7.

Wright, Claudia. 1979–80. Iraq: New Power in the Middle East. *Foreign Affairs* 58: 257–277.

———. 1980–81. Implications of the Iraq-Iran War. *Foreign Affairs* 59: 275–303.

Wurmser, David. 1999. *Tyranny's Ally: America's Failure to Defeat Saddam Hussein.* Washington, DC: AEI Press.

Yahia, Latif, and Karl Wendl. 1997. *I Was Saddam's Son*. New York: Arcade Publishing.

Yamami, Mai. 2003. Saudi Arabia; The Arab Street: The Media and Popular Agitation since September 11. *Asian Affairs* 34: 143–147.

Yaniv, Avner. 1993. Israel Faces Iraq: The Politics of Confrontation. In *Iraq's Road to War*, ed. Amazia Baram and Barry Rubin. New York: St. Martin's Press. 233–254.

Yaphe, Judith S. 2004. Reclaiming Iraq from the Baathists. *Current History* 103 (January): 11–16.

Zimmerman, Peter D. 1994. Proliferation: Bronze Medal Technology Is Enough. *Orbis* 38: 67–82.

Zimmerman, Tim. 1996. CIA Study: Why Do Countries Fall Apart? Al Gore Wanted to Know. *US News and World Report*, March 12.

Zola. 1998. The Cunnilingual Bomber Returns. *Laissez Faire City Times*, December 21.

Index